Lecture Notes in Computer Science 12173

More information about this series at http://www.springer.com/series/7408

Víctor Gutiérrez-Basulto ·
Tomáš Kliegr · Ahmet Soylu ·
Martin Giese · Dumitru Roman (Eds.)

Rules and Reasoning

4th International Joint Conference, RuleML+RR 2020
Oslo, Norway, June 29 – July 1, 2020
Proceedings

 Springer

Editors
Víctor Gutiérrez-Basulto
School of Computer Science and Informatics
Cardiff University
Cardiff, UK

Ahmet Soylu
Norwegian University of Science
and Technology
Gjøvik, Norway

SINTEF AS
Oslo, Norway

Dumitru Roman
SINTEF AS
Oslo, Norway

University of Oslo
Oslo, Norway

Tomáš Kliegr ⓘ
University of Economics, Prague
Prague, Czech Republic

Martin Giese ⓘ
Department of Informatics
University of Oslo
Oslo, Norway

ISSN 0302-9743   ISSN 1611-3349 (electronic)
Lecture Notes in Computer Science
ISBN 978-3-030-57976-0   ISBN 978-3-030-57977-7 (eBook)
https://doi.org/10.1007/978-3-030-57977-7

LNCS Sublibrary: SL2 – Programming and Software Engineering

This Springer imprint is published by the registered company Springer Nature Switzerland AG
The registered company address is: Gewerbestrasse 11, 6330 Cham, Switzerland

Preface

These are the proceedings of the 4th International Joint Conference on Rules and Reasoning (RuleML+RR 2020). RuleML+RR joined the efforts of two well-established conference series: the International Web Rule Symposia (RuleML) and the Web Reasoning and Rule Systems (RR) conferences.

The RuleML symposia have been held since 2002 and the RR conferences since 2007. The RR conferences have been a forum for discussion and dissemination of new results on Web Reasoning and Rule Systems, with an emphasis on rule-based approaches and languages. The RuleML symposia were devoted to disseminating research, applications, languages, and standards for rule technologies, with attention to both theoretical and practical developments, to challenging new ideas, and to industrial applications. Building on the tradition of both, RuleML and RR, the joint conference series RuleML+RR aims at bridging academia and industry in the field of rules, and at fostering the cross-fertilization between the different communities focused on the research, development, and applications of rule-based systems. RuleML+RR aims at being the leading conference series for all subjects concerning theoretical advances, novel technologies, and innovative applications about knowledge representation and reasoning with rules.

To leverage these ambitions, RuleML+RR 2020 was organized as part of the virtual event Declarative AI 2020: Rules, Reasoning, Decisions, and Explanations, that was held between June 29 – July 1, 2020. This event was co-organized by SINTEF AS, University of Oslo, and Norwegian University of Science and Technology, under the umbrella of the SIRIUS Centre for Scalable Data Access. With its general topic "Declarative Artificial Intelligence," a core objective of the event was to present the latest advancements in AI and rules, reasoning, decisions, and explanations and their adoption in IT systems. To this end, Declarative AI 2020 brought together co-located events with related interests. In addition to RuleML+RR, this included DecisionCAMP 2020 and the Reasoning Web Summer School (RW 2020).

The RuleML+RR 2020 conference moreover included three subevents:

1. Doctoral Consortium – an initiative to attract and promote student research in rules and reasoning, with the opportunity for students to present and discuss their ideas, and benefit from close contact with leading experts in the field.
2. International Rule Challenge – an initiative to provide competition among work in progress and new visionary ideas concerning innovative rule-oriented applications, aimed at both research and industry.
3. Industry Track – a forum for all sectors of industry and business (as well as public sector) to present, discuss, and propose existing or potential rule-based applications.

The program of the main track of RuleML+RR 2020 included the presentation of seven full research papers and six short papers. These contributions were carefully selected by the Program Committee (PC) from 30 high-quality submissions to the event. Each paper was carefully reviewed and discussed by at least three members of the PC. The technical program was then enriched with the additional contributions from its subevents as well as from DecisionCAMP 2020, a co-located event aimed at practitioners.

At RuleML+RR 2020 and DecisionCAMP 2020, four invited keynotes were presented by experts in the field:

- Dieter Fensel (University of Innsbruck Austria): "Knowledge Graphs: Methodologies, Tools, and Selected Use Cases"
- Eyke Hüllermeier (Paderborn University, Germany): "Multilabel Rule Learning"
- Derek Miers, (Gartner, UK): "What the Real World Needs From Decision Management, Reasoning and AI"
- Arild Waaler (University of Oslo, Norway): "Requirements as Rules"

The chairs sincerely thank the keynote speakers for their contribution to the success of the event. The chairs also thank the PC members and the additional reviewers for their hard work in the careful assessment of the submitted papers. Further thanks go to all authors of contributed papers, in particular, for their efforts in the preparation of their submissions and the camera-ready versions within the established schedule. Sincere thanks are due to the chairs of the Doctoral Consortium, the Rule Challenge, and the Industry Track, and to the chairs of all co-located Declarative AI 2020 events. The chairs finally thank the entire organization team including the publicity, proceedings, and sponsorship chairs, who actively contributed to the organization and the success of the event.

A special thanks goes to all the sponsors of RuleML+RR 2020 and Declarative AI 2020: SINTEF AS, University of Oslo, Norwegian University of Science and Technology, SIRIUS Centre for Scalable Data Access, RuleML Inc., RR Association, and Springer. A special thanks also goes to the publisher, Springer, for their cooperation in editing this volume and publication of these proceedings. We are grateful to the sponsors of the RuleML+RR 2020 Awards: the RR Association sponsored the Best Paper Award and the Best Presentation Award, and Springer sponsored the Best Student Paper Award and the Rule Challenge Award.

June 2020

Víctor Gutiérrez-Basulto
Tomáš Kliegr
Ahmet Soylu
Martin Giese
Dumitru Roman

Organization

Summit Chair (Declarative AI 2020)

Till C. Lech — SINTEF AS, Norway

General Chairs

Dumitru Roman — SINTEF AS, University of Oslo, Norway
Martin Giese — University of Oslo, Norway
Ahmet Soylu — NTNU, SINTEF AS, Norway

Program Chairs

Víctor Gutiérrez Basulto — Cardiff University, UK
Tomáš Kliegr — University of Economics, Prague, Czech Republic

Doctoral Consortium

Paul Fodor — Stony Brook University, USA
Daniela Inclezan — Miami University, USA

Rule Challenge Chairs

Sotiris Moschoyiannis — University of Surrey, UK
Jan Vanthienen — KU Leuven, Belgium

Industry Track Chairs

Francisco Martin-Recuerda — DNVGL, Norway
Nicolay Nikolov — SINTEF AS, Norway
Ioan Toma — Onlim, Austria

Posters and Interactions Chairs

Carlos A. Iglesias — Universidad Politécnica de Madrid, Spain
Dia Trambitas-Miron — UMFST, Romania, and John Snow Labs, USA

Publicity Chair

Jean Christoph Jung — Bremen University, Germany

Proceeding Chairs

Springer Proceedings

Dumitru Roman   SINTEF AS, University of Oslo, Norway

CEUR Proceedings

Sotiris Moschoyiannis   University of Surrey, UK

Program Committee

Pablo Barceló   Pontificia Universidad Católica de Chile, Chile
Petr Berka   University of Economics, Prague, Czech Republic
Leopoldo Bertossi   Adolfo Ibáñez University, Chile, and RelationalAI Inc.,
                               USA
Mehul Bhatt   Örebro University, Sweden
Andreas Billig   Fraunhofer FOKUS, Germany
Pedro Cabalar   University of Corunna, Spain
Diego Calvanese   Free University of Bozen-Bolzano, Italy
Iliano Cervesato   Carnegie Mellon University, USA
Horatiu Cirstea   Loria, France
Ioana-Georgiana Ciuciu   Babes-Bolyai University, Romania
Stefania Costantini   DISIM, University of L'Aquila, Italy
Giovanni De Gasperis   DISIM, University of L'Aquila, Italy
Cristina Feier   University of Bremen, Germany
Paul Fodor   Stony Brook University, USA
Thom Fruehwirth   Ulm University, Germany
Johannes Fürnkranz   Johannes Kepler University Linz, Austria
Víctor Gutiérrez-Basulto   Cardiff University, UK
Martin Holena   Institute of Computer Science, Czech Republic
Ernesto Jimenez-Ruiz   City, University of London, UK
Tomas Kliegr   University of Economics, Prague, Czech Republic
Matthias Klusch   DFKI, Germany
Michael Kohlhase   FAU Erlangen-Nürnberg, Germany
Roman Kontchakov   Birkbeck, University of London, UK
Egor V. Kostylev   University of Oxford, UK
John Krogstie   NTNU, Norway
Jaroslav Kuchař   Czech Technical University in Prague, Czech Republic
Mark Law   Imperial College, UK
Francesca Alessandra Lisi   Università degli Studi di Bari Aldo Moro, Italy
Thomas Lukasiewicz   University of Oxford, UK
Marco Manna   University of Calabria, Italy
Marco Maratea   DIBRIS, University of Genova, Italy
Angelo Montanari   University of Udine, Italy
Sotiris Moschoyiannis   University of Surrey, UK
Filip Murlak   University of Warsaw, Poland

Grzegorz J. Nalepa	AGH University of Science and Technology, Poland
Magdalena Ortiz	Vienna University of Technology, Austria
Matteo Palmonari	University of Milano-Bicocca, Italy
Adrian Paschke	Freie Universität Berlin, Germany
Heiko Paulheim	University of Mannheim, Germany
Rafael Peñaloza	University of Milano-Bicocca, Italy
Andreas Pieris	The University of Edinburgh, UK
Livia Predoiu	Free University of Bozen-Bolzano, Italy
Luca Pulina	University of Sassari, Italy
Jan Rauch	University of Economics, Prague, Czech Republic
Sebastian Rudolph	TU Dresden, Germany
Emanuel Sallinger	University of Oxford, UK
Stefan Schlobach	Vrije Universiteit Amsterdam, The Netherlands
Ute Schmid	University of Bamberg, Germany
Martin G. Skjæveland	University of Oslo, Norway
Giorgos Stoilos	Huawei Technologies, UK
Umberto Straccia	ISTI-CNR, Italy
Theresa Swift	NOVALINKS, Universidade Nova de Lisboa, Portugal
Sergio Tessaris	Free University of Bozen-Bolzano, Italy
Kia Teymourian	Boston University, USA
Dia Trambitas-Miron	UMFST, Romania, and John Snow Labs, USA
Guillermo Vega-Gorgojo	University of Valladolid, Spain
Frank Wolter	The University of Liverpool, UK
Riccardo Zese	ENDIF, University of Ferrara, Italy

Additional Reviewers

Kevin Angele
Luca Geatti Luca
Dag Hovland
Matthew Karlsen
Leszek Kolodziejczyk
Davide Lanti
John Mollas
George Papagiannis
Sascha Rechenberger
Blerina Spahiu
Jürgen Umbrich
Bjørn Marius Von Zernichow

Sponsors

 UiO **:** **University of Oslo**

Keynote Abstracts

Knowledge Graphs: Methodology, Tools and Selected Use Cases

Dieter Fensel

University of Innsbruck, STI Innsbruck, Austria
dieter.fensel@sti2.at

Abstract. Smart speakers such as Alexa and later Google Home introduced Artificial Intelligence (AI) in billions of households making AI an everyday experience. We can now look for information and order products and services without leaving the house or touching a computer. We just talk to a box and this thing will kindly perform the desired tasks for us. These new communication channels define a new challenge for successful eMarketing and eCommerce. Just running a traditional website with many colorful pictures is no longer state of the art. Actually, the web is currently reinventing itself by applying schema.org. Data, content, and services (i.e., resources) become semantically annotated allowing software agents, so-called bots, to search through the web understanding its content. The user nowadays consults their personal bot to find, aggregate, and personalize information, to reserve, book, or buy products and services. In consequence, it becomes increasingly important for providers of information, products, and services to be highly active and visible in these new online channels to ensure their future economic maturity.

In our talk, we discuss methods and tools helping to achieve these goals. The core is the development and application of machine processable (semantic) annotations of online resources as well as their aggregation in large Knowledge Graphs. This enables bots to not only understand a question but be able to answer a question in a knowledgeable way and to organize a useful dialogue. We discuss the process of knowledge generation, hosting, curation, and deployment, focusing on the use of the Knowledge Graph to support dialogue-based interfaces. We also provide an outlook on the broader application context of cyber-physical systems and physical agents.

Dieter Fensel—With the help of Umutcan Şimşek, Kevin Angele, Elwin Huaman, Elias Kärle, Oleksandra Panasiuk, Ioan Toma, Jürgen Umbrich, and Alexander Wahler.

Requirements as Rules

Arild Waaler

University of Oslo, Norway
arild@ifi.uio.no

Abstract. A requirement is a statement to the effect that some function or quality shall be fulfilled. The concept of a requirement, and the associated concept of verification, suggests an interpretation in logical terms, with requirement statements represented as rules and verification conditions expressed in terms of logical consequence. This talk presents an industry-driven initiative to implement this idea for the digitalization of requirement handling along the value chain of the oil and gas industry. I will sketch an OWL-based approach that is simple, standards-based, and scalable – features that are vital for implementation in industry. I will then address shortcomings of the model along with constraints for solutions.

Contents

Invited Paper

Rule-Based Multi-label Classification: Challenges and Opportunities

Eyke Hüllermeier[1]([✉]), Johannes Fürnkranz[2], Eneldo Loza Mencia[3],
Vu-Linh Nguyen[1], and Michael Rapp[3]

[1] Paderborn University, Paderborn, Germany
eyke@upb.de
[2] Johannes Kepler University, Linz, Austria
[3] Technical University Darmstadt, Darmstadt, Germany

Abstract. In the context of multi-label classification (MLC), rule-based learning algorithms have a number of appealing properties that are not, at least not as a whole, shared by other approaches. This includes the potential interpretability of rules, their ability to model (local) label dependencies in a flexible way, and the facile customization of a predictor to different loss functions. In this paper, we present a modular framework for rule-based MLC and discuss related challenges and opportunities for multi-label rule learning.

Keywords: Multi-label classification · Rule learning

1 Introduction

The setting of multi-label classification (MLC), which generalizes standard multi-class classification by relaxing the assumption of mutual exclusiveness of classes, has received a lot of attention in the recent machine learning literature—we refer to (Tsoumakas et al. 2010) and (Zhang and Zhou 2014) for survey articles on this topic. The motivation for MLC originated in the field of text categorization (Hayes and Weinstein 1991; Lewis 1992, 2004), but nowadays multi-label methods are used in applications as diverse as music categorization (Trohidis et al. 2008), semantic scene classification (Boutell et al. 2004), and protein function classification (Elisseeff and Weston 2001).

Rule induction is a well-established approach to supervised learning in general (Fürnkranz et al. 2012; Fürnkranz and Kliegr 2015). Since rules can be understood, analyzed, and qualitatively evaluated by domain experts, rule learning algorithms are often considered as a viable alternative when, in addition to predictive accuracy, criteria such as interpretability, transparency, and explainability are considered important. Ideally, by revealing patterns and regularities in the data, a rule-based theory yields new insights in the application domain.

This motivation applies to MLC as well as to any other machine learning problem. In addition, rule induction exhibits a number of other features that

© Springer Nature Switzerland AG 2020
V. Gutiérrez-Basulto et al. (Eds.): RuleML+RR 2020, LNCS 12173, pp. 3–19, 2020.
https://doi.org/10.1007/978-3-030-57977-7_1

might be useful in the context of MLC. In particular, rules allow for modeling *label dependencies* in a very flexible manner—the goal to improve predictive accuracy by exploiting such dependencies is at the core of research in MLC (Dembczyński et al. 2012), as opposed to the obvious idea of reducing multi-label to binary classification by learning a single binary classifier for each class label separately. Besides, a rule-based approach may well comply with the existence of a wide spectrum of *loss functions* in MLC, because rules can be tailored to different losses in a flexible way. For example, an existing rule-based model could be adapted to a new loss function by modifying the predictions in the head of the rules, without the need for relearning a complete model from scratch.

In this paper, we present elements of a general framework for multi-label rule learning, which is developed by the authors in the course of a joint research project on the topic. In particular, we highlight the potential of a rule-based approach to MLC and the opportunities it offers, but also the challenges it raises from a methodological point of view, especially compared to rule learning for standard classification. In preparation of this discussion, we start with a brief refresher on the two main topics, multi-label classification and rule learning.

2   Multi-label Classification

Let $\mathcal{X}$ denote an instance space, and let $\mathcal{L} = \{\lambda_1, \ldots, \lambda_K\}$ be a finite set of class labels. We assume that an instance $\boldsymbol{x} \in \mathcal{X}$ is (probabilistically) associated with a subset of labels $\Lambda = \Lambda(\boldsymbol{x}) \in 2^{\mathcal{L}}$; this subset is often called the set of *relevant* labels, while the complement $\mathcal{L} \setminus \Lambda(\boldsymbol{x})$ is considered to be irrelevant for $\boldsymbol{x}$. We identify a set Λ of relevant labels with a binary vector $\boldsymbol{y} = (y_1, \ldots, y_K)$, where $y_k = [\![\lambda_k \in \Lambda]\!]$.[1] By $\mathcal{Y} = \{0,1\}^K$ we denote the set of possible labelings.

We assume observations to be realizations of random variables generated independently and identically (i.i.d.) according to a probability measure P on $\mathcal{X} \times \mathcal{Y}$ (with density/mass function p), i.e., an observation $\boldsymbol{y} = (y_1, \ldots, y_K)$ is the realization of a corresponding random vector $\mathbf{Y} = (Y_1, \ldots, Y_K)$. We denote by $p(\mathbf{Y} \mid \boldsymbol{x})$ the conditional distribution of $\mathbf{Y}$ given $\mathbf{X} = \boldsymbol{x}$, and by $p_k(Y_k \mid \boldsymbol{x})$ the corresponding marginal distribution of the k-th label Y_k:

$$p_k(b \mid \boldsymbol{x}) = \sum_{\boldsymbol{y} \in \mathcal{Y}: y_k = b} p(\boldsymbol{y} \mid \boldsymbol{x}). \tag{1}$$

Given training data in the form of a finite set of observations

$$\mathcal{D} = \big\{(\boldsymbol{x}_n, \boldsymbol{y}_n)\big\}_{n=1}^{N} \subset \mathcal{X} \times \mathcal{Y}, \tag{2}$$

drawn independently from $P(\mathbf{X}, \mathbf{Y})$, the goal in MLC is to learn a predictive model that generalizes well beyond these observations, i.e., which yields predictions that minimize the expected risk with respect to a specific loss function. In this regard, we need to clarify what type of predictions are sought and how these predictions are assessed.

---

[1] $[\![\cdot]\!]$ is the indicator function, i.e., $[\![A]\!] = 1$ if the predicate A is true and $= 0$ otherwise.

2.1   Predictive Models in MLC

A multi-label classifier h is a mapping $\mathcal{X} \longrightarrow \mathcal{Y}$ that assigns a (predicted) label subset to each instance $x \in \mathcal{X}$. Thus, the output of a classifier h is a vector

$$h(x) = (h_1(x), \ldots, h_K(x)) \in \{0,1\}^K. \tag{3}$$

Predictions of this kind will also be denoted $\hat{y} = (\hat{y}_1, \ldots, \hat{y}_K)$.

Sometimes, MLC is treated as a *ranking* (instead of a subset selection) problem, in which the labels are sorted according to their degree or probability of relevance. Then, the prediction takes the form of a *scoring function*:

$$s(x) = (s_1(x), s_2(x), \ldots, s_K(x)) \in \mathbb{R}^K. \tag{4}$$

A prediction of that kind encodes a ranking $\pi : [K] \longrightarrow [K]$, such that $\pi(k)$ is the position of label λ_k. This ranking is obtained by sorting the labels λ_k in decreasing order of their scores $s_k(x)$, i.e., $\pi(k) < \pi(j)$ iff $s_k(x) > s_j(x)$.

2.2   MLC Loss Functions

In the literature, various MLC loss functions have been proposed. Commonly used are the subset 0/1 loss ℓ_S and the Hamming loss ℓ_H, which both generalize the standard 0/1 loss for multi-class classification, albeit in very different ways:

$$\ell_S(y, \hat{y}) = [\![y \neq \hat{y}]\!], \tag{5}$$

$$\ell_H(y, \hat{y}) = \frac{1}{K} \sum_{k=1}^{K} [\![y_k \neq \hat{y}_k]\!]. \tag{6}$$

While ℓ_H measures the fraction of incorrectly predicted labels, ℓ_S indiscriminately assigns the maximal error of 1 if one or more of the labels have been incorrectly predicted.

Besides, other performance metrics are often reported in experimental studies. For example, the (instance-wise) F-measure is defined in terms of the harmonic mean of precision and recall, and can be written as follows:

$$F(y, \hat{y}) = \frac{2 \sum_{k=1}^{K} \hat{y}_k y_k}{\sum_{k=1}^{K} \hat{y}_k + \sum_{k=1}^{K} y_k}.$$

The F-measure takes values in the unit interval and can be turned into a loss function by setting $\ell_F(y, \hat{y}) = 1 - F(y, \hat{y})$.

2.3   Label Dependence

The goal of classification algorithms in general is to capture dependencies between input features X_i and the target variable Y. In fact, the prediction of a scoring classifier is often regarded as an approximation of the conditional probability $p(Y = \hat{y} \mid \boldsymbol{x})$, i.e., the probability that $\hat{y}$ is the true label for the given instance $\boldsymbol{x}$. In MLC, dependencies may not only exist between the features X_i and each target, but also between the targets $Y_1, \ldots, Y_K$ themselves. The idea to improve predictive accuracy by capturing such dependencies is a driving force in research on multi-label classification.

One can distinguish between *unconditional* and *conditional independence* of labels (Dembczyński et al. 2012). In the first case, the joint distribution $p(\mathbf{Y})$ in the label space factorizes into the product of the marginals $p(Y_k)$, i.e.,

$$p(\mathbf{Y}) = p(Y_1) \times p(Y_2) \times \cdots \times p(Y_K),$$

whereas in the latter case, the factorization

$$p(\mathbf{Y} \mid \boldsymbol{x}) = p(Y_1 \mid \boldsymbol{x}) \times p(Y_2 \mid \boldsymbol{x}) \times \cdots \times p(Y_K \mid \boldsymbol{x})$$

holds conditioned on $\boldsymbol{x}$, for every instance $\boldsymbol{x}$. In other words, unconditional dependence is a kind of global dependence (for example originating from a hierarchical structure on the labels), whereas conditional dependence is a dependence locally restricted to a single point in the instance space.

It turns out that there is a close connection between label dependence and the *decomposability* of loss functions: A decomposable loss can be reduced to the sum of label-wise losses $\ell_k : \{0, 1\}^2 \longrightarrow \mathbb{R}$, i.e.,

$$\ell(\boldsymbol{y}, \hat{\boldsymbol{y}}) = \sum_{k=1}^{K} \ell_k(y_k, \hat{y}_k), \tag{7}$$

whereas a non-decomposable loss does not permit such a representation. Clearly, ℓ_H in (6) is decomposable, whereas ℓ_S in (5) is not. It can be shown that, to produce optimal predictions $\hat{\boldsymbol{y}} = \boldsymbol{h}(\boldsymbol{x})$ which minimize the expected loss, knowledge about the marginals $p_k(Y_k \mid \boldsymbol{x})$ is sufficient in the case of a decomposable loss, but not in the case of a non-decomposable loss (Dembczyński et al. 2012). Instead, if a loss is non-decomposable, probabilities for larger label subsets are needed, and in the extreme case even the entire distribution $p(\mathbf{Y} \mid \boldsymbol{x})$ (like in the case of ℓ_S). On an algorithmic level, this means that decomposable losses can be tackled by binary relevance learning (i.e., learning one binary classifier for each label individually), whereas non-decomposable losses call for more sophisticated learning methods that are able to take label-dependencies into account.

3 Rule-Based MLC Models

A rule-based classifier in the context of MLC is understood as a collection $\mathcal{R} = \{r_1, \ldots, r_M\}$ of individual rules r_m, where each rule $r_m : H_m \leftarrow B_m$ is characterized by a *head* H_m and a *body* B_m. Roughly speaking, the rule head makes an assertion about the relevance or irrelevance of individual labels λ_k or larger subsets of labels, whereas the rule body specifies conditions under which this assertion is valid. Table 1 shows examples of different types of MLC rules for

Table 1. Examples of different types of rules in a hypothetical newspaper subscription domain (Loza Mencía et al. 2018), which captures a hypothetical relation between customers (characterized by their educational level, sex, marital status, and whether they have children or not) and the types of magazine or newspapers they subscribe to (tabloid, quality newspaper, sports, or fashion magazine). Attribute names in italic denote label attributes, attributes with an overline denote negated conditions.

Head		Body	Example rule
Single-label	Positive	Label-independent	*quality* ← University, Female
	Negative		$\overline{tabloid}$ ← Secondary, Divorced
Single-label	Positive	Mixed representation	*quality* ← *tabloid*, University
	Negative		*quality*← *sports*, *tabloid*, Primary
Single-label	Positive	Label-dependent	*quality* ← *fashion*, *sports*
	Negative		$\overline{sports}$ ← *fashion*
Multi-label	Partial	Label-independent	*quality*, *fashion* ← University, Female
	Complete		*quality*, $\overline{tabloid}$, *fashion*, $\overline{sports}$← University, Female
Multi-label	Partial	Mixed representation	*tabloid*, $\overline{sports}$ ← *fashion*, Children
		Label-dependent	*fashion*, $\overline{sports}$ ← *quality*, *tabloid*

a hypothetical newspaper subscription domain. The rule body typically appears in the form of a logical predicate that specifies conditions on a query instance x, for example a logical conjunction of restrictions on some of the features. The concrete type of restriction naturally depends on the type of feature (e.g., categorical, numerical), though equality and inequality constraints are often used.

Interestingly, in the context of MLC, one may think of allowing a rule to specify conditions on instance features and *labels* simultaneously. This is a natural and very appealing way to capture label dependencies. We call rules of that kind *mixed representation rules*, because they mix conditions on features with conditions on class labels (cf. Table 1). Stated differently, they use labels in two different roles: as target variables to be predicted and as auxiliary input features to accomplish such predictions (for some example rules, we refer to Table 1 in Sect. 4.6). Note that this is very much in line with the idea of classifier chains (Read et al. 2011) as well as the generalizations of binary relevance learning proposed by Montañés et al. (2014). In passing, we also note that these approaches are not uncritical from a theoretical point of view, because the auxiliary input features are only available for training. At prediction time, they constitute missing values that have to be imputed by corresponding estimates, which may cause attribute noise and deteriorate predictive accuracy (Senge et al. 2013).

As for the rule head, the following distinctions can be made.

– *Partial versus complete*: A head H_m may predict relevancy or irrelevancy for every label or only for a subset of labels. In the first case, we call the head (or the rule) complete. In the second case, where the rule only predicts on some of the labels but abstains on the others, we speak about a partial rule. In the special—but not uncommon—case of rules predicting on exactly one label, we refer to them as single-label rules.

– *Binary versus soft*: Information might be given in the form of deterministic (e.g., $\hat{y}_k = 1$) or probabilistic predictions (e.g., $p(y_k = 1) = 0.7$). Besides, other types of representations are of course conceivable. For example, instead of using standard probability, uncertainty about a prediction could be specified in terms of generalized formalisms, such as possibility or imprecise probability distributions, or simply in terms of certain statistics on label distributions (e.g., the number of positive and negative examples for each label). We make a broad distinction between binary rules (with deterministic predictions) and "soft" rules (with non-deterministic predictions).

– *Interactive versus non-interactive*: The information may refer to individual labels (in which case the rule could be split into several rules, one for each label, and all with the same body) or capture interaction between labels. For example, in the case of probabilistic predictions, instead of specifying one distribution per label, a *joint* distribution (different from the product of the corresponding marginal distributions) could be specified over a subset or even the entire set of labels.

Eventually, a rule set $\mathcal{R}$ shall be associated with a predictive model, either a classifier $h_{\mathcal{R}}$ of the form (3) or a scoring function $s_{\mathcal{R}}$ of the form (4). Obviously, this requires a suitable interpretation of $\mathcal{R}$. In Sect. 4.3, we discuss two possible strategies, namely to order $\mathcal{R}$ into a rule list, which is processed sequentially until a final prediction is obtained, or to combine the (soft) predictions of the individual rules in the set into an overall predictions.

4   Learning Rule-Based MLC Models

Learning multi-label rules and rule-based models comes with a number of challenges that are specific to this problem. In the following, we briefly review important problems and some proposed solutions, focusing on the differences to conventional rule learning.

4.1   Rule Evaluation

At the core of essentially all rule learning methods is the search for "good" (candidate) rules $r_m : H_m \leftarrow B_m$, which are then combined into a global model (cf. Sect. 4.3). But what qualifies a rule as being good?

In conventional (single-target) classification, individual rules are typically assessed according to their *coverage* and *precision*: Ideally, a rule is general in the sense of covering a large part of the instance space and, correspondingly, many training examples. At the same time, the rule allows for making accurate predictions, i.e., most of the instances it covers belong to the same class (which then defines the head of the rule). Obviously, these two criteria tend to be in conflict with each other. Evaluation measures commonly used as search heuristics in this regard, such as the m-estimate or the F-measure, quantify both aspects and combine them into a single (compromise) metric (Fürnkranz and Flach 2005).

	y_1	y_2	y_3	y_4	y_5	y_6	y_7	y_8	y_9
x_1	0	0	1	0	1	0	0	0	0
x_2	1	0	0	0	0	0	0	0	0
x_3	1	0	0	0	0	1	0	0	1
x_4	1	1	1	1	0	0	0	0	0
x_5	1	1	0	0	0	1	1	0	0
x_6	1	0	0	0	0	0	0	0	1
x_7	0	0	1	0	1	0	1	1	0
H_m	1	$\perp$	0	$\perp$	0	$\perp$	0	0	$\perp$

Fig. 1. Illustration of a rule which covers instances x_3, x_4, x_5, and x_6 (*instance coverage*) and for these makes predictions for labels y_1, y_3, y_5, y_7, and y_8 (*label coverage*), as indicated by the gray background. A "good" rule has a high coverage (gray region) while making only a few mistakes (indicated by red boxes). (Color figure online)

In the context of MLC, a third criterion comes into play, because while rules in the standard, multi-class setting always predict one particular class value or label (i.e., the head of a rule is always λ_k or, equivalently, $y_k = 1$ for some k), the head of a multi-label rule can predict the relevance of a different number of labels. Complete rules predict the relevance ($y_k = 1$) or irrelevance ($y_k = 0$) for all K labels. In general, however, the head may "cover" only a subset of labels, i.e., it predicts positive or negative for some of the labels while making no prediction on others (which we denote as $y_k = \perp$). To distinguish the two types of coverage, we denote the examples covered by the rule body as *instance coverage* and the labels covered by the rule head as *label coverage*. As sketched in Fig. 1, the goal is then to find a rule that correctly covers many instances and many labels, i.e., that covers a large area in this instance/label matrix.

As an aside, note that negative predictions ($y_k = 0$) are not very common in conventional rule learning, where a rule head is normally positive; in other words, a rule body normally specifies conditions under which a class is present, not absent. Then, however, no distinction between predicting negative and "not knowing" is possible: An instance that is not predicted positive, as it is not covered by any rule, is automatically predicted negative. In the context of MLC, however, such a distinction is arguably important, and the learner should be allowed to (partially) "abstain": Having to deal with many label simultaneously, it might be more certain on some of them and less on others.

The specification of a search heuristic that quantifies and combines instance coverage, label coverage, and precision further complicates the evaluation compared to conventional classification and calls for another compromise, namely a trade-off between precise predictions on a few labels and presumably less precise predictions on many labels. For example, Klein et al. (2019) extend a standard rule evaluation measure multiplying it with a factor $\rho(|H_m|)$, where $|H_m|$ is the length of the head (the number of predicted labels) and ρ a monotonically increasing function (or a function peaked at a certain value, thereby encouraging rule heads of a specific length).

As already said, the local nature of rules has a number of advantages, but it may also cause difficulties in the context of MLC, especially due to the highly imbalanced distribution of positive and negative labels, which is a characteristic property of MLC. In many cases, only a tiny fraction of the labels is relevant (positive), while the majority is irrelevant (negative). In general, this makes it difficult to find a good rule with positive predictions in its head. On the contrary, the learner has a strong incentive to make negative predictions, especially for loss functions such as Hamming. For example, since most labels will be irrelevant, even the default rule (with empty body) predicting all labels to be always negative will often have a very low Hamming loss. In fact, with a high precision and an even higher coverage (both in the instance and label space), this rule will have a strong evaluation. The coverage of a rule with positive predictions will necessarily be much smaller and probably lead to a worse evaluation, even with a slightly better precision. Evaluation measures for multi-label rules should be aware of this problem and avoid a strong bias in favor of negative rules.

Indeed, while negative predictions might be favored by Hamming loss, they will yield poor predictions in terms of other loss functions, such as subset 0/1. In fact, a possible disadvantage of general evaluation measures and rule learning heuristics is that they are not necessarily adapted to an underlying multi-label loss ℓ to be minimized—for example, Rapp et al. (2019) show that, depending on the loss ℓ, the coverage and precision of single-label rules should be weighed differently. Optimizing precision on individual labels is in line with minimizing the Hamming loss, however, this correspondence will not necessarily hold for other loss functions, especially non-decomposable losses. Therefore, another approach to rule evaluation is to consider its (empirical) performance on the training data in terms of the loss ℓ, i.e., the smallest loss that can be achieved on the instance/label region covered by the rule. Constructing an optimal predictor, i.e., finding a loss minimizing head for a given rule body, may be computationally challenging though (as discussed in Sect. 4.2). A flexible way to directly optimize for a broad class of multi-label losses is gradient boosting, which was successfully used in decision tree learning. Recently, it was adapted to learning ensembles of boosted multi-label rules (BOOMER), including the ability to optimize for decomposable and non-decomposable losses (Rapp et al. 2020).

4.2   Rule Generation

Learning a rule-based model often starts with generating a relatively large set of candidate rules, which substantially exceeds the size of the model $\mathcal{R}$ eventually produced. As explained above, different types of rules are conceivable (partial/complete, binary/soft, interactive/non-interactive, etc.) in this regard.

Search Space. Like in traditional rule learning, the search space of possible bodies B_m can be explored in a systematic way in order to overcome the exponential size, e.g., in a top-down manner. However, in MLC, we face the additional difficulty that both the body and the head of a rule can be refined, and that the space of possible heads H_m also grows exponentially with the number of available labels. To reduce the computational complexity of a search for multi-label heads, certain properties of commonly used multi-label evaluation measures—namely anti-monotonicity and decomposability—can be exploited for pruning the search space (Rapp et al. 2018). Although this allows for efficiently selecting appropriate multi-label heads in theory, experiments have revealed that most of the rules learned on real data sets have heads with a single label. The reason is that these measures neglect the additional quality dimension of rules introduced by the occurrence of multiple labels. More precisely, a high label coverage is not especially rewarded. A better trade-off between label coverage and precision can be achieved, for instance, by explicitly introducing a bias towards larger heads (Klein et al. 2019). However, a more natural approach would be to incorporate the trade-off directly into the measure, as discussed in Sect. 4.1.

Search Strategies. The space of possible multi-label rules r_m can be searched in different ways. The most obvious and commonly used choice is a general-to-specific hill climbing search that greedily refines the current rule in order to approach the best rule. Alternatively, more costly search techniques such as evolutionary algorithms can be employed for finding strong multi-label classification rules (Allamanis et al. 2013; Arunadevi and Rajamani 2011; Ávila et al. 2010).

Exhaustive search guarantees to find the optimal, loss-minimizing rule in the search space, but is usually intractable. A possible compromise is to adapt association rule discovery, which finds all rules in a search space constrained by minimum support and minimum confidence constraints, for finding multi-label rules. To this end, one can use the union of labels and features as the basic itemset, discover all frequent itemsets, and derive all association rules with minimum confidence from these frequent itemsets, as most association rule discovery algorithms do. The only modification is that only rules with labels in the head are allowed, whereas potential rules with features in the head will be disregarded. Such approaches are, e.g., followed by Thabtah et al. (2006) and Bosc et al. (2016). Thabtah et al. (2004) and similarly Li et al. (2008) first induce only single-label association rules, which are then merged to create multi-label rules. Veloso et al. (2007) have proposed a lazy algorithm, which finds rules from the neighborhood of a test instance during prediction. Some works have focused on using association rule discovery in the label space for discovering global dependencies, with the idea of using them for improving the predictions of a conventional MLC classifier (Park and Fürnkranz 2008; Charte et al. 2014).

4.3   Model Formation

Constructing a rule-based MLC model typically involves the *selection* of a suitable subset of rules $\mathcal{R}$ and their *aggregation* into a classifier $h_{\mathcal{R}}$ or a ranker $s_{\mathcal{R}}$. The aggregation essentially addresses the question of how to combine the predictions of individual rules $r_m(x)$ into an overall prediction (cf. Sect. 4.5). In this regard, it is worth mentioning that the type of prediction of the final classifier is not necessarily the same as the predictions of the individual rules; for example, the former might be binary although the latter are soft.

In inductive rule learning, two types of models are commonly used: ordered *rule lists* (also known as decision lists) and *rule sets*. Both can be learned with various strategies, but the former are typically learned using a sequential covering strategy whereas the latter are often learned by ensemble algorithms. In the following, we will briefly review both approaches in the context of multi-label rule learning.

Learning Rule Lists. In the single-label case, rule lists are typically learned one rule at a time, removing all covered examples after each rule has been learned. Although it may seem quite straightforward, an adaptation of this simple covering or separate-and-conquer learning strategy (Fürnkranz 1999) to the multi-label case is not entirely trivial. In fact, in the multi-label case, this strategy can only be used if rules with complete heads are learned, which corresponds to learning a rule list with the label powerset strategy, i.e., where each subset of the labels that occurs in the training data is tackled as a separate meta-class. This, however, comes with the disadvantage of losing flexibility and the possibility of tailoring rules to individual labels. Indeed, the examples of a specific class often share some common properties and could be covered by a single rule. Additional labels could be added by additional partial-head rules. For this case, however, the covering strategy needs to be generalized.

A possible adaptation of this strategy is to remove all covered *labels* from these examples (the gray region in Fig. 1), so that each example remains in the training set until all of its labels are covered by at least one rule. However, in such an approach, it is difficult to model label dependencies. As a remedy, Loza Mencía and Janssen (2016) proposed a method that learns single-head rules by a layer-wise binary relevance algorithm, where the rules in each layer can use the labels that have been predicted in previous layers. Nevertheless, this method still has its shortcomings, most notably the restriction to single-label rules.

Learning Rule Sets. For learning rule sets, ideas from ensemble learning, in particular from stagewise additive modeling or boosting, have previously been adapted to single-label rule learning (see, e.g., (Dembczynski et al. 2010)). Along these lines is BOOMER (cf. Sect. 4.2), a multi-label variant of this family of rule learning algorithms, which provides a general framework for finding rule sets that optimize any multi-label loss functions. Following the stagewise procedure commonly used in gradient boosting, a rule set is built incrementally by adding partial or complete rules. For prediction, the "soft" information provided in the heads of the rules are aggregated using a weighted voting procedure that is tailored to the loss function at hand. BOOMER's versatility has been demonstrated on both decomposable and non-decomposable loss functions.

Learning rule sets in this way avoids many of the problems caused by rule lists, because the rules can be learned and evaluated in isolation, independently of the others. Then, however, multiple rules may cover a query instance at prediction time. In such cases, a suitable aggregation strategy for multi-label predictions needs to be found, which will be discussed in Sect. 4.5.

4.4   Partial Abstention

As already discussed in Sect. 4.1, a single MLC rule r_m is not necessarily obliged to predict on all labels, i.e., not all labels are necessarily covered by the rule head H_m. In other words, a rule is allowed to *abstain* on a certain subset of labels, and the choice—in particular the size—of this subset is (indirectly) controlled by the rule evaluation measure, which reflects a preference in favor of a higher label coverage.

The idea of (partial) abstention is actually more general and connected to standard (multi-class) classification with a reject option (Cortes et al. 2016; Franc and Prusa 2019). The basic notion is to make predictions more *reliable* by allowing the learner to restrict to those labels on which it feels sufficiently confident. In rule-based MLC, the possibility to abstain is of course not restricted to single rules, but may also apply to the model as a whole, i.e., abstention might also be allowed for the overall prediction $h_{\mathcal{R}}(x)$. The following cases could be distinguished:

- Abstention is neither allowed for individual rules nor the overall prediction.
- Abstention is allowed for individual rules, but not for the overall prediction. In this case, abstention cannot be decided for each rule independently, because each label must be covered by at least one rule.
- Abstention is not allowed for individual rules but for the overall prediction. In this case, given a query x, the former could be used to produce an estimation of $p(\cdot \mid x)$, and the overall prediction $h_{\mathcal{R}}(x)$ can then be obtained via (10).
- Abstention is allowed for both individual rules and the overall prediction.

In spite of being an interesting extension of the standard setting, there is surprisingly little work on abstention in multi-label classification so far—the first we are aware of is (Pillai et al. 2013), which considers a specific variant of the problem with a focus on the F-measure as a performance metric. Nguyen and Hüllermeier (2020) introduce a generalized setting of MLC with abstention, in which the classifier is allowed to produce partial predictions of the form

$$\hat{y} = h(x) \in \mathcal{Y}_{pa} = \{0, \bot, 1\}^K, \tag{8}$$

where $\hat{y}_i = \bot$ indicates an abstention on the label λ_i. As already said, the basic idea is to let the learner abstain on those labels on which it feels uncertain. On the other side, complete predictions are of course preferred to less complete ones. Consequently, there is a conflict between the objectives of reliability and completeness. To capture this aspect, Nguyen and Hüllermeier (2020) introduce a generalized class of loss functions

$$L : \mathcal{Y} \times \mathcal{Y}_{pa} \longrightarrow \mathbb{R}_+, \tag{9}$$

which compare a partial prediction $\hat{y}$ with a ground-truth labeling y. This is essentially done by applying a standard MLC loss ℓ to the predicted part of the labeling and adding a *penalty* for abstention, where the latter depends on the number of labels on which the learner abstains. Given such a loss, and assuming a probabilistic prediction for a query instance $\boldsymbol{x}$, i.e., a probability $p(\cdot \mid \boldsymbol{x})$ on the set of labelings (or at least an estimation thereof), an optimal prediction can be determined by expected loss minimization, i.e., by finding

$$h(\boldsymbol{x}) = \hat{\boldsymbol{y}} \in \operatorname*{argmin}_{\hat{\boldsymbol{y}} \in \mathcal{Y}_{pa}} \sum_{\boldsymbol{y} \in \mathcal{Y}} L(\boldsymbol{y}, \hat{\boldsymbol{y}}) \cdot p(\boldsymbol{y} \mid \boldsymbol{x}). \tag{10}$$

Thus, finding an optimal partial prediction, for example the head of a single rule, eventually comes down to solving an optimization problem. The difficulty of this problem depends on several choices, most notably the underlying MLC loss ℓ and its extension L. In any case, this approach based on expected generalized loss minimization allows for controlling the learner's propensity for abstention by means of the penalty: Increasing the penalty will increase the expected loss of a more partial compared to a less partial prediction, and therefore lead to less abstention.

4.5   Aggregation of Predictions

An important problem when dealing with rule sets is the aggregation or combination of the predictions $r_m(\boldsymbol{x})$ produced by different rules into an overall prediction $h_{\mathcal{R}}(\boldsymbol{x})$. In fact, a given query $\boldsymbol{x} \in \mathcal{X}$ will normally be covered by more than a single rule. The need for aggregation becomes especially apparent in the case of ensemble learning, i.e., where not only a single predictor $h_{\mathcal{R}}$ but a set of multi-label classifiers $h_1, \ldots, h_M$ his considered. Note that the distinction between these two cases becomes rather blurry in the case of learning rule sets, because each single rule r_m in a set $\mathcal{R}$ can also be seen as an individual predictor h_m, at least a partial predictor or a predictor that abstains on queries not covered by its rule body.

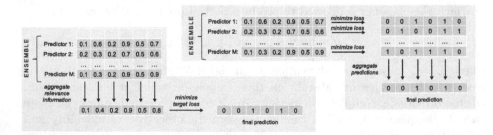

Fig. 2. Illustration of the "combine then predict" (left) and "predict then combine" (right) approaches for the case where relevance information consists of marginal probabilities.

In any case, the aggregation of predictions in MLC is arguably more challenging and less straightforward than in single-target prediction, where simple techniques such as majority voting for classification and averaging for regression are commonly used. In the case of MLC, predictions $\hat{\boldsymbol{y}}_1, \ldots, \hat{\boldsymbol{y}}_M$ are elements of $\mathcal{Y}$, or perhaps $\mathcal{Y}_{pa}$ if abstention is allowed, and hence of a more complex nature. Moreover, it is clear that a single aggregation cannot be assumed to be optimal for different MLC loss functions. Instead, different losses ℓ will call for different types of aggregation.

Nguyen et al. (2020) tackle the problem of aggregation from the general perspective of ensemble learning. More specifically, they introduce a formal framework of ensemble multi-label classification, in which two principal approaches are distinguished (cf. Fig. 2):

- In "predict then combine" (PTC), the ensemble members first make (loss minimizing) predictions $\hat{\boldsymbol{y}}_1, \ldots, \hat{\boldsymbol{y}}_M \in \mathcal{Y}$, which are subsequently combined into an overall prediction $\boldsymbol{y}$.
- In "combine then predict" (CTP), (label) *relevance information* produced by the individual ensemble members is aggregated first, and a final prediction is then derived from this aggregation afterward. An example of relevance information is a probabilistic prediction, i.e., (estimated) marginal probabilities $\hat{\boldsymbol{p}} = (\hat{p}_1, \ldots, \hat{p}_K) \in [0,1]^K$ for the relevance of the different labels, or, more generally, real-valued scores $\hat{\boldsymbol{s}} = (\hat{s}_1, \ldots, \hat{s}_K) \in \mathbb{R}^K$ quantifying the evidence in favor or against the relevance of a label. Such kind of information is produced (at least as an intermediate) step by most multi-label learners.

While both approaches generalize (label-wise) voting techniques commonly used for multi-label ensembles (Gharroudi 2017; Madjarov et al. 2012; Shi et al. 2011; Tsoumakas 2007), they allow for explicitly taking the target performance measure (MLC loss function) into account. Therefore, concrete instantiations of CTP and PTC can be tailored to concrete loss functions ℓ. Experimentally, we show that standard voting techniques are indeed outperformed by suitable instantiations of CTP and PTC, and provide some evidence that CTP performs well for decomposable loss functions, whereas PTC is the better choice for non-decomposable losses (Nguyen et al. 2020).

4.6   Interpretability

Rule learning algorithms are typically employed when one is not only interested in accurate predictions but also requires an interpretable theory that can be understood, analyzed, and qualitatively evaluated by domain experts. Ideally, by revealing the patterns and regularities that are implicitly captured in the data, a rule-based theory yields new insights in the application domain. Arguably, inductive rule learning is a promising approach for solving MLC problems in an interpretable way (Loza Mencía et al. 2018). In particular, rules provide an interpretable model for mapping inputs to outputs, and allow for tightly integrating input variables and labels into coherent comprehensible theories.

As an illustration, recall the toy domain introduced by Loza Mencía et al. (2018), which captures a hypothetical relation between customers and the types of magazine or newspapers they subscribe to. Table 1 illustrates various types of rules which mix input features and labels in a seamless manner. Conventional rules would map input features to the labels, such as a rule suggesting that university-educated female readers tend to subscribe to a fashion magazine and a quality newspaper (line 4). However, in addition, global dependencies between labels can be explicitly modeled and expressed in the form of rules such as that subscribers to a fashion magazine do not subscribe to a sports magazine (line 3). Mixed-representation rules can also capture local dependencies, which include regular input features as a local context in which a label dependency holds, such as that readers with a university education, who subscribe to a tabloid, also subscribe to a quality newspaper (line 2). Such rules mix labels and features, and are directly interpretable and comprehensible for humans. Even if complex and long rules are generated, the implication between labels can be easily grasped by focusing on the part of the rules that actually considers the labels. Hence, in contrast to many other types of models that capture label dependencies implicitly, such dependencies can be analyzed and interpreted more directly.

Nevertheless, surprisingly little attention has been devoted to the aspect of interpretability in multi-label learning in general, and in multi-label rule learning in particular. Loza Mencía et al. (2018) present learned rules of several types for various real-world benchmark datasets. While these examples nicely illustrate the potential of rule-based explanations in multi-label domains, it also became clear that learning powerful general rules, which mix multiple labels with input features, is still a challenging and largely unsolved problem.

We note in passing that, while rules are commonly perceived to be more comprehensible than other types of representations and hypothesis languages in machine learning, the topic of learning *interpretable* rules is still not very well explored either (Freitas 2014). For example, in many studies, the comprehensibility of learned rules is assumed to be negatively correlated with their complexity, a point of view that has been questioned more recently (Allahyari and Lavesson 2011; Fürnkranz et al. 2020).

In any case, we believe that mixed-dependency rules like those sketched above, which combine input data and labels in an explicit way, have a strong potential for increasing the interpretability of multi-label learning. A particularly promising direction is to use rule-based local models for explaining powerful yet opaque multi-label classifiers. While several such approaches have been proposed recently, such as LIME (Ribeiro et al. 2016) and SHAP (Lundberg and Lee 2017), or LORE (Guidotti et al. 2018) as a variant specifically tailored to learning local rule-based explanations, we are not aware of any work that tries to adapt these frameworks to the multi-label case.

5   Conclusion

In this paper, we have given an overview of the state of the art in multi-label rule learning, specifically focusing on an ongoing research project of the authors. The main goal of this project it to elaborate on the potential of rule learning in the context of MLC, and to develop a generic framework for constructing rule-based multi-label algorithms in a flexible manner. Our interim results so far are rather promising, although a couple of challenging problems still remain to be solved.

Acknowledgements. This work was supported by the German Research Foundation (DFG) under grant no. 400845550.

References

Allahyari, H., Lavesson, N.: User-oriented assessment of classification model understandability. In: Proceedings of 11th Scandinavian Conference on Artificial Intelligence (SCAI), pp. 11–19. IOS Press (2011)

Allamanis, M., Tzima, F.A., Mitkas, P.A.: Effective rule-based multi-label classification with learning classifier systems. In: Tomassini, M., Antonioni, A., Daolio, F., Buesser, P. (eds.) ICANNGA 2013. LNCS, vol. 7824, pp. 466–476. Springer, Heidelberg (2013). https://doi.org/10.1007/978-3-642-37213-1_48

Arunadevi, J., Rajamani, V.: An evolutionary multi label classification using associative rule mining. Int. J. Soft Comput. **6**, 20–25 (2011)

Ávila-Jiménez, J.L., Gibaja, E., Ventura, S.: Evolving multi-label classification rules with gene expression programming: a preliminary study. In: Corchado, E., Graña Romay, M., Manhaes Savio, A. (eds.) HAIS 2010. LNCS (LNAI), vol. 6077, pp. 9–16. Springer, Heidelberg (2010). https://doi.org/10.1007/978-3-642-13803-4_2

Bosc, G., et al.: Local subgroup discovery for eliciting and understanding new structure-odor relationships. In: Calders, T., Ceci, M., Malerba, D. (eds.) DS 2016. LNCS (LNAI), vol. 9956, pp. 19–34. Springer, Cham (2016). https://doi.org/10.1007/978-3-319-46307-0_2

Boutell, M.R., Luo, J., Shen, X., Brown, C.M.C.M.: Learning multi-label scene classification. Pattern Recogn. **37**(9), 1757–1771 (2004)

Charte, F., Rivera, A.J., del Jesús, M.J., Herrera, F.: LI-MLC: a label inference methodology for addressing high dimensionality in the label space for multilabel classification. IEEE Trans. Neural Netw. Learn. Syst. **25**(10), 1842–1854 (2014)

Cortes, C., DeSalvo, G., Mohri, M.: Learning with rejection. In: Ortner, R., Simon, H.U., Zilles, S. (eds.) ALT 2016. LNCS (LNAI), vol. 9925, pp. 67–82. Springer, Cham (2016). https://doi.org/10.1007/978-3-319-46379-7_5

Dembczynski, K., Kotlowski, W., Slowinski, R.: ENDER: a statistical framework for boosting decision rules. Data Min. Knowl. Disc. **21**(1), 52–90 (2010)

Dembczyński, K., Waegeman, W., Cheng, W., Hüllermeier, E.: On label dependence and loss minimization in multi-label classification. Mach. Learn. **88**(1–2), 5–45 (2012)

Elisseeff, A., Weston, J.: A kernel method for multi-labelled classification. In: Dietterich, T.G., Becker, S., Ghahramani, Z. (eds.) Advances in Neural Information Processing Systems (NeurIPS), vol. 14, pp. 681–687. MIT Press (2001)

Franc, V., Prusa, D.: On discriminative learning of prediction uncertainty. In: Proceedings of 36th International Conference on Machine Learning (ICML), pp. 1963–1971 (2019)

Freitas, A.A.: Comprehensible classification models: a position paper. SIGKDD Explor. **15**(1), 1–10 (2014)

Fürnkranz, J.: Separate-and-conquer rule learning. Artif. Intell. Rev. **13**(1), 3–54 (1999)

Fürnkranz, J., Flach, P.A.: ROC 'n' rule learning - towards a better understanding of covering algorithms. Mach. Learn. **58**(1), 39–77 (2005)

Fürnkranz, J., Gamberger, D., Lavrač, N.: Foundations of Rule Learning. Springer, Heidelberg (2012). https://doi.org/10.1007/978-3-540-75197-7

Fürnkranz, J., Kliegr, T.: A brief overview of rule learning. In: Bassiliades, N., Gottlob, G., Sadri, F., Paschke, A., Roman, D. (eds.) RuleML 2015. LNCS, vol. 9202, pp. 54–69. Springer, Cham (2015). https://doi.org/10.1007/978-3-319-21542-6_4

Fürnkranz, J., Kliegr, T., Paulheim, H.: On cognitive preferences and the plausibility of rule-based models. Mach. Learn. **109**(4), 853–898 (2020)

Gharroudi, O.: Ensemble multi-label learning in supervised and semi-supervised settings. Ph.D. thesis, Université de Lyon (2017)

Guidotti, R., Monreale, A., Ruggieri, S., Pedreschi, D., Turini, F., Giannotti, F.: Local rule-based explanations of black box decision systems. arXiv:1805.10820 (2018)

Hayes, P.J., Weinstein, S.P.: CONSTRUE/TIS: a system for content-based indexing of a database of news stories. In: Rappaport, A.T., Smith, R.G. (eds.) Proceedings of 2nd Conference on Innovative Applications of Artificial Intelligence (IAAI 1990), Washington, DC, USA, pp. 49–64. AAAI Press (1991)

Klein, Y., Rapp, M., Loza Mencía, E.: Efficient discovery of expressive multi-label rules using relaxed pruning. In: Kralj Novak, P., Šmuc, T., Džeroski, S. (eds.) DS 2019. LNCS (LNAI), vol. 11828, pp. 367–382. Springer, Cham (2019). https://doi.org/10.1007/978-3-030-33778-0_28

Lewis, D.D.: An evaluation of phrasal and clustered representations on a text categorization task. In: Proceedings of 15th Annual International Conference on Research and Development in Information Retrieval (SIGIR), pp. 37–50 (1992)

Lewis, D.D.: Reuters-21578 text categorization test collection distribution 1.0. README file (V 1.3), May 2004

Li, B., Li, H., Wu, M., Li, P.: Multi-label classification based on association rules with application to scene classification. In: Proceedings of 9th International Conference for Young Computer Scientists (ICYCS), pp. 36–41. IEEE (2008)

Mencía, E.L., Fürnkranz, J., Hüllermeier, E., Rapp, M.: Learning interpretable rules for multi-label classification. In: Escalante, H.J., et al. (eds.) Explainable and Interpretable Models in Computer Vision and Machine Learning. TSSCML, pp. 81–113. Springer, Cham (2018). https://doi.org/10.1007/978-3-319-98131-4_4

Loza Mencía, E., Janssen, F.: Learning rules for multi-label classification: a stacking and a separate-and-conquer approach. Mach. Learn. **105**(1), 77–126 (2016)

Lundberg, S.M., Lee, S.: A unified approach to interpreting model predictions. In: Guyon, I., et al. (eds.) Advances in Neural Information Processing Systems, Long Beach, CA, USA, vol. 30, pp. 4765–4774 (2017)

Madjarov, G., Kocev, D., Gjorgjevikj, D., Džeroski, S.: An extensive experimental comparison of methods for multi-label learning. Pattern Recogn. **45**(9), 3084–3104 (2012)

Montañés, E., Senge, R., Barranquero, J., Quevedo, J.R., del Coz, J.J., Hüllermeier, E.: Dependent binary relevance models for multi-label classification. Pattern Recogn. **47**(3), 1494–1508 (2014)

Nguyen, V., Hüllermeier, E., Rapp, M., Mencía, E.L., Fürnkranz, J.: On aggregation in ensembles of multilabel classifiers. CoRR abs/2006.11916 (2020). http://arxiv.org/abs/2006.11916

Nguyen, V.L., Hüllermeier, E.: Reliable multi-label classification: prediction with partial abstention. In: Proceedings of the Thirty-Fourth AAAI Conference on Artificial Intelligence (AAAI), pp. 5264–5271 (2020)

Park, S.H., Fürnkranz, J.: Multi-label classification with label constraints. In: Hüllermeier, E., Fürnkranz, J. (eds.) Proceedings of ECML-PKDD-08 Workshop on Preference Learning (PL 2008), Antwerp, Belgium, pp. 157–171 (2008)

Pillai, I., Fumera, G., Roli, F.: Multi-label classification with a reject option. Pattern Recogn. **46**(8), 2256–2266 (2013)

Rapp, M., Loza Mencía, E., Fürnkranz, J.: Exploiting anti-monotonicity of multi-label evaluation measures for inducing multi-label rules. In: Phung, D., Tseng, V.S., Webb, G.I., Ho, B., Ganji, M., Rashidi, L. (eds.) PAKDD 2018. LNCS (LNAI), vol. 10937, pp. 29–42. Springer, Cham (2018). https://doi.org/10.1007/978-3-319-93034-3_3

Rapp, M., Loza Mencía, E., Fürnkranz, J.: On the trade-off between consistency and coverage in multi-label rule learning heuristics. In: Kralj Novak, P., Šmuc, T., Džeroski, S. (eds.) DS 2019. LNCS (LNAI), vol. 11828, pp. 96–111. Springer, Cham (2019). https://doi.org/10.1007/978-3-030-33778-0_9

Rapp, M., Loza Mencía, E., Fürnkranz, J., Nguyen, V.L., Hüllermeier, E.: Learning gradient boosted multi-label classification rules. In: Proceedings of European Conference on Machine Learning and Knowledge Discovery in Databases (ECML/PKDD). Springer (2020)

Read, J., Pfahringer, B., Holmes, G., Frank, E.: Classifier chains for multi-label classification. Mach. Learn. **85**(3), 333–359 (2011)

Ribeiro, M.T., Singh, S., Guestrin, C.: "Why should I trust you?": explaining the predictions of any classifier. In: Krishnapuram, B., Shah, M., Smola, A.J., Aggarwal, C.C., Shen, D., Rastogi, R. (eds.) Proceedings of 22nd International Conference on Knowledge Discovery and Data Mining (KDD), pp. 1135–1144. ACM (2016)

Senge, R., del Coz, J.J., Hüllermeier, E.: Rectifying classifier chains for multi-label classification. In: Henrich, A., Sperker, H. (eds.) Proc. Lernen, Wissen & Adaptivität (LWA), pp. 151–158. Bamberg, Germany (2013)

Shi, C., Kong, X., Yu, P.S., Wang, B.: Multi-label ensemble learning. In: Gunopulos, D., Hofmann, T., Malerba, D., Vazirgiannis, M. (eds.) ECML PKDD 2011. LNCS (LNAI), vol. 6913, pp. 223–239. Springer, Heidelberg (2011). https://doi.org/10.1007/978-3-642-23808-6_15

Thabtah, F.A., Cowling, P.I., Peng, Y.: MMAC: a new multi-class, multi-label associative classification approach. In: Proceedings of 4th International Conference on Data Mining (ICDM), pp. 217–224. IEEE (2004)

Thabtah, F.A., Cowling, P.I., Peng, Y.: Multiple labels associative classification. Knowl. Inf. Syst. **9**(1), 109–129 (2006)

Trohidis, K., Tsoumakas, G., Kalliris, G., Vlahavas, I.P.: Multilabel classification of music into emotions. In: Proceedings of 9th International Conference on Music Information Retrieval (ISMIR), pp. 325–330 (2008)

Tsoumakas, G., Vlahavas, I.: Random k-labelsets: an ensemble method for multilabel classification. In: Kok, J.N., Koronacki, J., Mantaras, R.L., Matwin, S., Mladenič, D., Skowron, A. (eds.) ECML 2007. LNCS (LNAI), vol. 4701, pp. 406–417. Springer, Heidelberg (2007). https://doi.org/10.1007/978-3-540-74958-5_38

Tsoumakas, G., Katakis, I., Vlahavas, I.P.: Mining multi-label data. In: Maimon, O., Rokach, L. (eds.) Data Mining and Knowledge Discovery Handbook, pp. 667–685. Springer, Boston (2010). https://doi.org/10.1007/978-0-387-09823-4_34

Veloso, A., Meira, W., Gonçalves, M., Zaki, M.: Multi-label lazy associative classification. In: Kok, J.N., Koronacki, J., Lopez de Mantaras, R., Matwin, S., Mladenič, D., Skowron, A. (eds.) PKDD 2007. LNCS (LNAI), vol. 4702, pp. 605–612. Springer, Heidelberg (2007). https://doi.org/10.1007/978-3-540-74976-9_64

Zhang, M., Zhou, Z.: A review on multi-label learning algorithms. IEEE Trans. Knowl. Data Eng. **26**(8), 1819–1837 (2014)

Full Papers

Full Papers

Tackling the DMN Challenges
with cDMN: A Tight Integration of DMN
and Constraint Reasoning

Bram Aerts, Simon Vandevelde$^{(\boxtimes)}$, and Joost Vennekens

Department of Computer Science, KU Leuven, De Nayer Campus,
Sint-Katelijne-Waver, Belgium
{b.aerts,s.vandevelde,joost.vennekens}@kuleuven.be

Abstract. This paper describes an extension to the Decision Model and Notation (DMN) standard, called cDMN. DMN is a user-friendly, table-based notation for decision logic. cDMN aims to enlarge the expressivity of DMN in order to solve more complex problems, while retaining DMN's goal of being readable by domain experts. We test cDMN by solving the most complex challenges posted on the DM Community website. We compare our own cDMN solutions to the solutions that have been submitted to the website and find that our approach is competitive, both in readability and compactness. Moreover, cDMN is able to solve more challenges than any other approach.

1 Introduction

The Decision Model and Notation (DMN) [4] standard, designed by the Object Management Group (OMG), is a way of representing data and decision logic in a readable, table-based way. It is intended to be used directly by business experts without the help of computer scientists.

While DMN is very effective in modeling deterministic decision processes, it lacks the ability to represent more complex kinds of knowledge. In order to explore the boundaries of DMN, the Decision Management Community website[1] issues a monthly decision modeling challenge. Community members can then submit a solution, using their preferred decision modeling tools or programming languages. This allows solutions for complex problems to be found and compared across multiple DMN-like representations. So far, none of the available solvers have been able to solve all challenges. Moreover, the available solutions sometimes fail to meet the readability goals of DMN, because the representation is either too complex or too large.

In this paper, we propose an extension to the DMN standard, called cDMN. It allows more complex problems to be solved, while remaining readable by business

---

[1] https://dmcommunity.org/.

This research received funding from the Flemish Government under the "Onderzoeksprogramma Artificiële Intelligentie (AI) Vlaanderen" programme.

ⓒ Springer Nature Switzerland AG 2020
V. Gutiérrez-Basulto et al. (Eds.): RuleML+RR 2020, LNCS 12173, pp. 23–38, 2020.
https://doi.org/10.1007/978-3-030-57977-7_2

users. The main features of cDMN are constraint modeling, quantification, and the use of concepts such as types and functions. We test the usability of cDMN on the decision modeling challenges.

In [3], we presented a preliminary version of constraint modeling in DMN. In the current paper, we extend this by adding quantification, types, functions, relations, data tables, optimization and by evaluating the formalism on the DMN challenges.

The paper is structured as follows. In Sect. 2 we briefly describe the DMN standard. Section 3 gives an overview of the challenges used in this paper. After this, we touch on the related work in Sect. 4. We discuss both syntax and semantics of our new notation in Sect. 5. Section 6 briefly discusses the implementation of our cDMN solver. We compare our notation with other notations and evaluate its added value in Sect. 7, and conclude in Sect. 8.

2   Preliminaries: DMN

The DMN standard [4] describes the structure of a DMN model. Such a model consists of two components: a Decision Requirements Diagram (DRD), which is a graph that expresses the structure of the model, and Decision Tables, which contain the in-depth business logic. An example of such a decision table can be found in Fig. 1. It consists of a number of input columns (darker green) and a single output column (lighter blue). Each row is read as: if the input conditions are met (e.g., if "Age of Person" satisfies the comparison "≥18"), then the output expression is assigned the value of the output entry (e.g. "Person is Adult" is assigned value "Yes"). Only single values, such as strings and numbers, can be used as output entries. In the case where no row matches the input, then each output is either set to the special value *null* (which is typically taken to indicate an error in the specification) or to the output's default value, if one was provided.

The behaviour of a decision table is determined by its hit policy. There are a number of *single hit* policies, which define that a table can have at most one output for each possible input, such as "Unique" (no overlap may occur), "Any" (if there is an overlap, the outputs must be the same) and "First" (if there is an overlap, the first applicable row should be selected). There exist also *multiple hit* policies such as C (collect the output of all applicable rows in a list) and C+ (sum the output of all applicable rows). Regardless of which hit policy is used, each decision table uniquely determines the value of its output(s).

Define adults		
U	Age of Person	Person is Adult
1	≥ 18	Yes
2	< 18	No

Fig. 1. Decision table to define whether a person is an adult. (Color figure online)

The entries in a decision table are typically written in the (Simple) Friendly Enough Expression Language, or (S-)FEEL, which is also part of the DMN standard. S-FEEL allows to express simple values, lists of values, numerical comparisons, ranges of values and calculations. Decision tables with S-FEEL are generally considered quite readable by domain experts.

In addition, DMN also allows more complex FEEL statements in combination with boxed expressions, as will be illustrated in Fig. 6. However, this also greatly increases complexity of the representation, which makes it unsuitable to be used by domain experts without the aid of knowledge experts.

3   Challenges Overview

Of all the challenges on the DM Community website, we selected those that did not have a straightforward DMN-like solution submitted. The list of the 21 challenges that meet this criterion can be found in the cDMN documentation[2].

We categorize these challenges according to four different properties. Table 1 shows the list of properties, and the percentage of challenges that have this property.

The most frequent property is the need for aggregates (57.14%), such as counting the number of violated constraints in *Map Coloring with Violations* or summing the number of calories of ingredients in *Make a Good Burger*. The second most frequent property is having constraints in the problem description (33.33%). E.g., in *Who Killed Agatha*, the killer hates the victim and is no richer than her; or the constraint in *Map Coloring* states that two bordering countries can not share the same color. The next property, universal quantification (28.75%), is that a statement applies to every element of a type, for example in *Who Killed Agatha?*: nobody hates everyone. The final property, optimization, occurs in 23.81% of the challenges. For example, in *Zoo, Buses and Kids* the cheapest set of buses must be found.

Table 1. Percentage of occurrence of properties in challenges.

Property	(%)
1. Aggregates needed	57.14
2. Constraints	33.33
3. Universal quantification	28.75
4. Optimization	23.81

4   Related Work

It has been recognized that even though DMN has many advantages, it is somewhat limited in expressivity [1,3]. This holds especially for decision tables with S-FEEL, the fragment of FEEL that is considered most readable. While full

---

[2] https://cdmn.readthedocs.io/en/latest/community.html.

FEEL is more expressive, it is not suitable to be used by domain experts without the aid of knowledge experts. Moreover, it does not provide a solution to other shortcomings, such as the lack of constraint reasoning and optimization.

One of the systems that does effectively support constraint solving in a readable DMN-like representation is the OpenRules system [5]. It enables users to define constraints over the solution space by allowing "Solver Tables" to be added alongside decision tables. In contrast to standard decisions, which assign a specific value to an output, Solver Tables allow for setting constraints on the output space. OpenRules offers a number of *DecisionTableSolve-Templates*, which can be used to specify these constraints. It is possible to either use these predefined templates, or define such a template manually if the predefined ones are not expressive enough. Even though this system extends the range of applications that can be handled, there are three reasons why it does not offer the ease of use for business users that we are after. First, because of the wide range of available templates for solver tables, which differ from that of standard decision tables, using the OpenRules constraint solver entails a steep learning curve. Second, the solver's functionality can only be accessed through the Java API, which goes against the DMN philosophy [4, p. 13]. Third, because of the lack of quantification in OpenRules, solutions are generally not independent of domain size, which reduces readability.

Another system that aims to increase expressiveness of DMN is Corticon [6]. It implements a basic form of constraint solving by allowing the user to filter the solution space. While this approach indeed improves expressiveness, it decreases readability. Moreover, some constraints can only be expressed by combining a number of rules and a number of filters. For example, when expressing "all female monkeys are older than 10 years", this is split up in two parts; (1) a rule that states `Monkey.gender = female & Monkey. Age < 10 THEN Monkey.illegal = True` and (2) a filter that states that a monkey cannot be illegal: `Monkey.illegal = False`. There are no clear guidelines about which part of the constraints should be in the filter and what should be a rule.

In [1], Calvanese et al. propose an extension to DMN which allows for expressing additional domain knowledge in Description Logic. They share our goal of extending DMN to express more complex real-life problems. However, they introduce a completely separate Description Logic formalism, which seems too complex for a domain expert to use. Unfortunately, they did not submit any solutions to the DMN Challenges, which leaves us unable to compare its expressiveness in practice.

5   cDMN: Syntax and Semantics

While DMN allows users to elegantly represent a deterministic decision process, it lacks the ability to specify constraints on the solution space. The cDMN framework extends DMN, by allowing constraints to be represented in a straightforward and readable manner. It also allows for representations that are independent of domain size by supporting types, functions, relations and quantification.

We now explain both the usage and the syntax of every kind of table present in cDMN.

5.1   Glossary

In logical terms, the "variables" used in standard DMN correspond to constants (i.e., 0-ary functions). cDMN extends these by adding n-ary functions and n-ary relations. Similarly to OpenRules and Corticon, we allow the user to define their vocabulary by means of a glossary. This glossary contains every symbol used in a cDMN model. It consists of at most five glossary tables, each enumerating a different kind of symbol. An example glossary for the *Who Killed Agatha?* challenge is given in Fig. 2.

Type				Relation
Name	Type	Values		Name
Person	string	Agatha, Butler, Charles		Person hates Person
Number	int	[0..100]		Person is richer than Person

Boolean	Constant		Function	
Name	Name	Type	Name	Type
Suicide	Killer	Person	Hatees of Person	Number

Fig. 2. An example cDMN glossary for the *Who Killed Agatha?* problem.

In the *Type* table, *type* symbols are declared. The value of each type is a set of domain elements, specified either in the glossary or in a data table (see Sect. 5.3). An example is the type `Person`, which contains the names of people.

In the *Function* table, a symbol can be declared as a *function* of one or more types to another. The infix operator of is used to apply the function to its argument(s). For example, the `Hatees of Person` function denotes how many people a person hates. It maps each element of type `Person` to an element of type `Number`. Functions with $n > 1$ arguments can be declared by separating the n arguments by the keyword and.

For each domain element, a constant with the same name is automatically introduced, which allows the user to refer to this domain element in constraint or decision tables. For instance, the user can use the constant `Agatha` to refer to the domain element `Agatha`. In addition, the *Constant* table allows other constants to be introduced. Recall that such logical constants correspond to standard DMN variables. In our example case, we use a constant `Killer` of the type `Person`, which means it can refer to any of the domain elements `Agatha`, `Butler` or `Charles`.

In the *Relation* table, a verb phrase can be declared as a *relation* on one or more given types. For instance, the relation `Person is Adult` denotes for each `Person` whether they are an adult. This relation translates to the unary predicate *isAdult*. n-ary predicates can be defined by using n arguments in the name, e.g. `Person is richer than Person` is a relation with two arguments (both of the type `Person`), that denotes whether one person is richer than another.

The *Boolean* table contains *boolean* symbols (i.e. propositions), which are either true or false. An example is the boolean `Suicide`, which denotes whether the murder is a suicide.

5.2 Decision Tables and Constraint Tables

As stated earlier in Sect. 2, a standard decision table uniquely defines the value of its outputs. We extend DMN by allowing a new kind of table, called a *constraint table*, which does not have this property.

Whereas decision tables only allow single values to appear in output columns, our constraint tables allow arbitrary S-FEEL expressions in output columns, instead of only single values. Each row of a constraint table represents a logical *implication*, in the sense that, if the conditions on the inputs are satisfied, then the conditions on the outputs must also be satisfied. This means that if, for instance, none of the rows are applicable, the outputs can take on an arbitrary value, as opposed to being forced to *null*. In constraint tables, no default values can be assigned. Because of these changes, a set of cDMN tables does not define a single solution, but rather a solution space containing a set of possible solutions.

We introduce a new *hit policy* to identify constraint tables. We call this the *Every* hit policy, denoted as E^*, because it expresses that every implication in the table must be satisfied. An example of this can be found in Fig. 3, which states that each person hates less than 3 people.

cDMN does not only introduce constraint tables, it also extends the expressions that are allowed in column headers, both in decision and constraint tables. Such a header can consist of the following expressions: (1) a type *Type*; (2) an expression of the form "*Type* called *name*"; (3) a constant; (4) an expression of the form "*Function* of arg_1 and ... and arg_n", where each of the arg_i is another header expression; (5) an arithmetic combination of header expressions (such as a sum).

The first two kinds of expressions are called *variable* header expressions. They allow *universal quantification* in cDMN. Each input column whose header consists of such a *variable* expression either introduces a new universally quantified variable (we call this a *variable-introducing* column), or refers back to a variable introduced in a preceding *variable-introducing* column. Subsequent uses of the same type name (in case of the first kind of variable-introducing expression) or of the variable name (in case of the second kind) then refer back to this universally quantified variable. Whenever a type or variable name appears in a header of a column that is itself not variable-introducing, a unique preceding variable-introducing column that has introduced this variable must exists.

The table in Fig. 3 shows an example of quantification in cDMN. It introduces a universally quantified variable of the type *Person*, stating that every person hates less than three others. To illustrate the use of named variables, Fig. 4 defines variables `c1` and `c2`, both of the type `Country`, and states that when those countries are bordering, they cannot have the same color.

In summary, this section has discussed three ways in which cDMN extends DMN. First, the hit policy E^* changes the semantics of the table. Second, constraint tables allow S-FEEL expressions in the output columns. Third, cDMN allows quantification, functions, predicates and calculations to be used in both decision tables and constraint tables.

Noone hates all		
E*	**Person**	**Hatees of Person**
1	-	<3

Fig. 3. Part of the implementation of "Nobody hates everyone" in *Who Killed Agatha?*.

Bordering countries can not share colors			
E*	**Country called c1**	**Country called c2**	**c1 and c2 are Bordering**	**Color of c1**
1	-	-	Yes	Not(Color of c2)

Fig. 4. Example of a constraint table with quantification in cDMN, defining that bordering countries can't share colors.

5.3 Data Tables

Typically, problems can be split up into two parts: (1) the general logic of the problem, and (2) the specific problem instance that needs to be solved. Take for example the map coloring problem: the general logic consists of the rule that two bordering countries cannot share a color, whereas the instance of the problem is the specific map (e.g. Western Europe) to color. cDMN extends the DMN standard to include *data tables*, which are used to represent the problem instances, separating them from the general logic. The format of a data table closely resembles that of a decision table, with a couple of exceptions. Instead of a hit policy, a data table has "data table" in its name. Furthermore, only basic values (integers, floats and domain elements) are allowed in data tables. It is also possible for columns to have more than one value in a certain row, in which case the row is instantiated for the combination of each of the values of the columns. As an example, a snippet of the data table for the *Map Coloring* challenge is shown in Fig. 5.

This use of data tables offers several advantages.

1. There is a methodological advantage: by separating the data tables from the decision tables, reusing the specification becomes easier.
2. If the user chooses to enumerate the domain of a type in the glossary, then the system checks that each value in a data table indeed belongs to the domain of the appropriate type. This helps to prevent errors or typos in the input data or glossary. If the user chooses not to enumerate a type in the glossary, then the type's domain defaults to the set of all values in the data table.
3. The cDMN solver is able to compute solutions faster, due to a different internal representation between data tables and decision tables.

Data Table: Declaring which countries border		
Country called c1	**Country called c2**	**c1 and c2 are Bordering**
1	Belgium	France, Luxembourg, Netherlands, Germany	Yes
2	Germany	France, Denmark, Luxembourg, Belgium, Netherlands	Yes

Fig. 5. Data table describing countries and their neighbours

5.4 Execute Table

A standard DMN model defines a deterministic decision procedure. It is typically always used in the same way: the external inputs are supplied by the user, after which the values of the output variables are computed by forward propagation.

In cDMN, this is no longer the case. We can fill in as many or as few variables as we want, and use the model to derive useful information about the not-yet-known variables. By employing an *execute table*, users can specify what the model is to be used for: model expansion or optimization. Model expansion creates a given number of solutions, and optimization looks for the solution with either the lowest or highest value for a given term.

5.5 Semantics of cDMN

We describe the semantics of cDMN by translating it to the $FO(\cdot)$ language used by the IDP system [2,7]. $FO(\cdot)$ is a rich extension of First Order Logic, adding concepts such as types, aggregates and inductive definitions. The semantics of cDMN is defined by the semantics of each of its sub-components.

It is straightforward to translate the glossary into an $FO(\cdot)$ vocabulary: types, functions, constants, relations and booleans are each translated to their $FO(\cdot)$ counterpart.

Decision tables retain their usual semantics as described by Calvanese [1]. We briefly recall this semantics. Each cell of a decision table (i, j) corresponds to a formula $F_{ij}(x)$ in one free variable x. For instance, a cell "≤ 50" corresponds to the formula "$x \leq 50$". A decision table with rows R, input columns I and output columns O is a conjunction of material implications:

$$\bigwedge_{i \in R} \left(\bigwedge_{j \in I} F_{ij}(H_j) \Rightarrow \bigwedge_{k \in O} F_{ik}(H_k) \right)$$

where H_j is the header of column j. For example, the table in Fig. 1 corresponds to the logical formula ($AgeOfPerson \geq 18 \Rightarrow PersonIsAdult = Yes$) $\wedge$ ($AgeOfPerson < 18 \Rightarrow PersonIsAdult = No$).

Data tables are simply a specific case of decision tables.

In [3], the semantics of simple constraint tables (without quantification and functions) is introduced, which is also a conjunction of implications. The semantics of constraint tables and decision tables differ in the interpretation of incomplete tables: when no rows are applicable in decision tables, the output is forced to *null* (i.e., the implicit default value is *null*), while the output in constraint tables can take any value.

Now we extend this semantics to take variables and quantification into account. Our first step is to define a function that maps cDMN expressions to terms. For the most part, this definition corresponds to that of Calvanese [1]. However, we extend it to take into account the fact that certain expressions – which we call *variable expressions* – must be translated to FO variables. There are three kinds of variable expressions. We now define a mapping ν that maps each of these three kinds of cDMN variable expressions to a typed FO variable x of type T, which we denote as $x[T]$:

- The name T of a type is a variable expression. We define $\nu(T) = x_T[T]$, with x_T a new variable of type T.
- An expression e of the form "*Type called v*" is a variable expression. We define $\nu(e) = v[Type]$.
- If the header of a column contains an expression "*Type called v*", then v is a variable expression in all subsequent columns of the table and in its body. We define $\nu(v)$ as $v[Type]$.

Given this function ν, we now define the following mapping $t_\nu(\cdot)$ of cDMN expressions to terms.

- For a constant c, $t_\nu(c) = c$; similarly, for an integer or floating point number n, $t_\nu(n) = n$;
- For an arithmetic expression e of the form $e_1 \theta e_2$ with $\theta \in \{+, \ , *, /\}$, we define $t_\nu(e) = t_\nu(e_1) \ \theta \ t_\nu(e_2)$;
- For a variable expression v, we define $t_\nu(v) = \nu(v)$.
- For a function expression, i.e. "*Function of arg$_1$ and ... and arg$_n$*":
  $t_\nu(X) = Function(t_\nu(arg_1), ..., t_\nu(arg_n))$.

Similarly to Calvanese, we translate each entry c in a cell (i, j) of a table into a formula $F_{ij}(x)$ in one free variable x:

- If c is of the form "θe" with θ one of the relational operators $\{\leq, \geq, =, \neq\}$, then $F_{ij}(x)$ is the formula $x \ \theta \ t(e)$;
- If c is of the form *Not e*, then F_{ij} is $x \neq t(e)$;
- If c is a list $e_1, \ldots, e_n$, then F_{ij} is $x = t(e_1) \vee \ldots \vee x = t(e_n)$. As a special case, if c consists of a single expression e, then F_{ij} is $x = t(e)$.
- If c is a range, e.g. $[e_1, e_2)$, then F_{ij} is $x \geq t(e_1) \wedge x < t(e_2)$.

We are now ready to define the semantics of a constraint table. If I is the set of input columns of the table, O the set of output columns and $V \subseteq I$ the set of variable introducing columns, we define the semantics of the table as:

$$\underset{l \in V}{\forall} \nu(H_l) : \bigwedge_{i \in R} \left(\bigwedge_{j \in I} F_{ij}(t_\nu(H_j)) \Rightarrow \bigwedge_{k \in O} F_{ik}(t_\nu(H_k)) \right)$$

For example, in Fig. 3, $\nu(H_1) = x[Person]$ and $t_\nu(H_1) = x$, $t_\nu(H_2) = Hatee(t_\nu(H_1)) = Hatee(x)$, which leads to the formula:

$$\forall x[Person] : Hatee(x) < 3.$$

The above transformation turns each decision or constraint table T into an FO($\cdot$) formula ϕ_T. The glossary and data tables together define a structure S for part of the vocabulary. The domain of S consists of the union of the interpretations I_t of all the types t. If t is enumerated in the glossary, then I_t is this enumeration. Otherwise, I_t consists of all the values that appear in a data table in a column of type t. The structure S interprets all the relations/functions for which a data table is provided, and it interprets them by the set of tuples/the mapping that is given in this table.

The set of "solutions" of a cDMN model is the set $MX(\Phi, S)$ of all model expansions of the structure S w.r.t. the theory $\Phi = \{\phi_T \mid T$ is a constraint or decision table$\}$, i.e., the set of all structures $S' \models \Phi$ that extend S to the entire vocabulary.

6 Implementation

This section gives an overview of the inner workings of the cDMN solver[3]. It is a brief overview, as the solver is not the main focus of this paper. The solver consists of two parts: a constraint solver (the IDP system), and a converter from cDMN to IDP input. In principle, any constraint solver could be used, but we chose the IDP system because of its flexibility.

The cDMN to IDP converter is built using Python3, and works in a two-step process. It first interprets all tables in a .xslx sheet and converts them into Python objects. For example, the converter parses all the glossary tables and converts them into a single `Glossary` object, which then creates `Type` and `Predicate` objects. The created Python objects are then converted into IDP blocks. More detailed information about this conversion can be found in the cDMN documentation[4], along with an explanation of the usage of the solver and concrete examples of cDMN implementations.

7 Results and Discussion

In this section we first look at three of the DM Community challenges, each showcasing a feature of cDMN. For each challenge, we compare the DMN implementations from the DM Community website with our own implementation in cDMN. Afterwards, we compare all challenges on size and quality.

---

[3] https://gitlab.com/EAVISE/cdmn/cdmn-solver.
[4] www.cdmn.be.

7.1   Constraint Tables

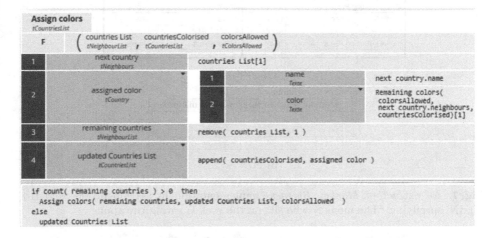

Fig. 6. An extract of the map coloring solution in standard DMN with FEEL

Constraint tables allow cDMN to model constraint satisfaction problems in a straightforward way. For example, in *Map Coloring*, a map of six European countries must be colored in such a way that no neighbouring countries share the same color. For this challenge, a pure DMN implementation was submitted, of which Fig. 6 shows an extract. The implementation uses complicated FEEL statements to solve the challenge. While these statements are DMN-compliant, they are nearly impossible for a business user to write without help. In cDMN, we can use a single straight-forward constraint table to solve this problem, as shown in Fig. 4. Together with the glossary and a data table (Fig. 5), this forms a complete yet simple cDMN implementation.

7.2   Quantification

Quantification is useful in the *Monkey Business* challenge. In this challenge, we want to know for four monkeys what their favorite fruit and their favorite resting place is, based on some information. There are two DMN-like submissions for this challenge: one using Corticon, and one using OpenRules.

One of the pieces of information is: **The monkey who sat on the rock ate the apple.** The OpenRules implementation has a table with a row for each monkey, which states that if this monkey's resting place was a rock, their fruit was an apple (Fig. 7a). In other words, for n monkeys, the OpenRules implementation of this rule requires n lines. Because of quantification, cDMN requires only one row, regardless of how many monkeys there are (Fig. 7b). The Corticon implementation also uses a similar quantification for this rule.

DecisionTable SituationRules					
ConditionVarOperValue			ConclusionVarOperValue		
String attribute	Oper op	String value	String attribute	Oper op	String value
...	...	...	...	...	...
Mike's Resting Place	=	Rock	Mike's Fruit	=	Apple
Sam's Resting Place	=	Rock	Sam's Fruit	=	Apple
Anna's Resting Place	=	Rock	Anna's Fruit	=	Apple
Harriet's Resting Place	=	Rock	Harriet's Fruit	=	Apple
...	...	...	...	...	...

(a) Open Rules

Monkey Constraints			
E*	Monkey	Place of Monkey	Fruit of Monkey
...	...	...	...
2	—	Rock	Apple
...	...	...	...

(b) cDMN

Fig. 7. An extract of *Monkey Business* implementation in (a) OpenRules and (b) cDMN, specifying "The monkey who sits on the rock is eating the apple".

Mike.fruit<>Sam.fruit	T
Mike.fruit<>Harriet.fruit	T
Mike.fruit<>Anna.fruit	T
Sam.fruit<>Harriet.fruit	T
Sam.fruit<>Anna.fruit	T
Harriet.fruit<>Anna.fruit	T

Mike.place<>Sam.place	T
Mike.place<>Harriet.place	T
Mike.place<>Anna.place	T
Sam.place<>Harriet.place	T
Sam.place<>Anna.place	T
Harriet.place<>Anna.place	T

(a) Corticon

Different Preferences				
E*	Monkey called m1	Monkey called m2	Place of m1	Fruit of m1
1	—	not(m1)	not(Place of m2)	not(Fruit of m2)

(b) cDMN

Fig. 8. An extract of the *Monkey Business* implementation in (a) Corticon and (b) cDMN, defining that no monkeys share fruit and no monkeys share the same place.

Another rule states that no two monkeys can have the same resting place or fruit. In both the Corticon and OpenRules implementations, this is handled by two tables with a row for each pair of monkeys. The Corticon tables are shown in Fig. 8a. Each row either states that two monkeys have different fruit, or that they have different place. Therefore, n monkeys require $\frac{n \times (n-1)}{2}$ rows. By contrast, the cDMN implementation seen in Fig. 8b requires only a single row to express the same.

7.3 Optimization

In the *Balanced Assignment* challenge, 210 employees need to be divided into 12 groups, so that every group is as diverse as possible. The department, location, gender and title of each employee is known. This is quite a complex problem to handle in DMN. As such, of the four submitted solutions, only one was DMN-like: an OpenRules implementation, using external CP/LP solvers. The logic for these external solvers is written in Java. Although the code is fairly compact, it cannot be written without prior programming knowledge. Because optimization is built-in in cDMN, we can solve the problem with two decision tables and one constraint table. The table *Diversity score*, shown in Fig. 9, adds 1 to the total diversity score if two similar people are in a different group. Maximizing this score then results in the most diverse groups.

Diversity score								
C+	Person called p1	Person called p2	Department of p1	Location of p1	Gender of p1	Title of p1	Group of p1	Score
1	-	-	= Department of p2	-	-	-	not(Group of p2)	1
2	-	-	-	= Location of p2	-	-	not(Group of p2)	1
3	-	-	-	-	= Gender of p2	-	not(Group of p2)	1
4	-	-	-	-	-	= Title of p2	not(Group of p2)	1

Execute
Maximize Score

Fig. 9. The decision tables and constraint table for Balanced Assignment.

7.4 Overview of All Challenges

Of the 21 challenges we considered, cDMN is capable of successfully modeling 19. In comparison, there were 12 OpenRules implementations and 12 Corticon implementations submitted. Note that we have not examined whether Open-Rules and Corticon might be capable of modeling more challenges than those for which a solution was submitted.

To compare cDMN to other approaches, we focus on two aspects: quantity (how big are they?) and quality (how readable and how scalable are they?). The size of implementations was measured by counting the number of cells used in all the decision tables. Glossaries, data tables and equivalents thereof were not included in the count. Table 2 shows that cDMN and Corticon alternate between having the fewest cells, and that OpenRules usually has the most. In general, OpenRules implementations require many cells because each cell is very simple. For instance, even an "=" operator is its own cell. The Corticon implementations, on the other hand, contain more complex cells, rendering them more compact.

Because of this, OpenRules implementations are usually easier to read than their Corticon counterparts. An example comparison between cDMN and Corticon can be seen in Fig. 10a and b. Each figure shows a snippet of their *Make a Good Burger* implementation, in which the food properties of a burger are calculated. While the Corticon implementation is more compact, it is less interpretable, less maintainable and dependent on domain size. If the user wants to add an ingredient to the burger, complex cells need to be changed. In cDMN, simply adding the ingredient to the data table suffices.

Table 2. Comparison of the number of cells used per implementation. Other implementations: 1. FEEL, 2. Blueriq, 3. Trisotech, 4. DMN

	Who Killed A.?	Change Making	A Good Burger	Define Dupl.	Coll. of Cars	Monkey Business	Vacation Days	Family Riddle	Cust. Greeting	Online Dating	Class. Employees	Reindeer Order	Zoo, Buses, Kids	Balanced Assign.	Vac. Days Adv.	Map Coloring	Map Color Viol.	Crack the Code	Numerical Haiku
cDMN	53	26	35	20	26	47	38	76	88	45	36	14	24	55	124	21	48	77	41
Corticon	54	14	20	19	45	64	32	22		78	21	64							
OpenRules	176		95	21		150	31		205		70	111	43	30	97				
Others			76[1]		48[1]		14[2]					34[3]	370[4]				31[4]		

A comparison between cDMN and OpenRules can be found in Fig. 11a and b. Here we show a part of their implementations of the *Who Killed Agatha?* challenge. They both show a translation of the following rule: "A killer always hates, and is no richer than his victim." By using constraints and a constant (`Killer`), cDMN allows us to form a more readable and more scalable table. If the police ever find a fourth suspect, they can easily add the person to the data table without needing to change anything else.

In Sect. 3, we identified four different problem properties. We now suggest that each property is tackled more easily by one or more of the additions cDMN proposes.

Aggregates Needed. Figure 10b shows how aggregates are both more readable and scalable when using quantification. Moreover, cDMN allows the use of aggregates for more complex operations such as optimization or defining constraints.

Conditions		1
a	beefPatties.count * 50 + bun.count * 330 + cheese.count * 310 + onion.count + ketchup_lettuce.count * (3+160) + pickle_tomato.count * (260+3)	< 3000
b	beefPatties.count * 17 + bun.count * 9 + cheese.count * 6 + onion.count*2	< 150
c	beefPatties.count * 220 + bun.count * 260 + cheese.count * 70 + onion.count*10 + ketchup_lettuce.count * (4+20) + pickle_tomato.count * (5+9)	< 3000

(a) Corticon

Determine Nutrition					
C+	Item	Total Sodium	Total Fat	Total Calories	Total Cost
1	-	Number of Item * Sodium of Item	Number of Item * Fat of Item	Number of Item * Calories of Item	Number of Item * Cost of Item

Nutrition Constraints			
E*	Total Sodium	Total Fat	Total Calories
1	<3000	<150	<3000

(b) cDMN

Fig. 10. Calculating the food properties of burger in Corticon and cDMN.

Constraints. Constraints can be conveniently modeled by constraint tables, such as the constraints in Fig. 11b, which states that the killer hates Agatha, but is no richer than her. The addition of constraint tables allows for an obvious translation from the rule in natural language to the table.

DecisionTable KillerHatesAndNoRicherHisVictim					
ConditionXoperY			ActionXoperY		
IF			THEN		
BUTLER KILLED AGATHA	=	1	Butler Hates Agatha	=	1
BUTLER KILLED AGATHA	=	1	Butler Richer Than Agatha	=	0
CHARLES KILLED AGATHA	=	1	Charles Hates Agatha	=	1
CHARLES KILLED AGATHA	=	1	Charles Richer Than Agatha	=	0
AGATHA KILLED AGATHA	=	1	Agatha Hates Agatha	=	1
AGATHA KILLED AGATHA	=	1	Agatha Richer Than Agatha	=	0

(a) OpenRules

Killer constraints		
E*	Killer hates Agatha	Killer richer than Agatha
1	Yes	No

(b) cDMN

Fig. 11. Implementation of "A killer always hates and is no richer than their victim" in OpenRules and cDMN

Universal Quantification. Problems which contain universal quantification can be compactly represented, as can, among others, be seen in Fig. 3. This table states that each person hates less than 3 people.

Optimization. Because cDMN directly supports optimization, problems containing this property are easily modeled. Furthermore, by the addition of more complex data types, optimization can be used in a more flexible manner. An example can be found in Fig. 9.

8   Conclusions

This paper presents an extension to DMN, which is able to solve complex problems while still maintaining DMN's level of readability. This extension, which we call cDMN, adds constraint modeling, more expressive data and quantification.

Constraint modeling allows a user to define a solution space instead of a single solution. A user can generate a desired number of models, or generate the model which optimizes the value of a specific term. Unlike DMN, which only knows constants, cDMN also supports the use of functions and predicates, which allow for more flexible representations. Together with quantification, this allows tables to be constructed in a compact and straightforward manner, while being independent of the size of the problem. This improves readability, maintainability and scalability of tables.

By comparing our cDMN implementations to the implementations of other state-of-the-art DMN-like solvers, we can conclude that cDMN succeeds in increasing expressivity while retaining the simplicity of standard DMN.

References

1. Calvanese, D., Montali, M., Dumas, M., Maggi, F.: Semantic DMN: formalizing and reasoning about decisions in the presence of background knowledge. Theory Pract. Logic Program. **19**(4), 536–573 (2019)
2. De Cat, B., Bogaerts, B., Bruynooghe, M., Janssens, G., Denecker, M.: Predicate logic as a modeling language: the IDP system. In: Declarative Logic Programming: Theory, Systems, and Applications, pp. 279–329. ACM Books (2018)
3. Deryck, M., Aerts, B., Vennekens, J.: Adding constraint tables to the DMN standard: preliminary results. In: Fodor, P., Montali, M., Calvanese, D., Roman, D. (eds.) RuleML+RR 2019. LNCS, vol. 11784, pp. 171–179. Springer, Cham (2019). https://doi.org/10.1007/978-3-030-31095-0_12
4. Object Modelling Group: Decision model and notation (2019). http://www.omg.org/spec/DMN/
5. OpenRules Inc.: Openrules (2017). http://openrules.com
6. Progress: Corticon (2019). progress.com/corticon
7. Wittocx, J., Mariën, M., Denecker, M.: The IDP system: a model expansion system for an extension of classical logic. In: Proceedings of the 2nd Workshop on Logic and Search, pp. 153–165. ACCO, Leuven (2008)

Query Answering in Fuzzy DL-Lite
with Graded Axioms

Gabriella Pasi and Rafael Peñaloza$^{(\boxtimes)}$

IKR3 Lab, University of Milano-Bicocca, Milan, Italy
{gabriella.pasi,rafael.penaloza}@unimib.it

Abstract. Fuzzy DL-Lite has been studied as a means to answer queries w.r.t. vague or imprecise knowledge and facts. Existing approaches consider only the Zadeh semantics or are limited to precise terminological knowledge, where only facts are graded. We study the problem of answering conjunctive queries over fuzzy DL-Lite$_R$ ontologies which allow also graded axioms, and whose semantics is based on mathematical fuzzy logic. We show that for the Gödel t-norm, the degree of an answer is computable through repeated calls to a classical query answering engine. For non-idempotent t-norms, we show the difficulty in dealing with degrees, and provide some partial solutions.

1 Introduction

Description logics [3] are a well known family of knowledge representation formalisms characterised by their formal logic-based semantics, and their decidable (usually with relatively low complexity) reasoning tasks. Within these logics, the DL-Lite family of light-weight DLs [2] is specially interesting, as it allows for very efficient query answering in terms of data and combined complexity. It is also the formalism underlying the OWL 2 QL profile of the standard ontology language for the semantic web [10]. For this reason, they have been used for many practical applications in various knowledge domains.

As the semantics are based on classical first-order logic, in their standard form DLs are not able to handle vague or imprecise knowledge and facts. For that reason, fuzzy extensions of DLs have been devised. Although most work has focused on extending more expressive DLs and solving standard reasoning services [8], some efforts have been made towards answering queries in DL-Lite. Specifically, Straccia [20] studied the problem of computing the answers with highest degree on a query w.r.t. some background knowledge. This was followed by Pan et al. [17], who considered more complex queries to be answered. Other work considering query answering in fuzzy DLs includes [21]. These three works were based on the so-called Zadeh semantics, and had the limitation that only the facts in the ontology could be graded, but not the terminological knowledge.

Later, Turhan and Mailis studied the problem from the point of view of fuzzy logic [12], where the semantics are based on the properties of continuous triangular norms. They developed a technique for computing the satisfaction

© Springer Nature Switzerland AG 2020
V. Gutiérrez-Basulto et al. (Eds.): RuleML+RR 2020, LNCS 12173, pp. 39–53, 2020.
https://doi.org/10.1007/978-3-030-57977-7_3

degrees of queries when the semantics were based on the Gödel t-norm [14]. This technique, which is based on the construction of a classical query, was later implemented and shown to be effective in [15]. However, it still suffered from two main drawbacks: (i) it was only capable to handle the idempotent t-norm and (ii) terminological knowledge had to still be precise. The latter condition is essential for the correctness of their approach: their reduction is unable to keep track of the degrees used by the terminological axioms, as this would require an unbounded memory use.

In this paper, we tackle these limitations over the well-known DL-Lite$_R$ logic. Considering the t-norm-based semantics, we show that every consistent fuzzy DL-Lite$_R$ ontology has a canonical model, which can be homomorphically embeded in every other model, and present an infinitary construction for obtaining it, based on the ideas of classical DL-Lite$_R$. Using this fact, we develop a method for finding the degree of an answer to a conjunctive query, which is also capable of dealing with fuzzy terminological axioms w.r.t. the Gödel t-norm. Indeed, despite being more general, our approach is much simpler than previous methods. We show that to verify a lower bound d of the degree, it suffices to consider only the subontology with all axioms and assertions with a degree at least d, and answer a classical query over it. Thus, one can use any off-the-shelf ontology-based query answering engine available [23]. The cost of our simpler method is that, to find the specific degree, the data complexity jumps from AC^0 to LogSpace. Whether the algorithm can be further improved or the LogSpace upper bound is tight remains open.

Considering other continuous t-norms, we show through several examples that query answering needs some more meticulous analysis. While deciding consistency w.r.t. the product t-norm is still easy, finding the precise degrees of an answer becomes more involved. In the case of the Łukasiewicz t-norm, we recall the fact that for a minimal extension of DL-Lite$_R$ consistency is already NP-hard in combined complexity, and hence unlikely to be decidable through a simple reduction to classical DL-Lite$_R$.

2   Preliminaries

We briefly introduce the syntax and semantics of fuzzy DL-Lite$_R$. Let N_C, N_R, and N_I be three mutually disjoint sets whose elements are called *concept names*, *role names*, and *individual names*, respectively. The sets of DL-Lite$_R$ *concepts* and *roles* are built through the grammar rules

$$B ::= A \mid \exists Q \qquad\qquad C ::= B \mid \neg B$$
$$Q ::= P \mid P^- \qquad\qquad R ::= Q \mid \neg Q$$

where $A \in N_C$ and $P \in N_R$. Concepts of the form B and roles of the form Q are called *basic*, and all others are called *general*.

A *fuzzy DL-Lite$_R$ TBox* is a finite set of *fuzzy axioms* of the form $\langle B \sqsubseteq C, d \rangle$ and $\langle Q \sqsubseteq R, d \rangle$, where d is a number in $[0, 1]$. An axiom is *positive* if it does not have negation on its right-hand side; note that negations can never occur on the left-hand side of an axiom. A *fuzzy DL-Lite$_R$ ABox* is a finite set of *fuzzy assertions* of the form $\langle B(a), d \rangle$ and $\langle P(a,b), d \rangle$, where $a, b \in N_I$. A *fuzzy DL-Lite$_R$ ontology* is a pair of the form $\mathcal{O} = (\mathcal{T}, \mathcal{A})$ where $\mathcal{T}$ is a TBox and $\mathcal{A}$ is an ABox. In the remainer of this paper, we will mostly exclude the qualifiers "fuzzy," and "DL-Lite" and simply refer to axioms, ontologies, etc.

Table 1. The three main continuous t-norms and related operations

Name	$d \otimes e$	$d \Rightarrow e$	$\ominus d$
Gödel	$\min\{d, e\}$	$\begin{cases} 1 & d \leq e \\ e & \text{ow} \end{cases}$	$\begin{cases} 1 & d = 0 \\ 0 & \text{ow} \end{cases}$
Łukasiewicz	$\max\{d + e - 1, 0\}$	$\min\{1 - d + e, 1\}$	$1 - d$
Product	$d \cdot e$	$\begin{cases} 1 & d \leq e \\ e/d & \text{ow} \end{cases}$	$\begin{cases} 1 & d = 0 \\ 0 & \text{ow} \end{cases}$

The semantics of fuzzy DL-Lite$_R$ is based on fuzzy interpretations, which provide a *membership degree* or *truth degree* for objects belonging to the different concept and role names. To fully define this semantics in the presence of other constructors according to the theory of mathematical fuzzy logic, we need the notion of a triangular norm (or *t-norm* for short).

A *t-norm* $\otimes$ is a binary operator over $[0, 1]$ that is commutative, associative, monotonic, and has as neutral operator 1 [13]. The t-norm is used to generalize the logical conjunction to the interval $[0, 1]$. Every continuous t-norm defines a unique *residuum* $\Rightarrow$ where $f \otimes d \leq e$ iff $f \leq d \Rightarrow e$. The residuum interprets implications. With the help of this operation, it is also possible to interpret other logical operators such as negation ($\ominus d := d \Rightarrow 0$). The three basic continuous t-norms are the *Gödel, Łukasiewicz*, and *product* t-norms, which are defined, with their residua and negations in Table 1. These t-norms are the fundamental ones in the sense that every other continuous t-norm is isomorphic to the ordinal sum of copies of them [12,16]. Hence, as usual, we focus our study to these three t-norms.

Note that the residuum always satisfies that $d \Rightarrow e = 1$ iff $d \leq e$, and that in the Gödel and product t-norms the negation is annihilating in the sense that it maps to 0 any positive value, while the negation of 0 is 1. In particular, this means that the negation is not involutive; that is, $\ominus \ominus d \neq d$ in general. From now on, unless specified explicitly otherwise, we assume that we have an arbitrary, but fixed, t-norm $\otimes$ which underlies the operators used. When the t-norm becomes relevant in the following sections, we will often use G, π, and Ł as prefixes to express that the underlying t-norm is Gödel, product, or Łukasiewicz, respectively, as usual in the literature.

We can now formally define the semantics of the logic. An *interpretation* is a pair $\mathcal{I} = (\Delta^{\mathcal{I}}, \cdot^{\mathcal{I}})$, where $\Delta^{\mathcal{I}}$ is a non-empty set called the *domain*, and $\cdot^{\mathcal{I}}$ is the *interpretation function* which maps every individual name $a \in N_I$ to an element $a^{\mathcal{I}} \in \Delta^{\mathcal{I}}$; every concept name $A \in N_C$ to a function $A^{\mathcal{I}} : \Delta^{\mathcal{I}} \to [0,1]$; and every role name $P \in N_R$ to a function $P^{\mathcal{I}} : \Delta^{\mathcal{I}} \times \Delta^{\mathcal{I}} \to [0,1]$. That is, concept names are interpreted as fuzzy unary relations and role names are interpreted as fuzzy binary relations over $\Delta^{\mathcal{I}}$. The interpretation function is extended to other constructors with the help of the t-norm operators as follows. For every $\delta, \eta \in \Delta^{\mathcal{I}}$,

$$(\exists Q)^{\mathcal{I}}(\delta) := \sup_{\delta' \in \Delta^{\mathcal{I}}} Q^{\mathcal{I}}(\delta, \delta') \qquad (\neg B)^{\mathcal{I}}(\delta) := \ominus B^{\mathcal{I}}(\delta) \qquad (\top)^{\mathcal{I}}(\delta) := 1$$

$$(P^-)^{\mathcal{I}}(\delta, \eta) := P^{\mathcal{I}}(\eta, \delta) \qquad (\neg Q)^{\mathcal{I}}(\delta, \eta) := \ominus Q^{\mathcal{I}}(\delta, \eta)$$

The interpretation $\mathcal{I}$ *satisfies* the axiom

- $\langle B \sqsubseteq C, d \rangle$ iff for every $\delta \in \Delta^{\mathcal{I}}$, $B^{\mathcal{I}}(\delta) \Rightarrow C^{\mathcal{I}}(\delta) \geq d$;
- $\langle Q \sqsubseteq R, d \rangle$ iff for every $\delta, \eta \in \Delta^{\mathcal{I}}$, $Q^{\mathcal{I}}(\delta, \eta) \Rightarrow R^{\mathcal{I}}(\delta, \eta) \geq d$.

It is a *model* of the TBox $\mathcal{T}$ if it satisfies all axioms in $\mathcal{T}$. $\mathcal{I}$ *satisfies* the assertion

- $\langle B(a), d \rangle$ iff $B^{\mathcal{I}}(a^{\mathcal{I}}) \geq d$;
- $\langle P(a, b), d \rangle$ iff $P^{\mathcal{I}}(a^{\mathcal{I}}, b^{\mathcal{I}}) \geq d$.

It is a *model* of the ABox $\mathcal{A}$ if it satisfies all axioms in $\mathcal{A}$, and it is a *model* of the ontology $\mathcal{O} = (\mathcal{T}, \mathcal{A})$ if it is a model of $\mathcal{T}$ and of $\mathcal{A}$.

We note that the classical notion of DL-Lite$_R$ [9] is a special case of fuzzy DL-Lite$_R$, where all the axioms and assertions hold with degree 1. In that case, it suffices to consider interpretations which map all elements to $\{0, 1\}$ representing the classical truth values. When speaking of classical ontologies, we remove the degree and assume it implicitly to be 1.

For this paper, we are interested in answering conjunctive queries, which consider whether a combination of facts can be derived from the knowledge in an ontology. Let N_V be a set of *variables*, which is disjoint from N_I, N_C, and N_R. A *term* is an element of $N_V \cup N_I$; that is, an individual name or a variable. An *atom* is an expression of the form $C(t)$ (concept atom) or $P(t_1, t_2)$ (role atom). Let $\mathbf{x}$ and $\mathbf{y}$ denote vectors of variables. A *conjunctive query* (CQ) is a first-order formula of the form $\exists \mathbf{y}. \phi(\mathbf{x}, \mathbf{y})$ where ϕ is a conjunction of atoms which only use the variables from $\mathbf{x}$ and $\mathbf{y}$. Let $\mathsf{At}(\phi)$ denote the set of all atoms appearing in ϕ. The variables $\mathbf{y}$ are called *existential variables*, and those in $\mathbf{x}$ are *answer variables*. A *union of conjunctive queries* (UCQ) is a finite set of CQs that use the same answer variables.

Given the CQ $q(\mathbf{x}) = \exists \mathbf{y}. \phi(\mathbf{x}, \mathbf{y})$, the interpretation $\mathcal{I}$, and a vector of individuals $\mathbf{a}$ of the same length as $\mathbf{x}$, a *match* is a mapping π which assigns to each $a \in N_I$ the value $a^{\mathcal{I}}$; to each variable in $\mathbf{x}$ the corresponding element of $\mathbf{a}^{\mathcal{I}}$; and to each variable in $\mathbf{y}$ an element $\delta \in \Delta^{\mathcal{I}}$. We extend the match π to apply to assertions as follows: $\pi(B(t)) = B(\pi(t))$ and $\pi(P(t_1, t_2)) = P(\pi(t_1), \pi(t_2))$. The *degree* of the CQ $q(\mathbf{x})$ w.r.t. the match π is

$$q^{\mathcal{I}}(\mathbf{a}^{\mathcal{I}}, \pi(\mathbf{y})) := \bigotimes_{\alpha \in \mathsf{At}(\phi)} (\pi(\alpha))^{\mathcal{I}}.$$

That is, a match maps all the variables in the query to elements of the interpretation domain, where the vector $\mathbf{a}$ is used to identify the mapping of the answer variables. The degree of the query is the (fuzzy) conjunction of the degrees of the atoms under this mapping. From now on, $\Pi(\mathcal{I})$ denotes the set of all matches of $q(\mathbf{x})$ w.r.t. the interpretation $\mathcal{I}$.

A tuple of individuals $\mathbf{a}$ is an *answer* of $q(\mathbf{x})$ to degree d w.r.t. the interpretation $\mathcal{I}$ (denoted by $\mathcal{I} \models q(\mathbf{a}) \geq d$) iff $q^{\mathcal{I}}(\mathbf{a}^{\mathcal{I}}) := \sup_{\pi \in \Pi(\mathcal{I})} q^{\mathcal{I}}(\mathbf{a}^{\mathcal{I}}, \pi(\mathbf{y})) \geq d$. It is a *certain answer* (or answer for short) of $q(\mathbf{x})$ over the ontology $\mathcal{O}$ to degree d (denoted as $\mathcal{O} \models q(\mathbf{a}) \geq d$) iff for every model $\mathcal{I}$ of $\mathcal{O}$ it holds that $\mathcal{I} \models q(\mathbf{a}) \geq d$. The set of certain answers of the query $q(\mathbf{x})$ w.r.t. $\mathcal{O}$ and their degree is denoted by $\mathsf{ans}(q(\mathbf{x}), \mathcal{O})$; that is,

$$\mathsf{ans}(q(\mathbf{x}), \mathcal{O}) := \{(\mathbf{a}, d) \mid \mathcal{O} \models q(\mathbf{a}) \geq d \text{ and for all } d' > d, \mathcal{O} \not\models q(\mathbf{a}) \geq d'\}.$$

It is important to keep in mind that the atoms in a CQ are not graded, but simply try to match with elements in the domain. The use of the truth degrees becomes relevant in the degree of the answers found.

A class of queries of special significance is that where the vector of answer variables $\mathbf{x}$ is empty. This means that the answer tuple of individuals must also be empty. In the classical setting, these are called *Boolean queries*, because they can only return a Boolean value: true if there is a match for the existential variables in every model, and false otherwise. In the fuzzy setting, the set of answers to such a query will only contain one element $((), d)$. Thus, in that case, we are only interested in finding the degree d, and call them *degree queries*. This degree is the tightest value for which we can find a satisfying matching. Formally, the ontology $\mathcal{O}$ *entails* the degree query $q()$ to degree d iff $\mathcal{O} \models q() \geq d$ and $\mathcal{O} \not\models q() \geq d'$ for all $d' > d$. Degree queries allow us to find the degree of a specific answer $\mathbf{a}$ without having to compute $\mathsf{ans}(q(\mathbf{x}), \mathcal{O})$: simply compute the degree of the degree query $q(\mathbf{a})$.

As typical in query answering for description logics, we consider two measures of complexity: *data complexity*, where only the size of the ABox is considered as part of the input, and *combined complexity* in which the size of the whole ontology (including the TBox) is taken into account.[1] For data complexity, it is relevant to consider sub-linear complexity classes. In particular, we consider AC^0 and LogSpace. For the formal definitions, see [4,18]; here we only mention briefly that evaluation of FO-queries over a database is in AC^0 on the size of the database [1] and AC^0 is strictly contained in LogSpace [11,19].

In classical DL-Lite, query answering w.r.t. an ontology is reduced to the standard problem of query answering over a database through a process known as query rewriting, and thus is in AC^0 w.r.t. data complexity. The main idea is to include in the query all the information that is required by the TBox, in such a way that only assertions from the ABox need to be considered. Since there are many possible choices to create the matches that comply with the TBox,

---

[1] Note that *combined complexity* does not include the query as part of the input, but only the ontology. This is in line with the terminology used in ontology-based query answering; e.g. [2]. It is typically only used in combination of simple fixed queries.

this method results in a UCQ. At this point, the ABox is treated as a database, which suffices to find all the certain answers. Similarly, a special UCQ can be used to verify that the ontology is *consistent*; that is, whether it is possible to build a model for this ontology. For the full details on how these query rewritings work in classical DL-Lite, see [9]. In terms of combined complexity, consistency can be decided in polynomial time; in fact, it is NLOGSPACE-complete [2].

3   The Canonical Interpretation

A very useful tool for developing techniques for answering queries in DL-Lite$_R$ is the canonical interpretation. We first show that the same idea can be extended to fuzzy ontologies, independently of the t-norm underlying its semantics.

Let $\mathcal{O} = (\mathcal{T}, \mathcal{A})$ be a DL-Lite ontology and assume w.l.o.g. that there are no axioms of the form $\langle \exists Q_1 \sqsubseteq \exists Q_2, d \rangle \in \mathcal{T}$; any such axiom can be substituted by the two axioms $\langle \exists Q_1 \sqsubseteq A, 1 \rangle, \langle A \sqsubseteq \exists Q_2, d \rangle$ where A is a concept name not appearing in $\mathcal{T}$. The *canonical interpretation* of $\mathcal{O}$ is the interpretation $\mathcal{I}_{\mathsf{can}}(\mathcal{O})$ over the domain $\Delta^{\mathcal{I}_{\mathsf{can}}} := N_I \cup N_N$, where N_N is a countable set of *constants* obtained through the following (infinite) process. Starting from the *empty* interpretation which sets $A^{\mathcal{I}_{\mathsf{can}}}(\delta) = 0$ and $P^{\mathcal{I}_{\mathsf{can}}}(\delta, \eta) = 0$ for every $A \in N_C, P \in N_R$ and $\delta, \eta \in \Delta^{\mathcal{I}_{\mathsf{can}}}$, exhaustively apply the following rules:

- if $\langle A(a), d \rangle \in \mathcal{A}$ and $A^{\mathcal{I}_{\mathsf{can}}}(a) < d$, then update $A^{\mathcal{I}_{\mathsf{can}}}(a) := d$;
- if $\langle P(a, b), d \rangle \in \mathcal{A}$ and $P^{\mathcal{I}_{\mathsf{can}}}(a, b) < d$, then update $P^{\mathcal{I}_{\mathsf{can}}}(a, b) := d$;
- if $\langle A_1 \sqsubseteq A_2, d \rangle \in \mathcal{T}$ and $A_2^{\mathcal{I}_{\mathsf{can}}}(\delta) < A_1^{\mathcal{I}_{\mathsf{can}}}(\delta) \otimes d$, then update the value $A_2^{\mathcal{I}_{\mathsf{can}}}(\delta) := A_1^{\mathcal{I}_{\mathsf{can}}}(\delta) \otimes d$;
- if $\langle A \sqsubseteq \exists P, d \rangle \in \mathcal{T}$ and for every $\eta \in \Delta^{\mathcal{I}_{\mathsf{can}}}$, $P^{\mathcal{I}_{\mathsf{can}}}(\delta, \eta) < A^{\mathcal{I}_{\mathsf{can}}}(\delta) \otimes d$ holds, then select a fresh element η_0 such that $P^{\mathcal{I}_{\mathsf{can}}}(\delta, \eta_0) = 0$ and update $P^{\mathcal{I}_{\mathsf{can}}}(\delta, \eta_0) := A^{\mathcal{I}_{\mathsf{can}}}(\delta) \otimes d$;
- if $\langle A \sqsubseteq \exists P^-, d \rangle \in \mathcal{T}$ and for every $\eta \in \Delta^{\mathcal{I}_{\mathsf{can}}}$ $P^{\mathcal{I}_{\mathsf{can}}}(\eta, \delta) < A^{\mathcal{I}_{\mathsf{can}}}(\delta) \otimes d$ holds, then select a fresh element η_0 such that $P^{\mathcal{I}_{\mathsf{can}}}(\eta_0, \delta) = 0$ and update $P^{\mathcal{I}_{\mathsf{can}}}(\eta_0, \delta) := A^{\mathcal{I}_{\mathsf{can}}}(\delta) \otimes d$;
- if $\langle \exists P \sqsubseteq A, d \rangle \in \mathcal{T}$ and $\exists \eta \in \Delta^{\mathcal{I}_{\mathsf{can}}}$ such that $A^{\mathcal{I}_{\mathsf{can}}}(\delta) < P^{\mathcal{I}_{\mathsf{can}}}(\delta, \eta) \otimes d$, then update $A^{\mathcal{I}_{\mathsf{can}}}(\delta) := P^{\mathcal{I}_{\mathsf{can}}}(\delta, \eta) \otimes d$;
- if $\langle \exists P^- \sqsubseteq A, d \rangle \in \mathcal{T}$ and $\exists \eta \in \Delta^{\mathcal{I}_{\mathsf{can}}}$ such that $A^{\mathcal{I}_{\mathsf{can}}}(\delta) < P^{\mathcal{I}_{\mathsf{can}}}(\eta, \delta) \otimes d$, then update $A^{\mathcal{I}_{\mathsf{can}}}(\delta) := P^{\mathcal{I}_{\mathsf{can}}}(\eta, \delta) \otimes d$;
- if $\langle Q_1 \sqsubseteq Q_2, d \rangle \in \mathcal{T}$ and $Q_2^{\mathcal{I}_{\mathsf{can}}}(\delta, \eta) < Q_1^{\mathcal{I}_{\mathsf{can}}}(\delta, \eta) \otimes d$, then update the value $Q_2^{\mathcal{I}_{\mathsf{can}}}(\delta, \eta) := Q_1^{\mathcal{I}_{\mathsf{can}}}(\delta, \eta) \otimes d$.

where the rules are applied in a fair manner; that is, an applicable rule is eventually triggered. The process of rule application is a monotone increasing function, and as such has a least fixpoint, which is the canonical interpretation $\mathcal{I}_{\mathsf{can}}(\mathcal{O})$.

Intuitively, $\mathcal{I}_{\mathsf{can}}(\mathcal{O})$ should be a minimal model of $\mathcal{O}$, which describes the necessary conditions of all other models of $\mathcal{O}$. Indeed, the first two rules ensure that the conditions imposed by the ABox are satisfied, while the remaining rules guarantee that all elements of the domain satisfy the positive axioms from the TBox, and each rule is as weak as possible in satisfying these constraints.

However, the construction of $\mathcal{I}_{\mathsf{can}}(\mathcal{O})$ does not take the negations into account. The effect of this is that $\mathcal{I}_{\mathsf{can}}(\mathcal{O})$ might not be a model of $\mathcal{O}$.

Example 1. Consider the fuzzy DL-Lite ontology $\mathcal{O}_0 = (\mathcal{T}_0, \mathcal{A}_0)$ where

$$\mathcal{T}_0 := \{\langle A_1 \sqsubseteq \neg A_2, 1\rangle\},$$
$$\mathcal{A}_0 := \{\langle A_1(a), 0.5\rangle, \langle A_2(a), 0.5\rangle\}.$$

Under the Gödel semantics, by application of the first rule, the canonical interpretation maps $A_1^{\mathcal{I}_{\mathsf{can}}}(a) = A_2^{\mathcal{I}_{\mathsf{can}}}(a) = 0.5$. However, this violates the axiom in $\mathcal{T}_0$, which requires that $A_1^{\mathcal{I}_{\mathsf{can}}}(a) \Rightarrow \ominus A_2^{\mathcal{I}_{\mathsf{can}}}(a) = 1$. That is, it requires that $A_1^{\mathcal{I}_{\mathsf{can}}}(a) < \ominus A_2^{\mathcal{I}_{\mathsf{can}}}(a)$, which is only possible when $A_1^{\mathcal{I}_{\mathsf{can}}}(a) = 0$ or $A_2^{\mathcal{I}_{\mathsf{can}}}(a) = 0$.

The issue is that the negative axioms may introduce inconsistencies, by enforcing upper bounds in the degrees used, which are not verified by the canonical interpretation. However, as long as there is a model, $\mathcal{I}_{\mathsf{can}}(\mathcal{O})$ is one.

Proposition 2. $\mathcal{I}_{\mathsf{can}}(\mathcal{O})$ *is a model of $\mathcal{O}$ iff $\mathcal{O}$ is consistent.*

It can be seen that $\mathcal{O}_0$ from Example 1 is inconsistent under the Gödel semantics. On the other hand, under the Łukasiewicz semantics, $\mathcal{O}_0$ is consistent which, by this proposition, means that $\mathcal{I}_{\mathsf{can}}(\mathcal{O})$ is a model of this ontology. This is easily confirmed by recalling that under the Łukasiewicz negation $\ominus 0.5 = 0.5$.

The name *canonical* comes from the fact that, as in the classical case, $\mathcal{I}_{\mathsf{can}}(\mathcal{O})$ can be homomorphically embedded in every model of $\mathcal{O}$. We show a similar result with the difference that in this case, the homomorphism needs to take into account the truth degrees from the interpretation function as well. This is described in the following proposition.

Proposition 3. *Let $\mathcal{O}$ be a consistent fuzzy DL-Lite ontology, $\mathcal{I} = (\Delta^{\mathcal{I}}, \cdot^{\mathcal{I}})$ a model of $\mathcal{O}$, and $\mathcal{I}_{\mathsf{can}}(\mathcal{O}) = (\Delta^{\mathcal{I}_{\mathsf{can}}}, \cdot^{\mathcal{I}_{\mathsf{can}}})$ its canonical interpretation. There is a function ψ from $\Delta^{\mathcal{I}_{\mathsf{can}}}$ to $\Delta^{\mathcal{I}}$ such that:*

1. for each $A \in N_I$ and $\delta \in \Delta^{\mathcal{I}_{\mathsf{can}}}$, $A^{\mathcal{I}_{\mathsf{can}}}(\delta) \leq A^{\mathcal{I}}(\delta)$; and
2. for each $P \in N_R$ and $\delta, \eta \in \Delta^{\mathcal{I}_{\mathsf{can}}}$, $P^{\mathcal{I}_{\mathsf{can}}}(\delta, \eta) \leq P^{\mathcal{I}}(\delta, \eta)$.

The consequence of this proposition is that $\mathcal{I}_{\mathsf{can}}(\mathcal{O})$ is complete for existential positive queries, and in particular for conjunctive queries.

Corollary 4. *If $\mathcal{O}$ is a consistent fuzzy DL-Lite ontology, then for every CQ $q(\mathbf{x})$ and answer tuple $\mathbf{a}$ it holds that $\mathcal{O} \models q(\mathbf{a}) \geq d$ iff $\mathcal{I}_{\mathsf{can}}(\mathcal{O}) \models q(\mathbf{a}) \geq d$.*

Obviously, answering queries through $\mathcal{I}_{\mathsf{can}}(\mathcal{O})$ is impractical, because it is an infinite model constructed through an infinitary process. Additionally, we still have the burden to prove that the ontology is consistent, before trying to use Corollary 4 to answer queries. Fortunately, for the Gödel and product t-norms, we resort to existing results from the literature.

Given a fuzzy DL-Lite ontology $\mathcal{O} = (\mathcal{T}, \mathcal{A})$, let $\widehat{\mathcal{O}}$ be its *classical version* defined as $\widehat{\mathcal{O}} := (\widehat{\mathcal{T}}, \widehat{\mathcal{A}})$ with

$$\widehat{\mathcal{T}} := \{B \sqsubseteq C \mid \langle B \sqsubseteq C, d \rangle \in \mathcal{T}, d > 0\} \cup \{Q \sqsubseteq R \mid \langle Q \sqsubseteq R, d \rangle \in \mathcal{T}, d > 0\},$$

$$\widehat{\mathcal{A}} := \{B(a) \mid \langle B(a), d \rangle \in \mathcal{T}, d > 0\} \cup \{P(a, b) \mid \langle P(a, b), d \rangle \in \mathcal{T}, d > 0\}.$$

That is, $\widehat{\mathcal{O}}$ contains all the axioms and assertions from $\mathcal{O}$ which hold with a positive degree—note that any fuzzy axiom or assertion with degree 0 could be removed w.l.o.g. anyway. The following result is a consequence of work on more expressive fuzzy DLs [7].

Proposition 5. *Let $\mathcal{O}$ be a G-DL-Lite$_R$ or π-DL-Lite$_R$ ontology. Then $\mathcal{O}$ is consistent iff $\widehat{\mathcal{O}}$ is consistent.*

In those cases, consistency checking can be reduced to the classical case, without the need to modify the query or the basic formulation of the ontology. For the ontology $\mathcal{O}_0$ in Example 1, we have $\widehat{\mathcal{O}_0} = (\{A_1 \sqsubseteq \neg A_2\}, \{A_1(a), A_2(a)\})$, which is inconsistent in the classical case. We note that the example also shows that Proposition 5 does not hold for the Łukasiewicz t-norm.

In particular, Proposition 5 shows that deciding consistency of G-DL-Lite$_R$ and π-DL-Lite$_R$ ontologies is in AC^0 w.r.t. data complexity and in NLogSpace w.r.t. combined complexity. Thus adding truth degrees does not affect the complexity of this reasoning task. We now turn our attention to the task of query answering with the different semantics, starting with the idempotent case of the Gödel t-norm.

Before studying how to answer queries over fuzzy DL-Lite$_R$ ontologies and its complexity, we note that in the case that an ontology is classical—i.e., it uses only degree 1 in all its axioms—its canonical interpretation constructed as described in this section is equivalent to the classical canonical interpretation from [9]. This fact will be used in the following section.

4   Answering Queries over Gödel Ontologies

The Gödel semantics are very limited in their expressivity. On the one hand, $\ominus d \in \{0, 1\}$ for all $d \in [0, 1]$. This means that whenever we have an axiom of the form $\langle B \sqsubseteq \neg B', d \rangle$ or $\langle Q \sqsubseteq \neg Q', d \rangle$ with $d > 0$, we are in fact saying that for every element $\delta \in \Delta^{\mathcal{I}}$, if $B^{\mathcal{I}}(\delta) > 0$, then $B'^{\mathcal{I}}(\delta) = 0$—because $\ominus B'^{\mathcal{I}}(\delta) = 1$ (and similarly for role axioms). Thus, for this section we can assume w.l.o.g. that all negative axioms hold with degree 1. On the other hand, a positive axiom of the form $\langle B \sqsubseteq B', d \rangle$ requires that for every $\delta \in \Delta^{\mathcal{I}}$, $B'^{\mathcal{I}}(\delta) \geq \min\{B^{\mathcal{I}}(\delta), d\}$. That is, the only way to guarantee that an atom gets a high degree is to use axioms with a high degree. We use these facts to reduce reasoning tasks in this setting to the classical DL-Lite$_R$ scenario.

Consider a consistent G-DL-Lite$_R$ ontology $\mathcal{O}$. We can decide a lower bound for the degree of a CQ simply by querying a *cut* of $\mathcal{O}$. Given a value $d \in (0, 1]$, the d-*cut* of $\mathcal{O}$ is defined as the sub-ontology $\mathcal{O}_{\geq d} := (\mathcal{T}_{\geq d}, \mathcal{A}_{\geq d})$ where

$$\mathcal{T}_{\geq d} := \{\langle \gamma, e \rangle \in \mathcal{T} \mid e \geq d\},$$
$$\mathcal{A}_{\geq d} := \{\langle \alpha, e \rangle \in \mathcal{A} \mid e \geq d\}.$$

That is, $\mathcal{O}_{\geq d}$ is the subontology containing only the axioms and assertions that hold to degree at least d. To show that d-cuts suffice for answering queries, we use the canonical interpretation.

Note that including new axioms or assertions to an ontology results in an update of the canonical interpretation which only increases the degree of some of the elements of the domain. More precisely, if $\mathcal{I}_{\mathsf{can}}(\mathcal{O})$ is the canonical interpretation of $\mathcal{O} = (\mathcal{T}, \mathcal{A})$, then the canonical interpretation of $\mathcal{O}' = (\mathcal{T} \cup \{\langle B \sqsubseteq C, d \rangle\}, \mathcal{A})$ is the result of applying the construction rules starting from $\mathcal{I}_{\mathsf{can}}(\mathcal{O})$. Since $\mathcal{I}_{\mathsf{can}}(\mathcal{O})$ has already applied all the rules on axioms of $\mathcal{O}$ exhaustively, the only remaining rule applications will be based on the new axiom $\langle B \sqsubseteq C, d \rangle$ and new applications over $\mathcal{T}$. Under the Gödel semantics, all the updates increase the interpretation function up to the value d; that is, if $\cdot^{\mathcal{I}'_{\mathsf{can}}}$ is the interpretation function of $\mathcal{I}_{\mathsf{can}}(\mathcal{O}')$, the difference between $\mathcal{I}_{\mathsf{can}}(\mathcal{O})$ and $\mathcal{I}_{\mathsf{can}}(\mathcal{O}')$ is that there exist some elements such that $A^{\mathcal{I}_{\mathsf{can}}}(\delta) < A^{\mathcal{I}'_{\mathsf{can}}}(\delta) = d$, and similarly for roles. Moreover, if d_0 is the smallest degree appearing in the ontology $\mathcal{O}$, then its canonical interpretation uses only truth degrees in $\{0\} \cup [d_0, 1]$; that is, no truth degree in $(0, d_0)$ appears in $\mathcal{I}_{\mathsf{can}}(\mathcal{O})$. With these insights we are ready to produce our first results. For the rest of this section, we always consider that the semantics is based on the Gödel t-norm; i.e., we have a G-DL-Lite$_R$ ontology.

Lemma 6. *Let $\mathcal{O}$ be a consistent G-DL-Lite$_R$ ontology, $q(\mathbf{x})$ a query, $\mathbf{a}$ a vector of individuals, and $d \in (0, 1]$. Then $\mathcal{O} \models q(\mathbf{a}) \geq d$ iff $\mathcal{O}_{\geq d} \models q(\mathbf{a}) \geq d$.*

Proof. Since $\mathcal{O}_{\geq d} \subseteq \mathcal{O}$, every model of $\mathcal{O}$ is also a model of $\mathcal{O}_{\geq d}$. Hence, if $\mathcal{O}_{\geq d} \models q(\mathbf{a}) \geq d$, then $\mathcal{O} \models q(\mathbf{a}) \geq d$.

For the converse, assume that $\mathcal{O}_{\geq d} \not\models q(\mathbf{a}) \geq d$. By Corollary 4, this means that $\mathcal{I}_{\mathsf{can}}(\mathcal{O}_{\geq d}) \not\models q(\mathbf{a}) \geq d$. That is, $q^{\mathcal{I}_{\mathsf{can}}}(\mathbf{a}^{\mathcal{I}_{\mathsf{can}}}) < d$. Let $\mathcal{I}_{\mathsf{can}}(\mathcal{O}) = (\Delta^{\mathcal{I}_{\mathsf{can}}}, \cdot^{\mathcal{I}_{\mathsf{can}}})$ be the canonical interpretation of $\mathcal{O}$. Recall that the difference between $\mathcal{O}$ and $\mathcal{O}_{\geq d}$ is that the former has some additional axioms with degrees smaller than d. As argued before, this means that the difference between $\mathcal{I}_{\mathsf{can}}(\mathcal{O})$ and $\mathcal{I}_{\mathsf{can}}(\mathcal{O}_{\geq d})$ are just some degrees, which are all smaller than d; that is, for every $A \in N_C$, $P \in N_R$, and $\delta, \eta \in \Delta^{\mathcal{I}_{\mathsf{can}}}$, if $A^{\mathcal{I}_{\mathsf{can}}}(\delta) \geq d$, then $A^{\mathcal{I}_{\mathsf{can}}}(\delta) \geq d$ and if $P^{\mathcal{I}_{\mathsf{can}}}(\delta, \eta) \geq d$, then $P^{\mathcal{I}_{\mathsf{can}}}(\delta, \eta) \geq d$. By assumption, this means that $q^{\mathcal{I}'_{\mathsf{can}}}(\mathbf{a}^{\mathcal{I}'_{\mathsf{can}}}) < d$ and hence $\mathcal{I}_{\mathsf{can}}(\mathcal{O}) \not\models q(\mathbf{a}) \geq d$. Thus, $\mathcal{O} \not\models q(\mathbf{a}) \geq d$. □

What this lemma states is that in order to find a lower bound for the degree of a query, one can ignore all the axioms and assertions that provide a smaller degree. However, one still needs to answer a query for a fuzzy ontology, for which we do not have any solution. The next lemma solves this issue.

Lemma 7. *Let $\mathcal{O}$ be a consistent G-DL-Lite$_R$ ontology such that $\mathcal{O}_{\geq d} = \mathcal{O}$ for some $d > 0$. Then, $\mathcal{O} \models q(\mathbf{a}) \geq d$ iff $\widehat{\mathcal{O}} \models q(\mathbf{a})$.*

Algorithm 1: Compute the degree of an answer to a query

Data: Ontology $\mathcal{O}$, query q, answer $\mathbf{a}$, $\mathcal{D} = \{d_0, d_1, \ldots, d_{n+1}\}$
Result: The degree of $q(\mathbf{a})$ w.r.t. $\mathcal{O}$

1   $i \leftarrow n + 1$
2   $\mathcal{N} \leftarrow \widehat{\mathcal{O}}_{\geq 1}$
3   **while** $\mathcal{N} \not\models q(\mathbf{a})$ **and** $i > 0$ **do**
4      $i \leftarrow i - 1$
5      $\mathcal{N} \leftarrow \widehat{\mathcal{O}}_{\geq d_i}$
6   **return** d_i

Proof. Every model of $\widehat{\mathcal{O}}$ is also a model of $\mathcal{O}$, with the additional property that the interpretation function maps all elements to $\{0, 1\}$. If $\mathcal{O} \models q(\mathbf{a}) \geq d > 0$, then for every model $\mathcal{I}$ of $\widehat{\mathcal{O}}$ it holds that $q^{\mathcal{I}}(\mathbf{a}^{\mathcal{I}}) \geq d > 0$ and thus $q^{\mathcal{I}}(\mathbf{a}^{\mathcal{I}}) = 1$, which means that $\widehat{\mathcal{O}} \models q(\mathbf{a})$.

Conversely, if $\widehat{\mathcal{O}} \models q(\mathbf{a})$, the canonical interpretation $\mathcal{I}_{\mathsf{can}}(\mathcal{O})$ must be such that $q^{\mathcal{I}_{\mathsf{can}}}(\mathbf{a}^{\mathcal{I}_{\mathsf{can}}}) > 0$; but as argued before, since $\mathcal{O}$ only has axioms and assertions with degrees $\geq d$, it must be the case that all degrees of $\mathcal{I}_{\mathsf{can}}(\mathcal{O})$ are in $\{0\} \cup [d, 1]$, and hence $q^{\mathcal{I}_{\mathsf{can}}}(\mathbf{a}^{\mathcal{I}_{\mathsf{can}}}) \geq d$. This implies, by Corollary 4 that $\mathcal{O} \models q(\mathbf{a}) \geq d$. □

These two lemmas together provide a method for reducing bound queries in G-DL-Lite$_R$ to query answering in classical DL-Lite$_R$.

Theorem 8. *If $\mathcal{O}$ is a consistent G-DL-Lite$_R$ ontology and $d > 0$, then it holds that $\mathcal{O} \models q(\mathbf{a}) \geq d$ iff $\widehat{\mathcal{O}}_{\geq d} \models q(\mathbf{a})$.*

This means that we can use a standard ontology-based query answering system to answer fuzzy queries in DL-Lite$_R$ as well. Note that the approach proposed by Theorem 8 can only decide whether the degree of an answer to a query is at least d, but it needs the value d as a parameter. If, instead, we are interested in computing the degree of an answer, or $\mathsf{ans}(q(\mathbf{x}), \mathcal{O})$, we can proceed as follows.

Since the TBox $\mathcal{T}$ and the ABox $\mathcal{A}$ which compose the ontology $\mathcal{O}$ are both finite, the set $\mathcal{D} := \{d \mid \langle \alpha, d \rangle \in \mathcal{T} \cup \mathcal{A}\}$ of degrees appearing in the ontology is also finite; in fact, its size is bounded by the size of $\mathcal{O}$. Hence, we can assume that $\mathcal{D}$ is of the form $\mathcal{D} = \{d_0, d_1, \ldots, d_n, d_{n+1}\}$ where $d_0 \geq 0, d_{n+1} \leq 1$ and for all $i, 0 \leq i \leq n$, $d_i < d_{i+1}$. In order to find the degree of an answer $\mathbf{a}$ to a query q, we proceed as follows: starting from $i := n + 1$, we iteratively ask the query $\mathcal{O}_{\geq d_i} \models q(\mathbf{a})$ and decrease i until the query is answered affirmatively, or i becomes 0 (see Algorithm 1). In the former case, d_i is the degree for $q(\mathbf{a})$; in the latter, the degree is 0—i.e., $\mathbf{a}$ is not an answer of q.

During the execution of this algorithm, each classical query needed at line 3 can be executed in AC^0 (and in particular in LogSpace) in the size of the data; i.e., the ABox [2]. The iterations in the loop do not affect the overall space used, as one can simply produce a new query every time and clean up the previous information. Overall, this means that the degree of an answer can be computed in LogSpace in data complexity.

Corollary 9. *The degree of an answer* **a** *to a query q w.r.t. the G-DL-Lite$_R$ ontology $\mathcal{O}$ is computable in* LOGSPACE *in data complexity.*

Computing $\mathsf{ans}(q(\mathbf{x}), \mathcal{O})$ is, however, a more complex task. Although we can follow an approach similar to Algorithm 1, where the answers to $q(\mathbf{x})$ are computed for each ontology $\widehat{\mathcal{O}}_{\geq d_i}$, in order to assign the appropriate degree to each answer, we need to either keep track of all the answers found so far, or add a negated query which excludes the answers with a higher degree. In both cases, we end up outside the realm of LOGSPACE complexity. On the other hand, the whole set of answers $\mathsf{ans}(q(\mathbf{x}), \mathcal{O})$ will usually contain many answers that hold with a very low degree, which may not be of much interest to the user making the query. When dealing with degrees, a more meaningful task is to find the k answers with the highest degree, for some natural number k; i.e., the *top-k answers* of q.

Algorithm 1 once again suggests a way to compute the top-k answers. As in the algorithm, one starts with the highest possible degree, and expands the classical ontology by including the axioms and assertions with a lower degree. The difference is that one stops now when the query returns at least k tuples as answers. At that point, the tuples found are those with the highest degree for the query. As before, each of these queries can be answered in AC^0 in data complexity, which yields a LOGSPACE upper bound for answering top-k queries in data complexity.

Corollary 10. *Top-k queries over consistent G-DL-Lite$_R$ ontologies can be answered in* NLOGSPACE *in data complexity.*

5 Non-idempotent t-Norms

We now move our attention to the t-norms that are not idempotent; in particular the product and Łukasiewicz t-norms. Unfortunately, as we will see, the correctness of the reductions presented in the previous section relies strongly on the idempotency of the Gödel t-norm, and does not transfer directly to the other cases. However, at least for the product t-norm, it is still possible to answer some kinds of queries efficiently.

First recall that Proposition 5 holds for the product t-norm as well. Hence, deciding consistency of a π-DL-Lite$_R$ ontology remains reducible to the classical case and thus, efficient. We now show with simple examples that the other results do not transfer so easily.

Example 11. Let $\mathcal{O}_1 := (\mathcal{T}_1, \mathcal{A}_1)$ with $\mathcal{T}_1 := \{\langle A_i \sqsubseteq A_{i+1}, 0.9 \rangle \mid 0 \leq i < n\}$ and $\mathcal{A}_1 := \{\langle A_0(a), 1 \rangle\}$. Note that $\mathcal{O}_1 = \mathcal{O}_{1 \geq 0.9}$, but the degree for the query $q() = A_n(a)$ is 0.9^n which can be made arbitrarily small by making n large.

Similarly, it is not possible to find the top-k answers simply by layering the d-cuts for decreasing values of d until enough answers can be found.

Example 12. Let $\mathcal{O}'_1 := (\mathcal{T}_1, \mathcal{A}'_1)$, where $\mathcal{A}'_1 := \mathcal{A}_1 \cup \{\langle A_n(b), 0.85\rangle\}$ and $\mathcal{T}_1, \mathcal{A}_1$ are as in Example 11. The top answer for $q(x) = A_n(x)$ is b with degree 0.85, but from $\mathcal{O}'_{1 \geq 0.9}$ we already find the answer a, which is not the top one.

The main point with these examples is that, from the lack of idempotency of the t-norm $\otimes$, we can obtain low degrees in a match which arises from combining several axioms and assertions having a high degree. On the other hand, the product behaves well for positive values in the sense that applying the t-norm to two positive values always results in a positive value; formally, if $d, e > 0$, then $d \otimes e > 0$. Thus, if we are only interested in knowing whether the result of a query is positive or not, there is no difference between the Gödel t-norm and the product t-norm.

Definition 13. *A tuple* $\mathbf{a}$ *is a* positive answer *to the query* $q(\mathbf{x})$ *w.r.t. the ontology* $\mathcal{O}$ *(denoted* $\mathcal{O} \models q(\mathbf{a}) > 0$*) iff for every model* $\mathcal{I}$ *of* $\mathcal{O}$ *it holds that* $q^{\mathcal{I}}(\mathbf{a}^{\mathcal{I}}) > 0$.

Theorem 14. *If* $\mathcal{O}$ *is a consistent* π-DL-$Lite_R$ *ontology, then* $\mathcal{O} \models q(\mathbf{a}) > 0$ *iff* $\widehat{\mathcal{O}} \models q(\mathbf{a})$.

Proof. Every model of $\widehat{\mathcal{O}}$ is also a model of $\mathcal{O}$, with the additional property that the interpretation function maps all elements to $\{0, 1\}$. If $\mathcal{O} \models q(\mathbf{a}) > 0$, then for every model $\mathcal{I}$ of $\widehat{\mathcal{O}}$ it holds that $q^{\mathcal{I}}(\mathbf{a}^{\mathcal{I}}) > 0$ and thus $q^{\mathcal{I}}(\mathbf{a}^{\mathcal{I}}) = 1$, which means that $\widehat{\mathcal{O}} \models q(\mathbf{a})$.

Conversely, if $\widehat{\mathcal{O}} \models q(\mathbf{a})$, then the canonical interpretation is such that $q^{\mathcal{I}_{can}}(\mathbf{a}^{\mathcal{I}_{can}}) > 0$, and hence for every model $\mathcal{I}$ it also holds that $q^{\mathcal{I}}(\mathbf{a}^{\mathcal{I}}) > 0$. $\square$

This means that, for the sake of answering positive queries over the product t-norm, one can simply ignore all the truth degrees and answer a classical query using any state-of-the-art engine. In particular, this means that positive answers can be found in AC^0 in data complexity just as in the classical case.

We now briefly consider the Łukasiewicz t-norm, which is known to be the hardest to handle due to its involutive negation and nilpotence, despite being in many cases the most natural choice for fuzzy semantics [6]. As mentioned already, Proposition 5 does not apply to the Łukasiewicz t-norm. That is, there are consistent L-DL-Lite$_R$ ontologies whose classical version is inconsistent (see Example 1). As a result, there is currently no known method for deciding consistency of these ontologies, let alone answering queries. The culprits for this are the involutive negation, which is weaker than the negation used in the other two t-norms, but also the nilpotence, which may combine positive degrees to produce a degree of 0. The latter also means that, even if one could check consistency, it is still not clear how to answer even positive queries.

Example 15. Consider the ontology $\mathcal{O}_2 := (\mathcal{T}_2, \mathcal{A}_2)$ where

$$\mathcal{T}_2 := \{\langle A_0 \sqsubseteq A_1, 0.5\rangle, \langle A_1 \sqsubseteq A_2, 0.5\rangle\}$$
$$\mathcal{A}_2 := \{\langle A_0(a), 1\rangle\}.$$

Note that $\mathcal{O}_2$ is consistent, but there is a model $\mathcal{I}$ (e.g., the canonical interpretation) of this ontology which sets $A_2^{\mathcal{I}}(a^{\mathcal{I}}) = 0$. Hence, a is not a positive answer to the query $q(x) = A_2(x)$ even though it is an answer of $q(x)$ over $\widehat{\mathcal{O}_2}$.

Importantly, if we extend DL-Lite$_R$ with the possibility of using conjunctions in the right-hand side of axioms—which becomes only syntactic sugar in the classical case—one can show following the ideas from [5,6] that deciding consistency of a L-DL-Lite$_R$ ontology is NP-hard in combined complexity, going beyond the NLOGSPACE upper bound for the case considered in this work.

6   Conclusions and Future Work

We have introduced the first method for answering conjunctive queries over fuzzy DL-Lite$_R$ ontologies where also the axioms in the TBox are allowed to constrain the admissible truth degrees, and the semantics is based in the notions of mathematical fuzzy logic, with an underlying t-norm an operators.

We have shown that for the Gödel t-norm dealing with the truth degrees adds only a linear overhead to classical query answering, and can be solved through repeated calls to a classical QA engine, which can be chosen from any of the many efficient existing solutions. Moreover, checking consistency of an ontology is easily reduced to the classical case. Technically, this greatly improves the results from [14], where the query needed to be translated into a new one to handle the different degrees (and the TBox must be classical). In our case, we can take any existing solver, and use it without modification. The drawback is that, by not providing a direct translation, the data complexity of the query answering method jumps from AC^0 to LOGSPACE; consistency checking is still in AC^0 w.r.t. data complexity and in NLOGSPACE in combined complexity. Finding the k answers with the highest truth degree remains within the same complexity bounds. Importantly, the LOGSPACE upper bounds are not necessarily tight. It remains to be seen whether answering w.r.t. G-DL-Lite$_R$ ontologies is in fact LOGSPACE-hard, or can be solved in AC^0. On the other hand, if one is only interested in deciding whether the degree is greater or equal to a given bound, the complexity lowers to that of the classical case again.

The case of other continuous t-norms is, unfortunately, not as clear as Gödel. Although for any t-norm that is not nilpotent (that is, anyone which behaves as the Gödel or the product t-norms at the beginning of the interval $[0, 1]$) ontology consistency trivially reduces to the classical case as in Proposition 5, it is not clear how to handle other reasoning problems, and in particular query answering efficiently. It is important to note that as soon as the t-norm is not idempotent, query-rewriting techniques cannot work as usual; in fact, query rewritings are agnostic to the number of times a single axiom or assertion is used in a derivation, which affects the final result when degrees are accumulated. For t-norms with nilpotent elements, and in particular for the Łukasiewicz t-norm, even the question of consistency is open. In fact, for a minimal extension of L-DL-Lite$_R$ consistency can be shown to be NP-hard in combined complexity.

We emphasise that, despite both using degrees in $[0, 1]$ and similar operators, π-DL-Lite$_R$ ontologies are *not* probabilistic ontologies. In particular, in the context of query answering, even if we consider only the assertions in the ABox, the product semantics produce very different results to probabilistic databases [22]. The main difference is that a probabilistic fact spawns two possible worlds—one in which the fact is true, and one where it is false—which pushes the data complexity of query answering to #P-hard. In π-DL-Lite$_R$, graded facts only provide a truth degree, and cannot be considered possible worlds.

In the literature of fuzzy query answering, a usual task is to answer *threshold queries*, where each of the conjuncts in the CQ is associated with a lower truth degree. The technique introduced in this paper is unable to handle this task, and new techniques will need to be developed for it. The most promising approach for the Gödel semantics is a new rewriting, which uses graded facts in the database. We will explore this road in more detail in the future.

References

1. Abiteboul, S., Hull, R., Vianu, V.: Foundations of Databases. Addison Wesley, Boston (1994)
2. Artale, A., Calvanese, D., Kontchakov, R., Zakharyaschev, M.: The DL-Lite family and relations. J. Artif. Intell. Res. **36**, 1–69 (2009). https://doi.org/10.1613/jair.2820
3. Baader, F., Calvanese, D., McGuinness, D., Nardi, D., Patel-Schneider, P. (eds.): The Description Logic Handbook: Theory, Implementation, and Applications, 2nd edn. Cambridge University Press, Cambridge (2007)
4. Boppana, R.B., Sipser, M.: The complexity of finite functions. In: van Leeuwen, J. (ed.) Handbook of Theoretical Computer Science, Volume A: Algorithms and Complexity, pp. 757–804. Elsevier and MIT Press, Amsterdam, Cambridge (1990)
5. Borgwardt, S., Cerami, M., Peñaloza, R.: Many-valued horn logic is hard. In: Lukasiewicz, T., Peñaloza, R., Turhan, A. (eds.) Proceedings of the First Workshop on Logics for Reasoning about Preferences, Uncertainty, and Vagueness, PRUV 2014. CEUR Workshop Proceedings, vol. 1205, pp. 52–58. CEUR-WS.org (2014). http://ceur-ws.org/Vol-1205/00010052.pdf
6. Borgwardt, S., Cerami, M., Peñaloza, R.: The complexity of fuzzy EL under the Lukasiewicz t-norm. Int. J. Approx. Reason. **91**, 179–201 (2017). https://doi.org/10.1016/j.ijar.2017.09.005
7. Borgwardt, S., Distel, F., Peñaloza, R.: The limits of decidability in fuzzy description logics with general concept inclusions. Artif. Intell. **218**, 23–55 (2015). https://doi.org/10.1016/j.artint.2014.09.001
8. Borgwardt, S., Peñaloza, R.: Fuzzy description logics – a survey. In: Moral, S., Pivert, O., Sánchez, D., Marín, N. (eds.) SUM 2017. LNCS (LNAI), vol. 10564, pp. 31–45. Springer, Cham (2017). https://doi.org/10.1007/978-3-319-67582-4_3
9. Calvanese, D., De Giacomo, G., Lembo, D., Lenzerini, M., Rosati, R.: Tractable reasoning and efficient query answering in description logics: The DL-Lite family. J. Autom. Reason. **39**(3), 385–429 (2007)
10. Cuenca Grau, B., Horrocks, I., Motik, B., Parsia, B., Patel-Schneider, P., Sattler, U.: OWL 2: the next step for OWL. J. Web Semant. **6**, 309–322 (2008)

11. Furst, M.L., Saxe, J.B., Sipser, M.: Parity, circuits, and the polynomial-time hierarchy. Math. Syst. Theory **17**(1), 13–27 (1984). https://doi.org/10.1007/BF01744431
12. Hájek, P.: Metamathematics of Fuzzy Logic, Trends in Logic, vol. 4. Kluwer (1998). https://doi.org/10.1007/978-94-011-5300-3
13. Klement, E.P., Mesiar, R., Pap, E.: Triangular Norms, Trends in Logic, vol. 8. Springer, New York (2000). https://doi.org/10.1007/978-94-015-9540-7
14. Mailis, T., Turhan, A.-Y.: Employing $DL\text{-}lite_R$-reasoners for fuzzy query answering. In: Supnithi, T., Yamaguchi, T., Pan, J.Z., Wuwongse, V., Buranarach, M. (eds.) JIST 2014. LNCS, vol. 8943, pp. 63–78. Springer, Cham (2015). https://doi.org/10.1007/978-3-319-15615-6_5
15. Mailis, T.P., Turhan, A., Zenker, E.: A pragmatic approach to answering CQs over fuzzy DL-lite-ontologies - introducing flite. In: Calvanese, D., Konev, B. (eds.) Proceedings of the 2015 International Workshop on Description Logics (DL 2015). CEUR Workshop Proceedings, vol. 1350. CEUR-WS.org (2015). http://ceur-ws.org/Vol-1350/paper-56.pdf
16. Mostert, P.S., Shields, A.L.: On the structure of semigroups on a compact manifold with boundary. Ann. Math. **65**(1), 117–143 (1957)
17. Pan, J.Z., Stamou, G.B., Stoilos, G., Thomas, E.: Expressive querying over fuzzy DL-lite ontologies. In: Proceedings of the 2007 International Workshop on Description Logics (DL 2007). CEUR Workshop Proceedings, vol. 250. CEUR-WS.org (2007). http://ceur-ws.org/Vol-250/paper_47.pdf
18. Papadimitriou, C.H.: Computational Complexity. Addison Wesley, Boston (1994)
19. Reingold, O.: Undirected connectivity in log-space. J. ACM **55**(4), 17:1–17:24 (2008). https://doi.org/10.1145/1391289.1391291
20. Straccia, U.: Towards top-k query answering in description logics: the case of DL-lite. In: Fisher, M., van der Hoek, W., Konev, B., Lisitsa, A. (eds.) JELIA 2006. LNCS (LNAI), vol. 4160, pp. 439–451. Springer, Heidelberg (2006). https://doi.org/10.1007/11853886_36
21. Straccia, U.: Top-k retrieval for ontology mediated access to relational databases. Inf. Sci. **198**, 1–23 (2012). https://doi.org/10.1016/j.ins.2012.02.026
22. Suciu, D., Olteanu, D., Ré, C., Koch, C.: Probabilistic Databases. Synthesis Lectures on Data Management. Morgan & Claypool Publishers (2011). https://doi.org/10.2200/S00362ED1V01Y201105DTM016
23. Xiao, G., et al.: Ontology-based data access: a survey, pp. 5511–5519. ijcai.org (2018). https://doi.org/10.24963/ijcai.2018/777

New Rule Induction Method by Use of a Co-occurrence Set from the Decision Table

Yuichi Kato[1][(✉)] and Tetsuro Saeki[2]

[1] Shimane University,
1060 Nishikawatsu-cho, Matsue, Shimane 690-8504, Japan
ykato@cis.shimane-u.ac.jp
[2] Yamaguchi University,
2-16-1 Tokiwadai, Ube, Yamaguchi 755-8611, Japan
tsaeki@yamaguchi-u.ac.jp

Abstract. STRIM (Statistical Test Rule Induction Method) has been proposed as an if-then rule induction method from the decision table (DT) and has improved those methods by the conventional Rough Sets from a statistical view. The method recognizes condition attributes (CA) and the decision attribute (DA) in DT as random variables having the causality of an input-output relation, and uses the relation of transforming the inputs (outcomes of CA) into the outputs (those DA) through the rules for rule induction strategies. This paper reconsiders the conventional STRIM, proposes a new rule induction method and strategy named apriori-STRIM and confirms the validity and capacity by a simulation experiment. Specifically, the new method explores CA of causes after receiving outcomes of DA by use of co-occurrence sets of outcomes of CA. The co-occurrence set is a well-known concept in the association rule learning (ARL) field. This paper also clarifies the differences of rule induction methods and their capacities between apriori-STRIM and ARL by the same experiments.

Keywords: Rough Sets · If-then rule induction · apriori-STRIM · Simulation experiment

1 Introduction

The Rough Set (RS) theory was introduced by Pawlak [1] and used for inducing if-then rules from a dataset called the decision table (DT). To date, various methods and algorithms for inducing rules by the theory have been proposed [2–5] since the inducing rules are useful to simply and clearly express the structure of rating and/or knowledge hiding behind the table. The basic idea to induce rules is to approximate the concept in the DT by use of the lower and/or upper approximation sets which are respectively derived from the equivalence relations and their equivalence sets in the given DT. However, those methods and algorithms by RS paid little attention to the fact that the DT was just a sample set

© Springer Nature Switzerland AG 2020
V. Gutiérrez-Basulto et al. (Eds.): RuleML+RR 2020, LNCS 12173, pp. 54–69, 2020.
https://doi.org/10.1007/978-3-030-57977-7_4

gathered from the population of interest. If resampling the DT from the population or the DT by Bootstrap method for example, the new DT will change equivalence relations, their equivalence sets, and the lower and/or upper approximation sets, so the induced rules will change and fluctuate. Those methods and algorithms also had the problem that those induced rules were not arranged from the statistical views. Then, we proposed a rule induction method named STRIM (Statistical Test Rule Induction Method) taking the above mentioned problems into consideration [6–16]. Specifically, STRIM

(1) Proposed a data generation model for generating a DT. This model recognized the DT as an input-output system which transformed a tuple of the condition attribute's value occurred by chance (the input) into the decision attribute value (the output) through pre-specified if-then rules (generally unknown) under some hypotheses. That is, the input was recognized as an outcome of the random variables and the output was also the outcome of a random variable dependent on the input and the pre-specified rules. Accordingly, the pairs of input and output formed the DT containing rules.

(2) Assumed a trying proper condition part of if-then rules and judged whether it was a candidate of rules by statistically testing whether the condition caused bias in the distribution of the decision attribute's values.

(3) Arranged the candidates having inclusion relationships by representing them with one of the highest bias and finally induced if-then rules with a statistical significance level after systematically exploring the trying condition part of rules. The validity and capacity of STRIM have been confirmed by the simulation experiments that STRIM can induce pre-specified if-then rules from the DT proposed in (1). In this way, the conventional data generation model proposed in (1) also can be used for a verification system of a rule induction method (VSofRIM). The validity and capacity also secure a certain extent of the confidence of rules induced by STRIM from the DT of real-world datasets. The VSofRIM is also used for confirming the validity and capacity of other rule induction methods proposed previously [11, 14].

The conventional STRIM systematically explores the domain of the condition attributes looking for rule candidates causing the bias and statistically judges their validity by use of the DT which is accumulated by rules intervening between the inputs of the condition attributes and the corresponding outputs of the decision attribute. This paper reconsiders the process after (2) from the view of Bayes's law which generally infers the causes from the results, and proposes a new rule induction method named apriori-STRIM. Specifically, the method explores a co-occurrence set of the condition attribute's value in the DT against a specific decision attribute's value. The concept of the co-occurrence set plays an important role in the association rule learning (ARL) field [17] and the set can be effectively found using the well-known Apriori algorithm [18]. That is, apriori-STRIM focuses on the property that the specific decision attribute's value will occur with the specific condition attribute values by the rules' intervention, although the conventional STRIM focuses on the bias. The rules' intervention also can be judged by a statistical test using the co-occurrence set in the DT.

The validity and capacity of apriori-STRIM is also confirmed by the same experiment as the conventional and the two-way confirmations by both STRIMs secure the validity and capacity for the rule induction method. This paper also shows interesting features of ARL by applying it to VSofRIM and clarifies the differences between apriori-STRIM and ARL.

2   Conventional Rough Sets and STRIM

The Rough Set theory is used for inducing if-then rules from a decision table S. S is conventionally denoted by $S = (U, A = C \cup \{D\}, V, \rho)$. Here, $U = \{u(i)|i = 1, ..., |U| = N\}$ is a sample set, A is an attribute set, $C = \{C(j)|j = 1, ..., |C|\}$ is a condition attribute set, $C(j)$ is a member of C and a condition attribute, and D is a decision attribute. Moreover, V is a set of attribute values denoted by $V = \cup_{a \in A} V_a$ and is characterized by the information function $\rho\colon U \times A \to V$.

The conventional Rough Set theory first focuses on the following equivalence relation and the equivalence set of indiscernibility within the decision table S of interest:

$$I_B = \{(u(i), u(j)) \in U^2 | \rho(u(i), a) = \rho(u(j), a), \forall a \in B \subseteq C\}.$$

I_B is an equivalence relation in U and derives the quotient set $U/I_B = \{[u_i]_B | i = 1, 2, ..., |U| = N\}$. Here, $[u_i]_B = \{u(j) \in U | (u(j), u_i) \in I_B, u_i \in U\}$, $[u_i]_B$ is an equivalence set with the representative element u_i.

Let X be an arbitrary subset of U then X can be approximated as $B_*(X) \subseteq X \subseteq B^*(X)$ through the use of the equivalence set. Here, $B_*(X) = \{u_i \in U | [u_i]_B \subseteq X\}$, and $B^*(X) = \{u_i \in U | [u_i]_B \cap X \neq \phi\}$, $B_*(X)$ and $B^*(X)$ are referred to as the lower and upper approximations of X by B respectively. The pair of $(B_*(X), B^*(X))$ is usually called a rough set of X by B.

Specifically, let be $X = \{u(i)|\rho(u(i), D) = d\} = U(d) = \{u(i)|u^{D=d}(i)\}$ called the concept of $D = d$, and define a set of $u(i)$ as $U(CP) = \{u(i)|u^{C=CP}(i)$, meaning CP satisfies $u^C(i)$, where $u^C(i)$ is the tuple of the condition attribute values of $u(i)\}$ and let it be equal to $B_*(X)$, then CP can be used as the condition part of the if-then rule of $D = d$, with necessity. That is, the following expression of if-then rules with necessity is obtained: if $CP = \wedge_j (C(j_k) = v_{j_k})$ then $D = d$. In the same way, $B^*(X)$ derives the condition part CP of the if-then rule of $D = d$ with possibility.

However, the approximation of $X = U(d)$ by the lower or upper approximation is respectively too strict or loose so that the rules induced by the approximations are often of no use. Then, Ziarko expanded the original RS by introducing an admissible error in two ways [4]: $\underline{B}_\epsilon(U(d)) = \{u(i)|accuracy \geq 1 - \varepsilon\}$, $\overline{B}_\varepsilon(U(d)) = \{u(i)|accuracy > \varepsilon\}$, where $\varepsilon \in [0, 0.5)$. The pair of $(\underline{B}_\epsilon(U(d)), \overline{B}_\varepsilon(U(d)))$ is called a ε-lower and ε-upper approximation which satisfies the following properties: $B_*(U(d)) \subseteq \underline{B}_\epsilon(U(d)) \subseteq \overline{B}_\varepsilon(U(d)) \subseteq B^*(U(d))$, $\underline{B}_{\varepsilon=0}(U(d)) = B_*(U(d))$ and $\overline{B}_{\varepsilon=0}(U(d)) = B^*(U(d))$. The ε-lower and/or ε-upper approximation induce if-then rules with admissible errors in the same way as the lower and/or upper approximation.

As mentioned above, the conventional RS theory basically focuses on the equivalence relation I_B and its equivalence sets U/I_B in U given in advance and induces rules approximating the concept by use of the approximation sets derived from the U/I_B. However, I_B is very dependent on the DT provided. Accordingly, every DT obtained from the same population is different from each other and, I_B, U/I_B and the approximation sets are different from each other for each DT, which leads to inducing different rule sets. That is, the rule induction methods by the conventional RS theory lack statistical views.

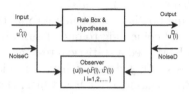

Fig. 1. A data generation model: Rule box contains if-then rules $R(d,k)$: if $sCP(d,k)$ then $D = d$ $(d = 1, 2, ..., k = 1, 2, ...)$.

Table 1. Hypotheses with regard to the decision attribute value.

Hypothesis 1	$u^C(i)$ coincides with $R(d,k)$, and $u^D(i)$ is uniquely determined as $D = d$ (uniquely determined data)
Hypothesis 2	$u^C(i)$ does not coincide with any $R(d,k)$, and $u^D(i)$ can only be determined randomly (indifferent data)
Hypothesis 3	$u^C(i)$ coincides with several $R(d,k)$ $(d = d1, d2, ...)$, and their outputs of $u^C(i)$ conflict with each other. Accordingly, the output of $u^C(i)$ must be randomly determined from the conflicted outputs (conflicted data)

Then, STRIM [6,9,10,12,15] has proposed a data generation model (DGM) for the DT and a rule induction method based on the model. Specifically, STRIM considers the decision table to be a sample dataset obtained from an input-output system including a rule box, as shown in Fig. 1, and hypotheses regarding the decision attribute values, as shown in Table 1. A sample $u(i)$ consists of its condition attribute values $u^C(i)$ and its decision attribute value $u^D(i)$. $u^C(i)$ is the input for the rule box, and is transformed into the output $u^D(i)$ using the rules (generally unknown) contained in the rule box and the hypotheses. The hypotheses consist of three cases corresponding to the input. They are uniquely determined, indifferent and conflicted cases (see Table 1). In contrast, $u(i) = (u^C(i), u^D(i))$ is measured by an observer, as shown in Fig. 1. The existence of NoiseC and NoiseD makes missing values in $u^C(i)$, and changes $u^D(i)$ to create another value for $u^D(i)$, respectively. Those noises bring the system closer to a real-world system. The data generation model suggests that a pair of $(u^C(i), u^D(i))$, $(i = 1, \ldots, N)$, i.e. a decision table is an outcome of these random variables: $(C, D) = ((C(1), \ldots, C(|C|), D)$ observing the population.

Based on the data generation model, STRIM (1) extracted significant pairs of a condition attribute and its value like $C(j_k) = v_{j_k}$ for rules of $D = d$ by the local reduct [10,12,13], (2) constructed a tentatively trying condition part of the rules like $CP = \wedge_j(C(j_k) = v_{j_k})$ by use of the reduct results, and (3) investigated whether $U(CP)$ caused a bias at n_d in the frequency distribution of the decision attribute values $f = (n_1, n_2, \ldots, n_{M_D})$ or not, where $n_m = |U(CP) \cap U(m)|$ $(m = 1, \ldots, |V_{a=D}| = M_D)$ and $U(m) = \{u(i)|u^{D=m}(i)\}$, since the $u^C(i)$ coinciding to $sCP(d, k)$ in the rule box is transformed into $u^D(i)$ based on Hypotheses 1 or 3. Accordingly, the CP coinciding to one of rules in the rule box produces bias in f. Specifically, STRIM used a statistical test method for the investigation specifying a null hypothesis $H0$: f does not have any bias, that is, CP is not a rule and its alternative hypothesis $H1$: f has a bias, that is, CP is a rule, and a proper significance level, and tested $H0$ by use of the sample dataset, that is, the decision table and the proper test statistics, for example,

$$z = \frac{(n_d + 0.5 - np_d)}{(np_d(1 - p_d))^{0.5}},$$

where $n_d = \max_m f = (n_1, \ldots, n_m, \ldots, n_{M_D})$, $p_d = P(D = d)$, $n = \sum_{j=1}^{M_D} n_j$. z obeys the standard normal distribution under test conditions: $np_d \geq 5$ and $n(1 - p_d) \geq 5$ [19] and is considered to be an index of the bias of f. (4) If $H0$ is rejected then the assumed CP becomes a candidate for the rules in the rule box. (5) After repeating the processes from (1) to (4) and obtaining the set of rule candidates, STRIM arranged their rule candidates and induced the final results (see literatures [12,13] for details).

To summarize, STRIM directly induces rules with statistical significance level assuming the condition part of rules: $CP = \wedge_j(C(j_k) = v_{j_k})$ and statistically testing it by use of U. STRIM does not require the basic concept of the approximation which is the point for the rule induction by RS theory. Conversely, RS theory has nothing directly to do with statistical significance.

3   Studies on STRIM by Simulation Experiment

We implemented the data generation process and verified the capacity of inducing the rules by the conventional STRIM as follows: (1) Specified the rules in Table 2 (the number of rules $(N_{rule}) = 10$) in the rule box in Fig. 1, where $|C| = 6$, $V_a = \{1, 2, \ldots, 5\}$ $(a = C(j), (j = 1, \ldots, |C|), a = D)$, and $sCP(1,1) = 110000$ denoted $sCP(1,1) = (C(1) = 1) \wedge (C(2) = 1)$ and was called a rule of the rule length 2 $(RL = 2)$, having two conditions. (2) Generated $v_{C(j)}(i)$ $(j = 1, \ldots, |C| = 6)$ with a uniform distribution and formed $u^C(i) = (v_{C(1)}(i), \ldots, v_{C(6)}(i))$ $(i = 1, \ldots, N = 10,000)$. (3) Transformed $u^C(i)$ into $u^D(i)$ using the pre-specified rules in Table 2 and hypotheses in Table 1,

Table 2. An example of pre-specified rules $R(d,k)$ in the rule box: if $sCP(d,k)$ then $D = d$ ($d = 1, \ldots, 5$, $k = 1, 2$).

$R(d,k)$	$sCP(d,k)$	$D = d$
$R(1,1)$	110000	$D = 1$
$R(1,2)$	001100	$D = 1$
$R(2,1)$	220000	$D = 2$
$R(2,2)$	002200	$D = 2$
$R(3,1)$	330000	$D = 3$
$R(3,2)$	003300	$D = 3$
$R(4,1)$	440000	$D = 4$
$R(4,2)$	004400	$D = 4$
$R(5,1)$	440000	$D = 5$
$R(5,2)$	004400	$D = 5$

Table 3. An example of estimated rules by the conventional STRIM for the DT with $N_B = 5{,}000$ generated by the data generation model in Fig. 1 and the pre-specified rules in Table 2.

Rule no.	Estimated rules $(C(1)\ldots C(6)D)$	$f = (n_1, n_2, n_3, n_4, n_5)$	p-value	Accuracy	Coverage
1	(0022002)	$(4, 216, 8, 5, 4)$	5.87E−173	0.911	0.223
2	(0011001)	$(207, 3, 4, 2, 3)$	8.26E−162	0.945	0.200
3	(0055005)	$(8, 4, 7, 5, 211)$	1.87E−159	0.898	0.212
4	(4400004)	$(5, 6, 5, 187, 4)$	5.73E−150	0.903	0.195
5	(1100001)	$(190, 1, 6, 3, 4)$	1.86E−145	0.931	0.184
6	(5500005)	$(5, 8, 6, 5, 191)$	2.73E−142	0.888	0.192
7	(0044004)	$(4, 3, 3, 167, 3)$	8.99E−140	0.928	0.174
8	(3300003)	$(5, 6, 193, 7, 3)$	1.98E−139	0.902	0.186
9	(2200002)	$(3, 167, 6, 1, 5)$	7.37E−136	0.918	0.172
10	(0033003)	$(3, 4, 185, 10, 2)$	6.03E−135	0.907	0.178

without generating NoiseC and NoiseD for a plain experiment and then generated the decision table. After randomly selecting samples by $N_B = 5{,}000$ samples, newly forming the DT and applying STRIM to the DT, Table 3 was obtained. The table shows us the following: For example, the estimated Rule No. 1 ($RN = 1$) "0022002" denotes if $(C(3) = 2) \wedge (C(4) = 2)$ then $D = 2$, has $f = (n_1, n_2, \ldots, n_5) = (4, 216, 8, 5, 4)$ and the bias at $D = 2$. The outcome probability to cause such a bias is around 5.87E-173 under $H0$, which leads to rejecting $H0$ and adopting $H1$. As the result, "0022002" was adopted as a rule. It should be noted that the reason it was adopted as the rule was not the high $accuracy = 216/237 = 0.911$. STRIM just induced all the pre-specified rules in

Table 2. This experiment suggests that conventional STRIM works well and the DGM in Fig. 1 can be useful as a verification system of a rule induction method.

4 New Rule Induction Method by Co-occurrence Set

As mentioned in Sect. 2, conventional STRIM regards the condition attributes C and the decision attribute D as random variables, and D of the output depends on C of the input, rules and hypotheses and the rule induction method focuses on $P(D = d|CP)$ of $P(CP, D = d) = P(CP)P(D = d|CP)$. That is, STRIM regards $P(D = d|CP)$ as $P($ if CP then $D = d)$ and explores $CP = \wedge_j(C(j_k) = v_{j_k})$ which causes bias at n_d in $f = (n_1, n_2, \ldots, n_{M_D})$. The bias can be detected by use of the DT and the statistical test.

Line No.	Algorithm to induce if-then rules by STRIM with apriori function
1	install.packages("arules") # import package arules
2	library(arules) # load package arules
3	input data # input Decision Table
4	for (iD in 1: M_D) {# proceed co-occurrence item set of iD
5	dataiD<-data[data[, (length(C) +1)]==iD,] # extract dataset of Decision attribute value of iD
6	dataCiD<-dataiD[1: length(C) ,] # extract its Condition attributes value part
7	CiD.tra<-transform dataCiD # CiD of transaction form
8	CiD.ap<-apriori(CiD.tra, parameter=list(support=supp0, target='frequent itemset')) # explore freqent item set more than supp0
9	SFIS<-inspect(CiD.ap) # output the set of frequent item set
10	for (iCo in 1: nrow(SFIS)) {# proceed each frequent item set
11	calculate p-value of SFIS(iCo)
12	if p-value < p-value0, save the SFIS(iCo) as a rule candidate with necessary index
13	}# end of for of iCo
14	arrange the rule candidates of iD
15	}# end of for of iD

Fig. 2. An algorithm for apriori-STRIM written in R language style.

From the view of Bayes's law, however, another strategy of focusing on $P(CP|D = d)$ of $P(CP, D = d) = P(D = d)P(CP|D = d)$ can be considered for the rule induction. That is, after receiving the outputs of $D = d$, the strategy exploring and estimating $CP = \wedge_j(C(j_k) = v_{j_k})$ of the corresponding inputs can be also valid. Specifically, when receiving the outputs, the corresponding inputs are classified into two cases: One is the uniquely determined and/or conflicted cases and the other is the indifferent case (see Table 1). Both cases can be easily distinguished from each other by use of a statistical test specifying the null hypothesis $H0$: the event $D = d$ has occurred by chance (the indifferent case) and the alternative hypothesis $H1$: the event $D = d$ hasn't occurred by chance (the uniquely and/or conflicted case). Under $H0$, $P(CP|D = d) = P(CP)$ and the intervention of rules transforming the inputs into the output is denied. If $H0$ is denied, $H1$ is adopted as a rule candidate, which means $P(CP|D = d) \neq P(CP)$. Such hypothesis testing can be easily executed by finding the co-occurrence set with the event $D = d$ since the concept of the co-occurrence set is well-known in

Table 4. An example of FIS extracted from $U(D = 1)$ of the DT corresponding to Table 3.

No. of FIS	Items	Support	Count
[1]	$\{15\}$	0.138	143
[2]	$\{22\}$	0.143	148
[27]	$\{11\}$	0.337	348
[31]	$\{15, 22\}$	0.032	33
[32]	$\{15, 24\}$	0.028	29
[350]	$\{11, 21\}$	0.184	190
[351]	$\{31, 41\}$	0.200	207
[353]	$\{21, 31\}$	0.101	104
[354]	$\{15, 31, 41\}$	0.029	30
[387]	$\{31, 52, 63\}$	0.024	25
[403]	$\{21, 31, 41\}$	0.044	45

the field of association rule learning (ARL) [17] and the finding is effectively executed by the Apriori algorithm [18]. Then, this paper names this rule induction method apriori-STRIM. The ARL and the Apriori algorithm are summarized in Appendix A and the differences of the idea for the rule induction method between ARL and apriori-STRIM are shown through the same experiment in Sect. 3, that is, by VSofRIM. See Appendix A to easily understand the following.

The specific procedure for apriori-STRIM is shown in Fig. 2 where the procedure is shown in R language style since the Apriori algorithm is already implemented by the language as an apriori() function which has a good reputation. The outline is the following: Line No. 1 ($LN = 1$) installs the package of ARL as "arules" [20] via the internet and $LN = 2$ loads it as the library "arules". $LN = 3$ inputs the DT as "data". From $LN = 4$ to $NL = 15$, every iD of the decision attribute ($= 1 \sim M_D$) is proceeded. $LN = 5$ substitutes $U(iD) = \{u(i)|u^{D=iD}(i)\}$ with dataiD, and its condition part dataCiD is extracted ($LN = 6$), and transformed into the transaction form $CiD.tra$ at $LN = 7$. $LN = 8$ extracts co-occurrence sets of $CiD.tra$, that is, co-occurrence sets of the condition attributes' values of $U(iD)$ as frequent item sets according to parameters which specify them as greater than or equal to $supp0$ and substitute them for $CiD.ap$. $LN = 9$ extracts the set of frequent item set ($SFIS$). From $LN = 10$ to $LN = 13$, every p-value of $SFIS(iCo)$ ($iCo = 1, \ldots, |SFIS|$) is calculated and tested for whether its p-value is less than a pre-specified p-value0 and $SFIS(iCo)$ is saved as a candidate if it satisfies the condition. $LN = 14$ arranges the candidates having inclusion relationship by representing the candidate with the least p-value and finally decides rules for iD.

5   Studies on Apriori-STRIM by Simulation Experiment

An experiment result for the rule induction by the conventional STRIM was shown in Table 3 by applying it to the DT containing the pre-specified rules. We also applied apriori-STRIM for the same DT and show the results with the process in Fig. 2.

Table 5. An example of rule candidates extracted from Table 4.

Rule no.	Estimated rules $(C(1)\ldots C(6)D)$	Count	p-value	Accuracy	Coverage
1	0011001	207	1.93E−81	0.945	0.200
2	1100001	190	1.48E−68	0.931	0.184
3	0100001	372	5.78E−33	0.360	0.360
4	0001001	366	7.14E−31	0.366	0.354
5	0010001	366	7.14E−31	0.366	0.354
6	0011031	57	4.44E−29	0.966	0.055
7	1000001	348	5.42E−25	0.360	0.337
8	0511001	52	7.38E−25	0.945	0.050
9	0011201	52	7.38E−25	0.963	0.050

Table 4 shows the part of $SFIS$ obtained at $LN = 8$ and 9 for $iD = 1$, that is, $D = 1$. Here, $supp0 = 5 \cdot |V_a|/|U(iD)|, \forall a \in C$ was used for exploring FIS. This specification secure $freq(FIS) \geq 5 \cdot |V_a| = count0$ for the hypothesis testing at $LN = 11$ and 12 and induced $|SFIS| = 403$. The table shows: No. of $FIS = 1 - 30$ ($NFIS = 1 - 30$) is $FIS(|items| = 1)$, $NFIS = 31 - 353$ is $FIS(|items| = 2)$ and $NFIS = 354 - 403$ is $FIS(|items| = 3)$, and for example, $NFIS = 387$ indicates that the co-occurrence set of $items = \{C(3) = 1, C(5) = 2, C(6) = 3\}$ that is, the pattern $CP = (C(3) = 1) \wedge (C(5) = 2) \wedge (C(6) = 3)$ occurred $count = 25$ times in $|U(D = 1) = \{u(i)|u^{D=1}(i)\}| = 1,033$. The pre-specified rules for $D = 1$ in Table 2 are $R(1,1)$ and $R(1,2)$, which appear in $NFIS = 350$ and 351 respectively.

$LN = 12$ induced significant FIS patterns in Table 4 by the hypothesis testing under $H0$. The frequency X of the co-occurrence pattern CP obeys Binominal distribution $Bn(n, p)$ having the expectation np where $n = |U(D = 1)|$ and $p = \prod_{a \in CP} \frac{1}{|V_a|}$. For example, $p = (\frac{1}{5})^3$ at $NFIS = 387$ due to $RL = 3$. One specification for $supp0$ was to satisfy the requirement $np = Xp \geq 5$ for $RL = 1$ as well as the conventional STRIM (see the test conditions [19] in Sect. 2). That is, $\min X = count0 = \frac{5}{p} = 5 \cdot |V_a|$. $count \geq count0 = 25$ is satisfied in Table 4. As shown in Appendix A, the small $count0$ tends to generate a large number of meaningless FIS, and conversely, the large increases the possibility to miss the valid FISs.

$LN = 12$ induced the number of 46 rule candidates from 403 in Table 4 using p-value $0 = 1.0E − 10$ this time and saved them with p-value, accuracy, coverage

Table 6. Finally estimated rules by apriori-STRIM for the DT corresponding to those of Table 3.

Rule no.	Estimated rules $(C(1)\ldots C(6)D)$	Count	p-value	Accuracy	Coverage
1	0011001	207	1.93E−81	0.945	0.200
2	1100001	190	1.48E−68	0.931	0.184
3	0022002	216	4.19E−94	0.911	0.223
4	2200002	167	2.65E−56	0.918	0.172
5	3300003	193	2.42E−70	0.902	0.186
6	0033003	185	1.64E−64	0.907	0.178
7	4400004	187	1.36E−71	0.903	0.195
8	0044004	167	6.91E−57	0.928	0.174
9	0055005	211	1.37E−87	0.898	0.212
10	5500005	191	6.45E−72	0.888	0.192

and so on. Table 5 shows the first nine candidates after sorting them in ascending order of p-value. $RN = 1$ and 2 coincide with $R(1, 2)$ and $R(1, 1)$ respectively. $RN = 3$ can be represented by $RN = 2$ with the smaller p-value and in the same manner all the following candidates were arranged and represented by $RN = 1$ or 2 at $LN = 14$. Table 6 shows the final rule induction results including those of $D = 2, \ldots, 5$ by apriori-STRIM.

To compare Table 6 by apriori-STRIM with Table 3 by the conventional STRIM, the following is seen:

(1) Both methods statistically induce the pre-specified rules in Table 2 in proper quantities and justly coincide with each other in corresponding figures.
(2) The differences between two tables are their surface caput of $f = (n_1, n_2, \ldots, n_5)$ and $count$. The former focuses on $P(D = d|CP)$ and adopts the strongest bias of the distribution of D by CP. The latter focuses on $P(CP|D = d)$ and adopts the strongest intervention by rules, which appears in the p-value of the co-occurrence set (pattern) in Table 5.

In the same way, to compare Table 6 and/or Table 3 with Table 9 and/or Table 10 by the associate rule learning (ARL), the following is seen:

(3) ARL first focuses on the co-occurrence set of (CP, D) and its count directly connects to $P(CP, D)$ and induces rules by use of parameters of support, confidence, and so on. However, ARL has no way of distinguishing the co-occurrence sets by rules from those by chance since ARL doesn't have any models for the distinction.
(4) Connecting to (3), ARL also has no way of arranging a large number of rule candidates as shown in Appendix A although it has useful indexes of support, confidence, lift, and so on. That is, ARL based on $P(CP, D)$ seems not to closely focus on inducing if-then rules although it can induce the co-occurrence set.

6   Conclusion

This paper summarized the rule induction methods by the conventional RS and their statistically improved method STRIM showing the validity and capacity of STRIM in VSofRIM. The conventional STRIM focused on $P(D = d|CP)$ which can be recognized as a probabilistic structure transforming the input CP into the corresponding output D, and used the structure and the DT for inducing the if-then rules that causes the bias in the distribution of D. From this view, another new rule induction method focusing on $P(CP|D = d)$ was proposed. Specifically, the method estimated the inputs after receiving the outputs by exploring the co-occurrence set of $U(d) = \{u(i)|u^{D=d}(i)\}$ and executing statistical testing with regard to the explored set under $H0$: $P(CP|D = d) = P(CP)$. The exploration was executed by Apriori algorithm developed in the field of ARL. The new method was named apriori-STRIM. The validity and capacity for apriori-STRIM was confirmed by applying it to the same DT as the conventional STRIM. The similarities and differences between the conventional, apriori-STRIM and ARL were clarified through the same simulation dataset, that is, VSofRIM.

Table 7. An example of transaction dataset.

Transaction	Record
$tr(1)$	$1, 2, 5, 6, 7, 9$
$tr(2)$	$2, 3, 4, 5$
$tr(3)$	$1, 2, 7, 8, 9$
$tr(4)$	$1, 7, 9$
$tr(5)$	$2, 3, 7, 9$

Table 8. An example of the set of FIS (SFIS) for Table 7 ($\theta_0 = 3$).

SFIS(1) = {{1}, {2}, {7}, {9}}
SFIS(2) = {{1, 2}, {1, 7}, {1, 9}, {2, 7}, {2, 9}, {7, 9}}
$\Rightarrow$ {{1, 7}, {1, 9}, {2, 7}, {2, 9}, {7, 9}}
SFIS (3) = {{1, 2, 7}, {1, 2, 9}, {1, 7, 9}, {2, 7, 9}}
$\Rightarrow$ {{1, 7, 9}, {2, 7, 9}}
SFIS(4) = {1, 2, 7, 9}
$\Rightarrow$ {ϕ}

Focus for future studies:

(1) The differences of performance evaluation between the above three methods were considered by the plain data generation model. To examine them in a much closer model to the real-world.
(2) To apply three methods to the real-world dataset after finishing the studies (1).
(3) To expand the DT to the transaction database and study if both STRIMs can be applied to such a database and work effectively.

A   Transaction Database and Association Rule Learning [21]

Transaction database (TrD) is defined as a set of records called transaction (tr): $TrD = \{tr(i)|i = 1, \ldots, m\}$. Here, each $tr(i)$ is a subset of an item set defined with $Itm = \{itm(j)|j = 1, \ldots, n\}$. One of the examples is shown in Table 7 where $m = 5$ and $Itm = \{itm(j) = j|j = 1, \ldots, n = 9\}$. Now let be $\forall X \subseteq Itm$ then $Occ(X) = \{tr(i)|X \subseteq tr(i)\}$ is called the occurrence set of X and its frequency is denoted $freq(X) = |Occ(X)|$. For example, let be $X = \{1\}$ in Table 7 then $Occ(X) = \{tr(1), tr(3), tr(4)\}$ and $freq(X) = 3$. $\exists X \subseteq Itm$ whose occurrence set is often found in TrD is called a frequent item set (FIS). Table 8 arranges FIS of X with $freq(X) \geq \theta_0 = 3$ in Table 7 and shows the set of FIS $(SFIS(|X|))$ every $|X|$. For example, $SFIS(|X| = 1)$ in Table 8 can be easily obtained by tallying the frequency of TrD with X. $SFIS(|X| = 2)$ should be constructed by every combination of the element of $SFIS(|X| = 1)$ and confirm them by use of TrD then $freq(\{1,2\}) = 2 \not\geq 3$ and $\{1,2\}$ is deleted. The result is shown after the symbol "$\Rightarrow$". In the same way, $SFIS(|X| = 3)$ should be constructed by every combination of items in $SFIS(|X| = 2)$. However, $\{1,2,7\}$ or $\{1,2,9\}$ should be deleted since $SFIS(|X| = 2)$ doesn't include $\{1,2\}$, which is called downward closure property of frequency $(DCPF)$. The rest of $FIS(|X| = 3)$ are confirmed by use of TrD. As well as the following.

The algorithm that effectively generates $SFIS(|X| = l+1)$ from $SFIS(|X| = l)$ by use of $DCPF$ is called Apriori algorithm [18] and implemented by R language as apriori() function in the library "arules" and is often used for association rule learning [17] problems.

Now let $\forall X, \forall Y \subseteq Itm$ and $X \cup Y \in FIS \subseteq SFIS$ then X and Y often simultaneously occur, which is called a co-occurrence set with $freq(X \cup Y)$ and induce rules called the association rule (AR): if X then Y, or: if Y then X. The following three indexes: support, confidence and lift are often referred as the quality of AR:

$$supp(X) = \frac{freq(X)}{|TrD|} = P(X),$$

$$conf(X \rightarrow Y) = \frac{supp(X \cup Y)}{supp(X)} = P(Y|X),$$

$$lift(X \rightarrow Y) = \frac{supp(X \cup Y)}{supp(X) \cdot supp(Y)} = \frac{conf(X \rightarrow Y)}{supp(Y)} = \frac{P(Y|X)}{P(Y)},$$

where "$\rightarrow$" denotes implication. Support is an index of how frequency the item set appears in the dataset and confidence how often the rule has been found to be true. Lift implies the degree to which X and Y are dependent on one another. If $lift(X \rightarrow Y) = 1$ then X and Y are independent of each other and AR has no sense.

For example, $\{1, 7, 9\}$ in Table 8 is a co-occurrence set with $freq(\{1, 7, 9\}) = 3$, which induces AR: if $\{1, 7\}$ has occurred then $\{9\}$ will occur with $supp(\{1, 7\}) = 3/5$. $conf(\{1, 7\} \rightarrow \{9\}) = 3/3 = 1$ and $lift(\{1, 7\} \rightarrow \{9\}) = 5/4$. This AR is valid to some extent since the $lift > 1$.

There are various kinds of $TrD = \{tr(i)|i = 1, \ldots, m\}$ and DT: $S = (U, A = C \cup \{D\}, V, \rho)$ can be regarded as one of TrD with corresponding relationships: $N \rightarrow m$, $u(i) = (\rho(u(i), C(1)) \ldots \rho(u(i), C(|C|)) \rho(u(i), D)) \rightarrow tr(i)$ and $V = \cup_{a \in A} V_a \rightarrow Itm$. For example, if $u(1) = (1234512)$ in the specification of Sect. 3 then $\{11, 22, 33, 44, 55, 61, 72\}$ corresponds to $tr(1)$. In this way, the U with $N = 5,000$ corresponding to Table 3 can be transformed into the TrD form: d.tran and the if-then rules behind the U can be induced by ARL of the following statement:

apriori(d.tran, parameter = list(support = 0.003, confidence = 0.80, maxlen = 5)).

This example induces rules satisfying $conf(X \rightarrow Y) \geq 0.80$ after finding the co-occurrence set satisfying the condition $supp(X \cup Y) \geq 0.003$ and $|X \cup Y| \leq 5$. The part of the number of 240 ARs induced is shown in Table 9 after sorting them in descending order of $lift$. In the surface caput of Table 9, Rule No. shows the descending order, lhs and rhs are abbreviations of left hand side and right hand side of an if-then rule respectively, and count is $freq(lhs \cup rhs)$.

Table 9. An example of estimated rules by apriori function for the dataset corresponding to that in Table 3.

Rule no.	lhs		rhs	Support	Confidence	Lift	Count
1	$\{24, 34, 44\}$	=>	$\{74\}$	0.008	1.000	5.20	40
5	$\{14, 24, 42, 65\}$	=>	$\{74\}$	0.003	1.000	5.20	15
6	$\{12, 22, 32\}$	=>	$\{72\}$	0.007	1.000	5.15	36
14	$\{15, 21, 32, 42\}$	=>	$\{72\}$	0.003	1.000	5.15	15
22	$\{15, 25, 55, 63\}$	=>	$\{75\}$	0.003	1.000	5.02	17
23	$\{11, 23, 35, 45\}$	=>	$\{75\}$	0.003	1.000	5.02	15
41	$\{24, 42, 63, 72\}$	=>	$\{32\}$	0.003	0.938	4.85	15
42	$\{11, 31, 41\}$	=>	$\{71\}$	0.010	1.000	4.84	49
55	$\{23, 33, 43\}$	=>	$\{73\}$	0.006	1.000	4.81	32
56	$\{13, 23, 43\}$	=>	$\{73\}$	0.006	1.000	4.81	29
75	$\{12, 22\}$	=>	$\{72\}$	0.033	0.918	4.73	167
76	$\{11, 21, 32\}$	=>	$\{71\}$	0.008	0.976	4.72	40

Table 9 shows the following: For example, $RN = 1$ indicates if $C(2) = 4 \wedge$ $C(3) = 4 \wedge C(4) = 4$ then $D = 4$ and $count = freq(lhs \cup rhs) = support \cdot$ $|TrD| = 0.008 \cdot 5000 = 40$. $RN = 41$ is an interesting case that lhs includes the decision attribute value 72 ($D = 2$) and rhs is the condition attribute 32 ($C(3) = 2$). Such rules should be deleted when inducing rules from DT by ARL since TrD has neither the explanatory nor response variables. When inducing rules from an information table which doesn't have such a distinction, ARL can be used. $RN = 75$ coincides with $R(2, 1)$ in Table 2. However, most of ARs from the DT is such rules adding a pair of the condition attribute and its value to the pre-specified rules in Table 2, that is, the part of pre-specified rules or those having no sense against them.

Table 10. An example of estimated rules of $D = 1$ by apriori function for the dataset corresponding to that in Table 3.

Rule No.	lhs	rhs	Support	Confidence	Lift	Count
42(1)	$\{11, 31, 41\}$ => $\{71\}$		0.010	1.000	4.84	49
47(6)	$\{11, 21, 31, 43\}$ => $\{71\}$		0.003	1.000	4.84	17
48(7)	$\{11, 21, 43, 52\}$ => $\{71\}$		0.003	1.000	4.84	15
49(8)	$\{14, 25, 31, 41\}$ => $\{71\}$		0.004	1.000	4.84	18
124(24)	$\{25, 31, 41\}$ => $\{71\}$		0.010	0.945	4.58	52
125(25)	$\{31, 41\}$ => $\{71\}$		0.041	0.945	4.58	207
143(30)	$\{11, 21\}$ -> $\{71\}$		0.038	0.931	4.51	190
208(46)	$\{11, 21, 63\}$ => $\{71\}$		0.008	0.891	4.31	41
211(47)	$\{11, 21, 43\}$ => $\{71\}$		0.010	0.889	4.30	48
231(48)	$\{11, 21, 53\}$ => $\{71\}$		0.006	0.857	4.15	30
237(49)	$\{11, 21, 33\}$ => $\{71\}$		0.006	0.829	4.01	29

Table 10 shows the part of 49 ARs of $D = 1$ extracted from the above 240 ARs where the number within parentheses in Rule No. shows the $lift$ order in the 49 ARs of $D = 1$. This table shows us the following:

(1) The pre-specified rules in Table 2 appears in $RN = 125(25)$ and $143(30)$ although there is no objective criterion or standard to adopt them by use of support, confidence or $lift$ and so on since ARL has no way of arranging a lot of ARs based on an objective principle.
(2) Accordingly, an analysist can't help but subjectively adopt several ARs by his own domain knowledge referring to indexes like $lift$ and so on. Incidentally, the above apriori() function also had difficulties specifying its parameters. For example, when specified $support = 0.001$ or 0.008 fixing the other parameters, the function induced ARs of the number of $1,893$ or 92. This example suggests that the specification for its parameters including their combinations will puzzle the analyst and he can't help but subjectively

specify them based on his domain knowledge after many trials when analyzing the real-world TrD.

References

1. Pawlak, Z.: Rough sets. Int. J. Comput. Sci. **11**(5), 341–356 (1982)
2. Skowron, A., Rauser, C.M.: The discernibility matrix and functions in information systems. In: Słowiński, R. (ed.) Intelligent Decision Support, Handbook of Application and Advances of Rough Set Theory, pp. 331–362. Kluwer Academic Publishers, Dordrecht (1992)
3. Grzymala-Busse, J.W.: LERS — a system for learning from examples based on rough sets. In: Słowiński, R. (ed.) Intelligent Decision Support, Handbook of Applications and Advances of the Rough Sets Theory, pp. 3–18. Kluwer Academic Publishers, Dordrecht (1992)
4. Ziarko, W.: Variable precision rough set model. J. Comput. Syst. Sci. **46**, 39–59 (1993)
5. Shan, N., Ziarko, W.: Data-based acquisition and incremental modification of classification rules. Comput. Intell. **11**(2), 357–370 (1995)
6. Matsubayashi, T., Kato, Y., Saeki, T.: A new rule induction method from a decision table using a statistical test. In: Li, T., et al. (eds.) RSKT 2012. LNCS (LNAI), vol. 7414, pp. 81–90. Springer, Heidelberg (2012). https://doi.org/10.1007/978-3-642-31900-6_11
7. Kato, Y., Saeki, T., Mizuno, S.: Studies on the necessary data size for rule induction by STRIM. In: Lingras, P., Wolski, M., Cornelis, C., Mitra, S., Wasilewski, P. (eds.) RSKT 2013. LNCS (LNAI), vol. 8171, pp. 213–220. Springer, Heidelberg (2013). https://doi.org/10.1007/978-3-642-41299-8_20
8. Kato, Y., Saeki, T., Mizuno, S.: Considerations on rule induction procedures by STRIM and their relationship to VPRS. In: Kryszkiewicz, M., Cornelis, C., Ciucci, D., Medina-Moreno, J., Motoda, H., Raś, Z.W. (eds.) RSEISP 2014. LNCS (LNAI), vol. 8537, pp. 198–208. Springer, Cham (2014). https://doi.org/10.1007/978-3-319-08729-0_19
9. Kato, Y., Saeki, T., Mizuno, S.: Proposal of a statistical test rule induction method by use of the decision table. Appl. Soft Comput. **28**, 160–166 (2015)
10. Kato, Y., Saeki, T., Mizuno, S.: Proposal for a statistical reduct method for decision tables. In: Ciucci, D., Wang, G., Mitra, S., Wu, W.-Z. (eds.) RSKT 2015. LNCS (LNAI), vol. 9436, pp. 140–152. Springer, Cham (2015). https://doi.org/10.1007/978-3-319-25754-9_13
11. Kitazaki, Y., Saeki, T., Kato, Y.: Performance comparison to a classification problem by the second method of quantification and STRIM. In: Flores, V., et al. (eds.) IJCRS 2016. LNCS (LNAI), vol. 9920, pp. 406–415. Springer, Cham (2016). https://doi.org/10.1007/978-3-319-47160-0_37
12. Fei, J., Saeki, T., Kato, Y.: Proposal for a new reduct method for decision tables and an improved STRIM. In: Tan, Y., Takagi, H., Shi, Y. (eds.) DMBD 2017. LNCS, vol. 10387, pp. 366–378. Springer, Cham (2017). https://doi.org/10.1007/978-3-319-61845-6_37
13. Kato, Y., Itsuno, T., Saeki, T.: Proposal of dominance-based rough set approach by STRIM and its applied example. In: Polkowski, L., et al. (eds.) IJCRS 2017. LNCS (LNAI), vol. 10313, pp. 418–431. Springer, Cham (2017). https://doi.org/10.1007/978-3-319-60837-2_35

14. Kato, Y., Kawaguchi, S., Saeki, T.: Studies on CART's performance in rule induction and comparisons by STRIM. In: Nguyen, H.S., Ha, Q.-T., Li, T., Przybyła-Kasperek, M. (eds.) IJCRS 2018. LNCS (LNAI), vol. 11103, pp. 148–161. Springer, Cham (2018). https://doi.org/10.1007/978-3-319-99368-3_12
15. Kato, Y., Saeki, T., Mizuno, S.: Considerations on the principle of rule induction by STRIM and its relationship to the conventional Rough Sets methods. Appl. Soft Comput. J. **73**, 933–942 (2018)
16. Kato, Y., Saeki, T.: Studies on reducing the necessary data size for rule induction from the decision table by STRIM. In: Mihálydeák, T., et al. (eds.) IJCRS 2019. LNCS (LNAI), vol. 11499, pp. 130–143. Springer, Cham (2019). https://doi.org/10.1007/978-3-030-22815-6_11
17. Piatetsky-Shapiro, G.: Discovery, analysis, and presentation of strong rules. In: Piatetsky-Shapiro, G., Frawley, W.J. (eds.) Knowledge Discovery in Databases. AAAI/MT Press, Cambridge (1991)
18. Agrawal, R., Srikant, R.: Fast algorithm for mining association rules in large databases. In: Proceedings of the 20th International Conference on Very Large Data Bases, VLDB 1994, pp. 487–499 (1994)
19. Walpole, R.E., Myers, R.H., Myers, S.L., Ye, K.: Probability and Statistics for Engineers and Scientists, 8th edn., pp. 187–191. Pearson Prentice Hall, Upper Saddle River (2007)
20. https://www.rdocumentation.org/packages/arules/versions/1.5-5
21. Witten, I.H., Frank, E., Hall, M.A., Pal, C.J.: Data Mining Practical Machine Learning Tools and Techniques, 4th edn., pp. 120–127. Morgan Kaufmann Publishers, Burlington (2017)

An ASP-Based Approach
to Counterfactual Explanations
for Classification

Leopoldo Bertossi[✉]

Faculty of Engineering and Sciences, Universidad Adolfo Ibañez, Santiago, Chile
leopoldo.bertossi@uai.cl

Abstract. We propose answer-set programs that specify and compute counterfactual interventions as a basis for causality-based explanations to decisions produced by classification models. They can be applied with black-box models and models that can be specified as logic programs, such as rule-based classifiers. The main focus is on the specification and computation of maximum responsibility causal explanations. The use of additional semantic knowledge is investigated.

1 Introduction

Providing explanations to results obtained from machine-learning models has been recognized as critical in many applications, and has become an active research direction in the broader area of *explainable AI*, and explainable machine learning, in particular [23]. This becomes particularly relevant when decisions are automatically made by those models, possibly with serious consequences for stake holders. Since most of those models are algorithms learned from training data, providing explanations may not be easy or possible. These models are or can be seen as *black-box models*.

In AI, explanations have been investigated in several areas, and in particular, under *actual causality* [16], where *counterfactual interventions* on a causal model are central [24]. They are hypothetical updates on the model's variables, to explore if and how the outcome of the model changes or not. In this way, explanations for an original output are defined and computed. Counterfactual interventions have been used with ML models, in particular with classification models [6,10,17,20,21,26,27].

In this work we introduce the notion of *causal explanation* as a set of feature value for the entity under classification that is *most responsible* for the outcome. The responsibility score is adopted and adapted from the general notion of responsibility used in actual causality [9]. Experimental results with the responsibility score, and comparisons with other scores are reported in [6]. We also introduce *answer-set programs* (ASPs) that specify counterfactual interventions

Leopoldo Bertossi—Member of the Data Observatory Foundation, the Millenium Institute of Foundations of Data (IMFD), Chile; and RelationalAI's Academic Network.

V. Gutiérrez-Basulto et al. (Eds.): RuleML+RR 2020, LNCS 12173, pp. 70–81, 2020.
https://doi.org/10.1007/978-3-030-57977-7_5

and causal explanations, and allow to specify and compute the responsibility score. The programs can be applied with black-box models, and with rule-based classification models.

As we show in this work, our declarative approach to counterfactual interventions is particularly appropriate for bringing into the game additional declarative semantic knowledge, which is much more complicated to do with purely procedural approaches. In this way, we can combine logic-based specifications, and use the generic and optimized solvers behind ASP implementations.

This paper is structured as follows. Section 2 introduces the background, and the notions of *counterfactual intervention* and *causal explanation*; and the *explanatory responsibility score*, x-resp, on their basis. Section 3 introduces ASPs that specify causal explanations, the *counterfactual ASPs*. Section 4 argues for the need to include semantic domain knowledge in the specification of causal explanations. Section 5 discusses several issues raised by this work and possible extensions.

2   Counterfactual Explanations

We consider *classification models*, C, that are represented by an input/output relation. Inputs are the so-called *entities*, $\mathbf{e}$, which are represented each by a record (or vector), $\mathbf{e} = \langle x_1, \ldots, x_n \rangle$, where x_i is the value $F_i(\mathbf{e}) \in Dom(F_i)$ taken on $\mathbf{e}$ by a *feature* $F_i \in \mathcal{F} = \{F_1, \ldots, F_n\}$, a set of functions. The output is represented by a *label function* L that maps entities $\mathbf{e}$ to 0 or 1, the binary result of the classification. That is, to simplify the presentation, we concentrate here on binary classifiers, but this is not essential. We also concentrate on features whose domains $Dom(F_i)$ take a finite number of categorical values. C.f. Sect. 4 for the transformation of numerical domains into categorical ones.

Building a classifier, C, from a set of training data, i.e. a set of pairs $T = \{\langle \mathbf{e}_1, c(\mathbf{e}_1) \rangle, \ldots, \langle \mathbf{e}_M, c(\mathbf{e}_M) \rangle\}$, with $c(\mathbf{e}_i) \in \{0, 1\}$, is one of the most common tasks in machine learning [13]. It is about learning the label function L for the entire domain of values, beyond T. We say that L "represents" the classifier C.

Classifiers may take many different internal forms. They could be decision trees, random forests, rule-based classifiers, logistic regression models, neural network-based (or deep) classifiers, etc. [13]. Some of them are more "opaque" than others, i.e. with a more complex and less interpretable internal structure and results [25]. Hence the need for explanations to their classification outcomes. In this work, we are not assuming that we have an explicit classification model, and we do not need it. All we need is to be able to invoke and use it. It could be a "black-box" model.

The problem is the following: Given an entity $\mathbf{e}$ that has received the label $L(\mathbf{e})$, provide an "explanation" for this outcome. In order to simplify the presentation, and without loss of generality, *we assume that label 1 is the one that has to be explained*. It is the "negative" outcome one has to justify, such as the rejection of a loan application.

Causal explanations are defined in terms of counterfactual interventions that simultaneously change feature values in $\mathbf{e}$ in such a way that the updated record gets a new label. A *causal explanation* for the classification of **e** is then a set of its original feature values that are affected by a *minimal counterfactual interventions*. These explanations are assumed to be more informative than others. Minimality can be defined in different ways, and we adopt an abstract approach, assuming a partial order relation $\preceq$ on counterfactual interventions.

Definition 1. Consider a binary classifier represented by its label function L, and a fixed input record $\mathbf{e} = \langle x_1, \ldots, x_n \rangle$, with $F_i(\mathbf{e}) = x_i$, $1 \leq i \leq n$, and $L(\mathbf{e}) = 1$.
(a) An *intervention* ι on **e** is a set of the form $\{\langle F_{i_1}, x'_{i_1} \rangle, \ldots, \langle F_{i_K}, x'_{i_K} \rangle\}$, with $F_{i_s} \neq F_{i_\ell}$, for $s \neq \ell$, $x_{i_s} \neq x'_{i_s} \in Dom(X_{i_s})$. We denote with $\iota(\mathbf{e})$ the record obtained by applying to **e** intervention ι, i.e. by replacing in **e** every $x_{i_s} = F_{i_s}(\mathbf{e})$, with F_{i_s} appearing in ι, by x'_{i_s}.
(b) A *counterfactual intervention* on **e** is an intervention ι on **e** such that $L(\iota(\mathbf{e})) = 0$. A $\preceq$-*minimal* counterfactual intervention is such that there is no counterfactual intervention ι' on **e** with $\iota' \prec \iota$ (i.e. $\iota' \preceq \iota$, but not $\iota \preceq \iota'$).
(c) A *causal explanation* for $L(\mathbf{e})$ is a set of the form $\epsilon = \{\langle F_{i_1}, x_{i_1} \rangle, \ldots, \langle F_{i_K}, x_{i_K} \rangle\}$ for which there is a counterfactual intervention $\iota = \{\langle F_{i_1}, x'_{i_1} \rangle, \ldots, \langle F_{i_K}, x'_{i_K} \rangle\}$ for **e**. Sometimes, to emphasize the intervention, we denote the explanation with $\epsilon(\iota)$.
(d) A causal explanation ϵ for $L(\mathbf{e})$ is $\preceq$-*minimal* if it is of the form $\epsilon(\iota)$ for a $\preceq$-minimal counterfactual intervention ι on **e**.   ☐

Several minimality criteria can be expressed in terms of partial orders, such as: (a) $\iota_1 \leq^s \iota_2$ iff $\pi_1(\iota_1) \subseteq \pi_1(\iota_2)$, with $\pi_1(\iota)$ the projection of ι on the first position. (b) $\iota_1 \leq^c \iota_2$ iff $|\iota_1| \leq |\iota_2|$. That is, minimality under set inclusion and cardinality, resp. In the following, we will consider only these; and mostly the second.

Example 1. Consider three binary features, i.e. $\mathcal{F} = \{F_1, F_2, F_3\}$, and they take values 0 or 1; and the input/output relation of a classifier $\mathcal{C}$ shown in Table 1. Let **e** be $\mathbf{e}_1$ in the table. We want causal explanations for its label 1. Any other record in the table can be seen as the result of an intervention on $\mathbf{e}_1$. However, only $\mathbf{e}_4, \mathbf{e}_7, \mathbf{e}_8$ are (results of) counterfactual interventions in that they switch the label to 0.

For example, $\mathbf{e}_4$ corresponds to the intervention $\iota_4 = \{\langle F_1, 1 \rangle, \langle F_2, 0 \rangle\}$ in that $\mathbf{e}_4$ is obtained from $\mathbf{e}_1$ by changing the values of F_1, F_2 into 1 and 0, resp. For ι_4, $\pi_1(\iota_4) = \{\langle F_1 \rangle, \langle F_2 \rangle\}$. From ι_4 we obtain the causal explanation $\epsilon_4 = \{\langle F_1, 0 \rangle, \langle F_2, 1 \rangle\}$, telling us that the values $F_1(\mathbf{e}_1) = 0$ and $F_2(\mathbf{e}_1) = 1$ are the joint cause for $\mathbf{e}_1$ to have been classified as 1. There are three causal explanations: $\epsilon_4 := \{\langle F_1, 0 \rangle, \langle F_2, 1 \rangle\}$, $\epsilon_7 := \{\langle F_2, 1 \rangle\}$, and $\epsilon_8 := \{\langle F_2, 1 \rangle, \langle F_3, 1 \rangle\}$. Here, $\mathbf{e}_4$ and $\mathbf{e}_8$ are incomparable under $\preceq^s$, $\mathbf{e}_7 \prec^s \mathbf{e}_4$, $\mathbf{e}_7 \prec^s \mathbf{e}_8$, and ϵ_7 turns out to be $\preceq^s$- and $\preceq^c$-minimal (actually, minimum).   ☐

Table 1. Entities, feature values and labels.

Entity (id)	F_1	F_2	F_3	L
e_1	0	1	1	1
e_2	1	1	1	1
e_3	1	1	0	1
e_4	1	0	1	0
e_5	1	0	0	1
e_6	0	1	0	1
e_7	0	0	1	0
e_8	0	0	0	0

Notice that, by taking a projection, the partial order $\preceq^s$ does not care about the values that replace the original feature values, as long as the latter are changed. Furthermore, given **e**, it would be good enough to indicate the features whose values are relevant, e.g. $\epsilon_7 = \{F_2\}$ in the previous example. However, the introduced notation emphasizes the fact that the original values are those we concentrate on when providing explanations.

Clearly, every $\preceq^c$-minimal explanation is also $\preceq^s$-minimal. However, it is easy to produce an example showing that a $\preceq^s$-minimal explanation may not be $\preceq^c$-minimal.

Notation: An *s-explanation* for $L(\mathbf{e})$ is a $\preceq^s$-minimal causal explanation for $L(\mathbf{e})$. A *c-explanations* $L(\mathbf{e})$ is a $\preceq^c$-minimal causal explanation for $L(\mathbf{e})$.

This definition characterizes explanations as sets of (interventions on) features. However, it is common that one wants to quantify the "causal strength" of a single feature value in a record representing an entity [6,20], or a single tuple in a database (as a cause for a query answer) [22], or a single attribute value in a database tuple [3,4], etc. Different *scores* have been proposed in this direction, e.g. SHAP in [20] and Resp in [6]. The latter has it origin in *actual causality* [16], as the *responsibility* of an actual cause [9], which we adapt to our setting.

Definition 2. Consider **c** to be an entity represented as a record of feature values $x_i = F_i(\mathbf{e})$, $F_i \in \mathcal{F}$.
(a) A feature value $v = F(\mathbf{e})$, with $F \in \mathcal{F}$, is a *value-explanation* for $L(\mathbf{e})$ if there is an s-explanation ϵ for $L(\mathbf{e})$, such that $\langle F, v \rangle \in \epsilon$.
(b) The *explanatory responsibility* of a value-explanation $v = F(\mathbf{e})$ is:

$$\mathsf{x\text{-}resp}_{\mathbf{e},F}(v) := max\{\frac{1}{|\epsilon|} : \epsilon \text{ is s-explanation with } \langle F, v \rangle \in \epsilon\}.$$

(c) If $v = F(\mathbf{e})$ is not a value-explanation, $\mathsf{x\text{-}resp}_{\mathbf{e},F}(v) := 0$.   □

Notice that (b) can be stated as $\mathsf{x\text{-}resp}_{\mathbf{e},F}(v) := \frac{1}{|\epsilon^*|}$, with $\epsilon^* = argmin\{|\epsilon| : \epsilon$ is s-explanation with $\langle F, v \rangle \in \epsilon\}$.

Adopting the usual terminology in actual causality [16], a *counterfactual value-explanation* for **e**'s classification is a value-explanation v with $\mathsf{x\text{-}resp}_{\mathbf{e}}(v) = 1$, that is, it suffices, without company of other feature values in **e**, to justify the classification. Similarly, an *actual value-explanation* for **e**'s classification is a value-explanation v with $\mathsf{x\text{-}resp}_{\mathbf{e}}(v) > 0$. That is, v appears in an s-explanation ϵ, say as $\langle F, v \rangle$, but possibly in company of other feature values in **e**. In this case, $\epsilon \smallsetminus \{\langle F, v \rangle\}$ is called a *contingency set* for v [22]. It turns out that maximum-responsibility value-explanations appear in c-explanations.

Example 2. (Example 1 cont.) ϵ_7 is the only c-explanation for entity e_1's classification. Its value 1 for feature F_2 is a value-explanation, and its explanatory responsibility is $\text{x-resp}_{e_1, F_2}(1) := 1$.   □

3   Specifying Causal Explanations in ASP

Entities will be represented by a predicate with $n+2$ arguments $E(\cdot; \cdots; \cdot)$. The first one holds a record (or entity) id (which may not be needed when dealing with single entities). The next n arguments hold the feature values.[1] The last argument holds an annotation constant from the set $\{o, do, \star, s\}$. Their semantics will be specified below, by the generic program that uses them.

Initially, a record $e = \langle x_1, \ldots, x_n \rangle$ has not been subject to interventions, and the corresponding entry in predicate E is of the form $E(e; \bar{x}; o)$, with $\bar{x}$ an abbreviation for $x_1, \ldots, x_n$, and constant o standing for "original entity".

When the classifier gives label 1 to e, the idea is to start changing feature values, one at a time. The intervened entity becomes then annotated with constant do in the last argument. When the resulting intervened entities are classified, we may not have the classifier specified within the program. For this reason, the program uses a special predicate $C[\cdot; \cdot]$, whose first argument takes (a representation of) an entity under classification, and whose second argument returns the binary label. We will assume this predicate can be invoked by an ASP as an external procedure, much in the spirit of HEX-programs [11,12]. Since the original instance may have to go through several interventions until reaching one that switches the label to 0, the intermediate entities get the "transition" annotation $\star$. This is achieved by a generic program.

The Counterfactual Intervention Program:

P1. The facts of the program are all the atoms of the form $Dom_i(c)$, with $c \in Dom_i$, plus the initial entity $E(e; \bar{f}; o)$, where $\bar{f}$ is the initial vector of feature values.

P2. The transition entities are obtained as initial, original entities, or as the result of an intervention: (here, e is a variable standing for a record id)

$$E(e; \bar{x}; \star) \longleftarrow E(e; \bar{x}; o).$$
$$E(e; \bar{x}; \star) \longleftarrow E(e; \bar{x}; do).$$

P3. The program rule specifying that, every time the entity at hand (original or obtained after a "previous" intervention) is classified with label 1, a new value has to be picked from a domain, and replaced for the current value. The new value is chosen via the non-deterministic "choice operator", a well-established mechanism in ASP [15]. In this case, the values are chosen from

---

[1] For performance-related reasons, it might be more convenient to use n 3-are predicates to represent an entity with an identifier, but the presentation here would be more complicated.

the domains, and are subject to the condition of not being the same as the current value:

$$E(\mathbf{e}; x_1', x_2, \ldots, x_n, \mathsf{do}) \vee \cdots \vee E(\mathbf{e}; x_1, x_2, \ldots, x_n', \mathsf{do}) \longleftarrow E(\mathbf{e}; \bar{x}; \star), \mathcal{C}[\bar{x}; 1],$$
$$Dom_1(x_1'), \ldots, Dom_n(x_n'), x_1' \neq x_1, \ldots, x_n' \neq x_n,$$
$$choice(\bar{x}; x_1'), \ldots, choice(\bar{x}; x_n').$$

For each fixed $\bar{x}$, $choice(\bar{x}; y)$ chooses a unique value y subject to the other conditions in the same rule body. The use of the choice operator can be eliminated by replacing each $choice(\bar{x}; x_i')$ atom by the atom $Chosen_i(\bar{x}, x_i')$, and defining each predicate $Chosen_i$ by means of "classical" rules [15], as follows:

$$Chosen_i(\bar{x}, y) \leftarrow E(\mathbf{e}; \bar{x}; \star), \mathcal{C}[\bar{x}; 1], Dom_i(y), y \neq x_i, not\ DiffChoice(\bar{x}, y).$$
$$DiffChoice(\bar{x}, y) \leftarrow Chosen_i(\bar{x}, y'), y' \neq y.$$

P4. The following rule specifies that we can "stop", hence annotation s, when we reach an entity that gets label 0:

$$E(\mathbf{e}; \bar{x}; \mathsf{s}) \longleftarrow E(\mathbf{e}; \bar{x}; \mathsf{do}), \mathcal{C}[\bar{x}; 0].$$

P5. We add a *program constraint* specifying that we prohibit going back to the original entity via local interventions:

$$\longleftarrow E(\mathbf{e}; \bar{x}; \mathsf{do}), E(\mathbf{e}; \bar{x}; \mathsf{o}).$$

P6. The causal explanations can be collected by means of predicates $Expl_i(\cdot; \cdot)$ specified by means of:

$$Expl_i(\mathbf{e}; x_i) \longleftarrow E(\mathbf{e}; x_1, \ldots, x_n; \mathsf{o}), E(\mathbf{e}; x_1', \ldots, x_n'; \mathsf{s}), x_i \neq x_i'.$$

Actually, each of these is a value-explanation. □

The program will have several stable models due to the disjunctive rule and the choice operator. Each model will hold intervened versions of the original entity, and hopefully versions for which the label is switched, i.e. those with annotation s. If the classifier never switches the label, despite the fact that local interventions are not restricted (and this would be quite an unusual classifier), we will not find a model with a version of the initial entity annotated with s. Due to the program constraint in P5., none of the models will have the original entity annotated with do, because those models would be discarded [19].

Notice that the use of the choice operator hides occurrences of non-stratified negation [15]. In relation to the use of disjunction in a rule head, the semantics of ASP, which involves model minimality, makes only one of the atoms in the disjunction true (unless forced otherwise by the program itself).

Example 3. (Example 1 cont.) Most of the *Counterfactual Intervention Program* above is generic. In this particular example, the have the following facts: $Dom_1(0)$, $Dom_1(1)$, $Dom_2(0)$, $Dom_2(1)$, $Dom_3(0)$, $Dom_3(1)$ and $E(\mathbf{e}_1; 0, 1, 1; \mathsf{o})$, with $\mathbf{e}_1$ a constant, the record id of the first row in Table 1.

In this very particular situation, the classifier is explicitly given by Table 1. Then, predicate $\mathcal{C}[\cdot; \cdot]$ can be specified with a set of additional facts: $\mathcal{C}[0, 1, 1; 1]$, $\mathcal{C}[1, 1, 1; 1]$, $\mathcal{C}[1, 1, 0; 1]$ $\mathcal{C}[1, 0, 1; 0]$ $\mathcal{C}[1, 0, 0; 1]$ $\mathcal{C}[0, 1, 0; 1]$ $\mathcal{C}[0, 0, 1; 0]$ $\mathcal{C}[0, 0, 0; 0]$.

The stable models of the program will contain all the facts above. One of them, say $\mathcal{M}_1$, will contain (among others) the facts: $E(\mathbf{e}_1; 0, 1, 1; \mathsf{o})$ and $E(\mathbf{e}_1; 0, 1, 1; \star)$. The presence of the last atom activates rule P3., because $\mathcal{C}[0, 1, 1; 1]$ is true (for $\mathbf{e}_1$ in Table 1). New facts are produced for $\mathcal{M}_1$ (the new value due to an intervention is underlined): $E(\mathbf{e}_1; \underline{1}, 1, 1; \mathsf{do})$, $E(\mathbf{e}_1; \underline{1}, 1, 1; \star)$. Due to the last fact and the true $\mathcal{C}[1, 1, 1; 1]$, rule P3. is activated again. Choosing the value 0 for the second disjunct, atoms $E(\mathbf{e}_1; \underline{1}, \underline{0}, 1; \mathsf{do})$, $E(\mathbf{e}_1; \underline{1}, \underline{0}, 1; \star)$ are generated. For the latter, $\mathcal{C}[1, 0, 1; 0]$ is true (coming from $\mathbf{e}_4$ in Table 1), switching the label to 0. Rule P3 is no longer activated, and we can apply rule P4., obtaining $E(\mathbf{e}_1; \underline{1}, \underline{0}, 1; \mathsf{s})$.

From rules P6., we obtain as explanations: $Expl_1(\mathbf{e}_1; 0)$, $Expl_2(\mathbf{e}_1; 1)$, showing the values in $\mathbf{e}_i$ that were changed. All this in model $\mathcal{M}_1$. There are other models, and one of them contains $E(\mathbf{e}_1; 0, \underline{0}, 1; \mathsf{s})$, the minimally intervened version of $\mathbf{e}_1$, i.e. $\mathbf{e}_7$. □

3.1   C-Explanations and Maximum Responsibility

There is no guarantee that the intervened entities $E(\mathbf{e}; c_1, \ldots, c_n; \mathsf{s})$ will correspond to c-explanations, which are the main focus of this work. In order to obtain them (and only them), we add *weak program constraints* (WCs) to the program. They can be violated by a stable model of the program (as opposed to (strong) program constraints that have to be satisfied). However, they have to be violated in a minimal way. We use WCs, whose *number* of violations have to be minimized, in this case, for $1 \leq i \leq n$ (This notation follows the standard in [7]):

$$:\sim E(\mathbf{e}; x_1, \ldots, x_n, \mathsf{o}), E(\mathbf{e}; x_1', \ldots, x_n', \mathsf{s}), x_i \neq x_i'.$$

Only the stable models representing an intervened version of $\mathbf{e}$ with a minimum number of value discrepancies with $\mathbf{e}$ will be kept.

In each of these "minimum-cardinality" stable models $\mathcal{M}$, we can collect the corresponding c-explanation for $\mathbf{e}$'s classification as the set $\epsilon^{\mathcal{M}} = \{ \langle F_i, c_i \rangle \mid Expl_i(\mathbf{e}; c_i) \in \mathcal{M} \}$. This can be done within a ASP system such as *DLV*, which allows set construction and aggregation, in particular, counting [1, 19]. Actually, counting comes handy to obtain the cardinality of $\epsilon^{\mathcal{M}}$. The responsibility of a value-explanation $Expl_i(\mathbf{e}; c_i)$ will then be: $\mathsf{x}\text{-}\mathsf{resp}_{\mathbf{e}, F_i}(c_i) = \frac{1}{|\epsilon^{\mathcal{M}}|}$.

4   Semantic Knowledge

Counterfactual interventions in the presence of semantic conditions requires consideration. As the following example shows, not every intervention, or combination of them, may be admissible [5]. It is in this kind of situations that declarative approaches to counterfactual interventions, like the one presented here, become particularly useful.

Example 4. A moving company makes automated hiring decisions based on feature values in applicants' records of the form $R = \langle appCode, abilitytolift, gender, weight, height, age \rangle$. Mary, represented by $R^\star = \langle 101, 1, F, 160\ pounds, 6\ feet, 28 \rangle$ applies, but is denied the job, i.e. the classifier returns: $L(R^\star) = 1$. To explain the decision, we can hypothetically change Mary's gender, from F into M, obtaining record $R^{\star\prime}$, for which we now observe $L(R^{\star\prime}) = 0$. Thus, her value F for *gender* can be seen as a counterfactual explanation for the initial decision.

As an alternative, we might keep the value of *gender*, and counterfactually change other feature values. However, we might be constrained or guided by an ontology containing, e.g. the denial semantic constraint $\neg(R[2] = 1 \wedge R[6] > 80)$ (2 and 6 indicating positions in the record) that prohibits someone over 80 to be qualified as fit to lift. We could also have a rule, such as $(R[3] = M \wedge R[4] > 100 \wedge R[6] < 70) \rightarrow R[2] = 1$, specifying that men who weigh over 100 pounds and are younger than 70 are automatically qualified to lift weight.

In situations like this, we could add to the ASP we had before: (a) program constraints that prohibit certain models, e.g. $\longleftarrow R(\mathsf{e}; x, 1, y, z, u, w; \star)$, $w > 80$; (b) additional rules, e.g. $R(\mathsf{e}; x, 1, y, z, u, w; \star) \longleftarrow R(\mathsf{e}; x, y, \mathsf{M}, z, u, w; \star)$, $z > 100, w < 70$, that may automatically generate additional interventions. In a similar way, one could accommodate certain preferences using weak program constraints. $\qquad\qquad\square$

Another situation where not all interventions are admissible occurs when features take continuous values, and their domains have to be discretized. The common way of doing this, namely the combination of *bucketization and one-hot-encoding*, leads to the natural and necessary imposition of additional constraints on interventions, as we will show. Through bucketization, a feature range is discretized by splitting it into finitely many, say N, usually non-overlapping intervals. This makes the feature basically categorical (each interval becoming a categorical value). Next, through one-hot-encoding, the original feature is represented as a vector of length N of indicator functions, one for each categorical value (intervals here) [6]. In this way, the original feature gives rise to N binary features. For example, if we have a continuous feature "External Risk Estimate" (ERE), its buckets could be: $[0, 64), [64, 71), [71, 76), [76, 81), [81, \infty)$. Accordingly, if for an entity e, $\mathsf{ERE}(\mathsf{e}) = 65$, then, after one-hot-encoding, this value is represented as the vector $[0, 1, 0, 0, 0, 0]$, because 65 falls into the second bucket.

In a case like this, it is clear that counterfactual interventions are constrained by the assumptions behind bucketization and one-hot-encoding. For example, the vector cannot be updated into, say $[0, 1, 0, 1, 0, 0]$, meaning that the feature value for the entity falls both in intervals $[64, 71)$ and $[76, 81)$. Bucketization and one-hot-encoding can make good use of program constraints, such as $\longleftarrow$ ERE(e; $x, 1, y, 1, z, w; \star$), etc. Of course, admissible interventions on predicate ERE could be easily handled with a disjunctive rule like that in P3., but without the "transition" annotation $\star$. However, the ERE record is commonly a component of a larger record containing all the feature values for an entity [6]. Hence the need for a more general and uniform form of specification.

5   Discussion

This work is about interacting with possibly external classifiers and reasoning with their results and potential inputs. That is, the classifier is supposed to have been learned by means of some other methodology. In particular, this is not about learning ASPs, which goes in a different direction [18].

We have treated classifiers as black-boxes that are represented by external predicates in the ASP. However, in some cases it could be the case that the classifier is given by a set of rules, which, if compatible with ASPs, could be appended to the program, to define the classification predicate $\mathcal{C}$. The domains used by the programs can be given explicitly. However, they can be specified and extracted from other sources. For example, for the experiments in [6], the domains were built from the training data, a process that can be specified and implemented in ASP.

The ASPs we have used are inspired by *repair programs* that specify and compute the repairs of a database that fails to satisfy the intended integrity constraints [8]. Actually, the connection between database repairs and actual query answer causality was established and exploited in [3]. ASPs that compute attribute-level causes for query answering were introduced in [4]. They are much simpler that those presented here, because, in that scenario, changing attribute values by nulls is good enough to invalidate the query answer (the "equivalent" in that scenario to switching the classification label here). Once a null is introduced, there is no need to take it into account anymore, and a single "step" of interventions is good enough.

Here we have considered only s- and c-explanations, specially the latter. Both embody specific and different, but related, minimization conditions. However, counterfactual explanations can be cast in terms of different optimization criteria [17, 26]. One could investigate in this setting other forms on preferences, the generic $\preceq$ in Definition 1, by using ASPs as those introduced in [14]. These programs could also de useful to compute (a subclass of) s-explanations, when c-explanations are, for some reason, not useful or interesting enough. The ASPs, as introduced in this work, are meant to compute c-explanations, but extending them is natural and useful.

This article reports on preliminary work that is part of longer term and ongoing research. In particular, we are addressing the following: (a) multi-task classification. (b) inclusion of rule-based classifiers. (c) scores associated to more than one intervention at a time [6], in particular, to full causal explanations. (d) experiments with this approach and comparisons with other forms of explanations. However, the most important direction to explore, and that is a matter of ongoing work, is described next.

5.1   From Ideal to More Practical Explanations

The approach to specification of causal explanations we described so far in this paper is in some sense *ideal*, in that the whole product space of the feature domains is considered, together with the applicability of the classifier over that space. This may be impractical or unrealistic. However, we see our proposal as a conceptual and specification basis that can be adapted in order to include more specific practices and mechanisms, hopefully keeping a clear declarative semantics. One way to go consists in restricting the product space; and this can be done in different manners. For instance, one can use constrains or additional conditions in rule bodies. An extreme case of this approach consists in replacing the product space with the entities in a *data sample* $S \subseteq \Pi_{i=1}^{n} Dom(F_i)$. We could even assume that this sample already comes with classification labels, i.e. $S^L = \{\langle \mathbf{e}'_1, L(\mathbf{e}'_1)\rangle, \ldots, \langle \mathbf{e}'_K, L(\mathbf{e}'_K)\rangle\}$. Actually, this dataset does not have to be disjoint from the training dataset T mentioned early in Sect. 2. The definition of causal explanation and the counterfactual ASPs could be adapted to these new setting without major difficulties.

An alternative and more sophisticated approach consists in using knowledge about the underlying population of entities, such a probabilistic distribution; and using it to define causal explanations, and explanation scores for them. This is the case of the Resp and SHAP explanation scores mentioned in Sect. 2 [6,20]. In these cases, it is natural to explore the applicability of probabilistic extensions of ASP [2]. In most cases, the underlying distribution is not known, and has to be estimated from the available data, e.g. a sample as S^L above, and the scores have to be redefined (or estimated) through by appealing to this sample. This was done in [6] for both Resp and SHAP. In these cases, counterfactual ASPs could be used, with extensions for set building and aggregations to compute the empirical scores, hopefully in interaction with a database containing the sample.

Acknowledgements. The thorough and useful comments provided by anonymous reviewers are greatly appreciated.

References

1. Alviano, M., et al.: The ASP system DLV2. In: Balduccini, M., Janhunen, T. (eds.) LPNMR 2017. LNCS (LNAI), vol. 10377, pp. 215–221. Springer, Cham (2017). https://doi.org/10.1007/978-3-319-61660-5_19
2. Baral, C., Gelfond, M., Rushton, N.: Probabilistic reasoning with answer sets. Theory Pract. Log. Program. **9**(1), 57–144 (2009)
3. Bertossi, L., Salimi, B.: From causes for database queries to repairs and model-based diagnosis and back. Theory Comput. Syst. **61**(1), 191–232 (2016). https://doi.org/10.1007/s00224-016-9718-9

4. Bertossi, L.: Characterizing and computing causes for query answers in databases from database repairs and repair programs. In: Ferrarotti, F., Woltran, S. (eds.) FoIKS 2018. LNCS, vol. 10833, pp. 55–76. Springer, Cham (2018). https://doi.org/10.1007/978-3-319-90050-6_4. Revised and extended version as Corr Arxiv Paper cs.DB/1712.01001

5. Bertossi, L., Geerts, F.: Data quality and explainable AI. ACM J. Data Inf. Qual. **12**(2), 1–9 (2020)

6. Bertossi, L., Li, J., Schleich, M., Suciu, D., Vagena, Z.: Causality-based explanation of classification outcomes. In: Proceedings of the 4th International Workshop on "Data Management for End-to-End Machine Learning" (DEEM) at ACM SIGMOD (2020). Posted as Corr Arxiv Paper arXiv:2003.0686

7. Calimeri, F., et al.: ASP-Core-2 input language format. Theory Pract. Log. Program. **20**(2), 294–309 (2020)

8. Caniupan, M., Bertossi, L.: The consistency extractor system: answer set programs for consistent query answering in databases. Data Knowl. Eng. **69**(6), 545–572 (2010)

9. Chockler, H., Halpern, J.Y.: Responsibility and blame: a structural-model approach. J. Artif. Intell. Res. **22**, 93–115 (2004)

10. Datta, A., Sen, S., Zick, Y.: Algorithmic transparency via quantitative input influence: theory and experiments with learning systems. In: Proceedings of the IEEE Symposium on Security and Privacy (2016)

11. Eiter, T., et al.: The DLVHEX system. KI - Künstl. Intell. **32**(2), 187–189 (2018). https://doi.org/10.1007/s13218-018-0535-y

12. Eiter, T., Kaminski, T., Redl, C., Schüller, P., Weinzierl, A.: Answer set programming with external source access. In: Ianni, G., et al. (eds.) Reasoning Web 2017. LNCS, vol. 10370, pp. 204–275. Springer, Cham (2017). https://doi.org/10.1007/978-3-319-61033-7_7

13. Flach, P.: Machine Learning. Cambridge University Press, Cambridge (2012)

14. Gebser, M., Kaminski, R., Schaub, T.: Complex optimization in answer set programming. Theory Pract. Log. Program. **11**(4–5), 821–839 (2011)

15. Giannotti, F., Greco, S., Sacca, D., Zaniolo, C.: Programming with nondeterminism in deductive databases. Ann. Math. Artif. Intell. **19**(12), 97–125 (1997). https://doi.org/10.1023/A:1018999404360

16. Halpern, J., Pearl, J.: Causes and explanations: a structural-model approach: part 1. Brit. J. Philos. Sci. **56**, 843–887 (2005)

17. Karimi, A.H., Barthe, G., Balle, B., Valera, I.: Model-agnostic counterfactual explanations for consequential decisions. In: Proceedings of the International Conference on Artificial Intelligence and Statistics (AISTATS) (2020). arXiv: 1905.11190

18. Law, M., Russo, A., Broda, K.: Logic-based learning of answer set programs. In: Krötzsch, M., Stepanova, D. (eds.) Reasoning Web. Explainable Artificial Intelligence. LNCS, vol. 11810, pp. 196–231. Springer, Cham (2019). https://doi.org/10.1007/978-3-030-31423-1_6

19. Leone, N., et al.: The DLV system for knowledge representation and reasoning. ACM Trans. Comput. Log. **7**(3), 499–562 (2006)

20. Lundberg, S., Lee, S.-I.: A unified approach to interpreting model predictions. In: Proceedings of the NIPS, pp. 4765–4774 (2017)

21. Martens, D., Provost, F.J.: Explaining data-driven document classifications. MIS Quart. **38**(1), 73–99 (2014)

22. Meliou, A., Gatterbauer, W., Moore, K.F., Suciu, D.: The complexity of causality and responsibility for query answers and non-answers. Proceedings of the VLDB, pp. 34–41 (2010)

23. Molnar, C.: Interpretable machine learning: a guide for making black box models explainable (2020). https://christophm.github.io/interpretable-ml-book
24. Pearl, J.: Causality: Models, Reasoning and Inference, 2nd edn. Cambridge University Press, Cambridge (2009)
25. Rudin, C.: Stop explaining black box machine learning models for high stakes decisions and use interpretable models instead. Nat. Mach. Intell. **1**, 206–215 (2019)
26. Russell, C.: Efficient search for diverse coherent explanations. In: Proceedings of the FAT, pp. 20–28 (2019). arXiv:1901.04909
27. Wachter, S., Brent, D., Mittelstadt, B.D., Chris Russell, C.: Counterfactual explanations without opening the black box: automated decisions and the GDPR. CoRR abs/1711.00399 (2017)

Benchmark for Performance Evaluation of SHACL Implementations in Graph Databases

Robert Schaffenrath$^{(\boxtimes)}$, Daniel Proksch, Markus Kopp, Iacopo Albasini,
Oleksandra Panasiuk, and Anna Fensel

Department of Computer Science, University of Innsbruck, Innsbruck, Austria
{robert.schaffenrath,daniel.proksch,markus.kopp,
iacopo.albasini}@student.uibk.ac.at,
{oleksandra.panasiuk,anna.fensel}@sti2.at

Abstract. Due to the rise in the commercial usage of knowledge graphs, the validation of graph-based data has gained importance over the past few years in the field of Semantic Web. In spite of this trend, the number of graph databases that support W3C's validation specification Shapes Constraint Language (SHACL) can still be regarded as low, and best practices for their SHACL implementations performance evaluation are lacking. In this paper, we propose a benchmark for performance evaluation of SHACL implementations and present an evaluation of five common graph databases using the benchmark.

Keywords: Benchmark · SHACL · Graph database

1 Introduction

The Semantic Web is a concept for an extension of the World Wide Web that was originally popularized through a 2001 article in the Scientific American by Berners-Lee, Hendler and Lassila [3]. The goal of the concept was to provide a new form of web content focusing on machine interpretability. This would enable the usage of autonomous task handling by software agents and by that enhance the user experience on the web.

Since the initial introduction of the concept, many developments have taken place. There has been a substantial increase in the amount of publicly available linked data on the web. Companies like Google and Facebook started to use semantic data structures and knowledge graphs to improve their services for the user [23,26]. The establishment of intelligent assistants, like Cortana by Microsoft or Siri by Apple that can act comparably to the in 2001 envisioned software agents to autonomously solve tasks basing on the semantic annotations [3], can be seen as a sign of the increasing importance of the Semantic Web.

With the increase in utilization of graph-based data on the web and the issues with the published data quality [13], the need for validation of this type of data has increased as well. To accommodate this need, the World Wide Web

© Springer Nature Switzerland AG 2020
V. Gutiérrez-Basulto et al. (Eds.): RuleML+RR 2020, LNCS 12173, pp. 82–96, 2020.
https://doi.org/10.1007/978-3-030-57977-7_6

Consortium (W3C) has provided a standardized Shapes Constraint Language (SHACL) [15] in 2017. The W3C recommendation represents a language for the validation of RDF graphs against a set of conditions. Moreover, with the increased velocity needs of applications, time is becoming an important factor for the data processing with SHACL.

In spite of the need for the type of validations SHACL provides, most popular graph databases currently do not offer an implementation of the standard or a different validation language. Depending on the size of the data graph and shapes graph, validation can entail substantial issues in terms of the memory consumption versus computation time. There are currently no benchmarks for SHACL validations in graph databases, which warrant an empirical evaluation of the available implementations. In this paper, we provide a SHACL performance evaluation benchmark and conduct the performance evaluation of SHACL implementations of different graph databases employing it.

This paper is structured as follows. Section 2 presents related work, which focuses on benchmarking of graph databases. Section 3 describes the methodology and construction of our benchmark. Section 4 presents the performance evaluation of five common graph databases we conducted using the benchmark. A detailed explanation for the results is provided in Sect. 5. Section 6 concludes the paper.

2 Related Work

There are multiple available evaluations of graph databases for various benchmark and instruction types. Jouili and Vansteenberghe [12] performed an empirical comparison of the graph databases Neo4j, Titan, OrientDB and DEX using the specifically developed benchmarking framework GDB. The framework focuses on benchmarking typical graph operations. The database management system Neo4j generally yielded the best result for the performed instructions.

McColl et al. [16] conducted a performance comparison of 12 different graph databases using the four fundamental graph algorithms SSSP, Connected Components, PageRank and Update Rate. The evaluation was performed on a network containing up to 256 million edges.

Dominguez-Sal et al. [6] evaluated the performance of the graph databases Neo4j, Apache Jena, HypergraphDB and DEX using the HPC Scalable Graph Analysis Benchmark. From the results, they concluded that DEX and Neo4j were the most efficient of the four tested graph databases.

Capotă et al. [5] developed a big data benchmark for graph-processing platforms. Using this benchmark, they evaluated the platforms Apache Giraph, MapReduce, GraphX and Neo4j for five different algorithms on three different datasets.

While these evaluations focused on ordinary graph operations, multiple evaluations based on benchmarks for SPARQL queries were conducted as well. Bizer and Schulz [4] developed the Berlin SPARQL Benchmark, which focuses on search and navigation patterns in a fictional use-case. Using this benchmark, they conducted a comparative evaluation of the RDF stores Sesame, Virtuoso, Jena TDB and Jena SDB to compare them to the performance of the SPARQL-to-SQL writers D2R Server and Virtuoso RDF.

Schmidt et al. [21] created another SPARQL performance benchmark based on generated data using the scenario of the DBLP dataset. Compared to the Berlin Benchmark, SP2Bench is less use-case driven and tries to address language-specific issues. The benchmark was conducted for the RDF stores Virtuoso, Sesame, Redland, ARQ and SDB.

The presented papers portray the availability of evaluations and benchmarks for multiple aspects of graph databases. These aspects however do not include SHACL validations at the current moment, which suggests the need for more research in this specific area.

3   The Benchmark

We propose a benchmark for performance evaluation of SHACL implementations in graph databases. The benchmark focuses on evaluating the performance of full SHACL validations on a dataset using the implementations and storages provided by the graph database management system. Using the benchmark, a comparative analysis of five common graph databases is performed. The validity of the validation processes is not part of our project scope.

As our dataset, we use a subset consisting of one million quads from the Tyrolean Knowledge Graph, which contains currently around eight billion triples, set up by Kärle et al. [14]. This dataset is very representative for the real-life data found currently on the Web, and is therefore suitable for a benchmark construction. Based on this dataset and domain specifications[1] defined by Panasiuk et al. [18,19], we constructed 58 different SHACL shapes that are suitable to be used as valid shapes to clean the data of this specific knowledge graph. The dataset combined with the defined shapes form the benchmark. These two inputs are used for the validation process to test the performance of SHACL implementations in graph databases. We have published the benchmark dataset, as well as the developed SHACL shapes as open research data[2], and discuss them further in detail.

3.1   The Benchmark Dataset

The Tyrolean Knowledge Graph is a knowledge graph that gathers and publicly provides tourism data in the Austrian region of Tyrol [14]. The knowledge graph currently contains more than eight billion triples based on schema.org

---

[1] A domain specification is a domain specific pattern that restricts and extends schema.org for domain and task specific needs. Currently, 84 domain specifications are available that focus on providing representations for tourism related data and can be used for validation purposes [22].

[2] Benchmark for SHACL Performance in Knowledge Bases, doi: 10.17632/jfrdpnb-945.1.

annotations collected from different sources such as destination management organizations and geographical information systems. Apart from service types relevant in tourism, like hotels, food and beverage establishments or events, the knowledge graph contains information on additional attributes, like geographic data. The vocabulary of the knowledge graph is schema.org [10], a de-facto standard for semantically annotating data, content, and services on the web.

The SHACL shapes of our benchmark were designed for a subset of the Tyrolean Knowledge Graph containing 30 million quads. Due to resource and software limitations that occurred throughout the evaluation process (described in Sect. 4.3), the size of the dataset had to be reduced to one million quads. This allows the usage of any subset of the 30 million quads dataset as valid input with a similar validation coverage. For different subsets of the Tyrolean Knowledge Graph or other datasets based on the schema.org ontology, the number of validated classes and properties can vary significantly. Especially the usage of other datasets can lead to an increase of violations, since many SHACL shapes are explicitly designed for properties in Tyrol, e.g. the latitude property of https://schema.org/GeoCoordinates has to be between the values 46.3 and 47.5.

3.2   The SHACL Shapes

In order to validate data, SHACL requires two different inputs. First, a data graph has to be available that may contain invalid or malformed entries. In our benchmark, this data graph is represented by the subset of the Tyrolean Knowledge Graph. The second required input is the shapes graph that declares constraints upon the given data from the data graph. It is worth mentioning that combining the data and shape graphs together into a single graph is possible, but this has a negative impact on the readability and compatibility, due to the limited support of SHACL by many databases.

There exist two types of shapes: node shapes and property shapes. A node shape specifies constraints that need to be fulfilled by focus nodes. A focus node is an RDF term from the data graph that is validated against a shape. This means that a node shape specifies a focus node for which the remaining constraints of the shape has to apply. A property shape specifies constraints on nodes that are reachable from a given focus node by following a property path. This allows to define clear restrictions on possible values for subjects of a triple or quad, e.g. cardinality constraints, value types and value ranges.

The design philosophy of the SHACL shapes for our benchmark was to validate most of the data in our dataset to make the evaluation accurate and computationally demanding. With that in mind we tried to cover a majority of the properties for each class that appears in the initial 30 million quads dataset, prioritising the most frequent appearing properties. In addition we specified the cardinality for each property according to the domain specifications of *Schema Tourism* [20].

The constructed by us 58 different SHACL shapes can be used as valid shapes to clean the data of this specific knowledge graph. Apart from the instrumental shape-based constraint components, the shapes include the cardinality constraint components sh:maxCount and sh:minCount, value type constraint components like sh:datatype, and string-based constraint components like sh:pattern and sh:maxLength. We also utilize the logical constraint component sh:or, which led to different results in the validation reports depending on the graph database. The goal of these constraints is to mimic a non-specific validation of a knowledge graph based on its vocabulary.

In addition to the domain related constraints, we approached a design of specific constraints for regional attributes of the Tyrolean Knowledge Graph. Since the dataset should only contain data about businesses and events from Austria and more specifically from Tyrol, values of many properties of that schema can be evaluated precisely. For instance, the property **addressCountry** must have the string "AT", which is the ISO 3166 code for Austria [11]. The shape for this specific example is depicted in Listing 1.1.

Listing 1.1. Shape for schema **PostalAddress**.

```
@prefix schema: <http://schema.org/> .
@prefix sh: <http://www.w3.org/ns/shacl#> .
@prefix xsd: <http://www.w3.org/2001/XMLSchema#> .

:AddressCountryShape a sh:NodeShape;
    sh:targetClass schema:PostalAddress;
        sh:property [
            sh:path schema:addressCountry;
            sh:datatype xsd:string;
            sh:pattern "AT";
            sh:maxCount 1;
        ].
```

Following the principles described above, the SHACL shapes can be constructed in a similar manner for different datasets. This ensures that our approach is sufficiently representative and generic.

4   Performance Evaluation

In this section, we explain the utilization of the evaluated graph databases for the validation of our dataset. We describe the ease of use, potential pitfalls of the current implementations and results of the overall evaluation.

4.1   Database Selection

To determine which graph databases offer SHACL implementations we performed keyword searches in the respective software documentations and in the source code of open source projects. We also searched for indications on the official database websites, in various forums and contacted some developers of the respective databases. Using this process, we were able to identify a number of graph databases that provide a SHACL implementation. For the project, we decided to use the free-to-use versions of the graph databases AllegroGraph by Franz Inc, Apache Jena by Apache, GraphDB by Ontotext, RDF4J, Stardog by Stardog Union Inc. We should point out that the most popular graph database according to DB-Engines [24], Neo4j, did not have native SHACL support at the time we conducted our evaluation. Furthermore, we determined the absence of SHACL support for more graph databases.

AllegroGraph [9] is a closed-source persistent RDF store with an additional graph database management system. It is developed and published by Franz Inc and solely supports RDFS as its data scheme. AllegroGraph uses SPARQL as its query language and is available for Linux, OS X and Windows. The problem with the usage lies in the limitations of the free-to-use community edition of the commercial product. This version is only able to store up to five million triples in its triplestore, which is not enough to work with our initial 30 million quads dataset. Since we had to reduce our dataset to one million quads, this restriction did not pose a problem.

Apache Jena is an open-source Java framework by Apache that offers the component TDB [2], which acts as an RDF store and query database management system. Jena is implemented in Java and available on every operating system with a Java virtual machine. SPARQL is supported as a query language.

GraphDB [17] is a commercial, closed-source graph database management system and RDF store by Ontotext. It is implemented in Java and supports OWL/RDFS-schema as an optional feature. SPARQL is used as the query language and it is available for all operating systems that support a Java virtual machine. While GraphDB is a commercial product, a free version with limited functionality exists and was deemed usable for this project. SHACL is not supported natively, instead it supports the validation language using the RDF4J API.

RDF4J [7] is an open-source Java framework and part of the Eclipse project. The functionality of the framework is focused on processing RDF data. It is implemented in Java and available for Linux, OS X, Unix and Windows. SPARQL is supported as a query language.

Stardog [25] is a closed-source graph database management system and RDF store by Stardog Union Inc. It is implemented in Java and supports OWL/RDFS-schema as an optional feature. It uses SPARQL as its query language and is available for Linux, macOS and Windows. Stardog is a commercial product, but its one-year fully-featured non-commercial use license for students renders it usable for our project.

4.2 Evaluation Methodology

The study was conducted by installing the graph databases on a single machine with the following specifications: Intel Core i7-6700K @ 4.00 GHz processor, 16 GB PC 3200 DDR4 RAM and a Kingston A400 240 GB SSD. Manjaro Linux 18.1.5 was used as the operating system for the evaluation. The criterion to assess performance is measuring the time it takes to generate a SHACL report. To measure the time the bash command time was used for all databases, since the entire validation process should be captured. The same holds for the tested Java frameworks, where our Java implementation could have an impact on the overall time. Therefore, these implementations were kept relatively simple. Since the structure and provided information of the generated reports differ between databases and the average size of the reports was 1.5 GB, we were not able to compare them in detail except from size and number of violations.

The method used in the evaluation was to measure the SHACL implementation eight times on the same database under the same conditions to increase the accuracy of the results. One requirement is that the dataset is stored in a native, indexed triplestore. The generated reports were piped to the null device (/dev/null) for the measurement to reduce the impact of system calls. In addition we provide information regarding the difficulty of using SHACL, the usefulness of the documentation and the quality of the SHACL report produced by the database. Unlike previous measurements, these are of a qualitative nature and consist of a textual description.

4.3   Evaluation Experience

In this subsection, we highlight our experiences in the performance evaluation of each individual database. We explain the usage of the respective implementations of SHACL validation and present certain challenges and pitfalls we encountered. In addition, an extract of the respective validation reports is presented to display the discrepancy of information in the reports. The presented violations occur through the defined property path from Listing 1.2.

Listing 1.2. The property path leading to the violations in this subsection.

```
@prefix schema: <http://schema.org/> .
@prefix sh: <http://www.w3.org/ns/shacl#> .
@prefix xsd: <http://www.w3.org/2001/XMLSchema#> .

:imagePath sh:path schema:image;
    sh:nodeKind sh:BlankNodeOrIRI;
    sh:maxCount 1;
    sh:or(
        [ sh:datatype schema:ImageObject;]
        [ sh:datatype xsd:string;
        sh:pattern "((?:http|https)://)?(?:www\\.)?
            [\\w\\d\\-_]+\\.\\w{2,3}(\\.\\w{2})?(/(?<=/)
            (?:[\\w\\d\\-./_]+)?)?+[.(jpg|jpeg|gif|tif|png|bmp)]?";]
    )
```

AllegroGraph. AllegroGraph provides two different usage options: command-line interface (CLI) and a graphical user interface called AGWebView. The graphical user interface has limited functionality and does not support SHACL validation. Neither the import of the dataset represented in the N-Quads format nor the SHACL shapes written in Turtle yielded any problems.

To use SHACL in AllegroGraph, the command-line program agtool has to be utilized, which offers a variety of utilities. We used agtool to create a new database, import our dataset and shapes and perform the SHACL validation to obtain the report. It is important to note that the AllegroGraph's SHACL implementation necessitates the explicit indication of all data graphs for the evaluation. The tool also allows to specify the output format of choice. We piped the output to the null device for a more precise time measurement. In Listing 1.3 the two generated violations can be seen. The only part missing from the generated violation is a `sh:resultMessage`, which could describe the violation in more detail.

Listing 1.3. Extract of the validation report from **AllegroGraph**.

```
prefix rdf: <http://www.w3.org/1999/02/22-rdf-syntax-ns#>
prefix sh: <http://www.w3.org/ns/shacl#>

_:bCDDA3ADEx4018736 sh:sourceConstraintComponent sh:OrConstraintComponent ;
  sh:value "asdasdasdas" ;
  sh:resultPath <http://schema.org/image> ;
  sh:resultSeverity sh:Violation ;
  sh:focusNode <https://smtfy.it/Skxm5Vi17> ;
  rdf:type sh:ValidationResult ;
  sh:sourceShape <http://gdb.benchmark.com/imagePath> .

_:bCDDA3ADEx4018737 sh:sourceConstraintComponent sh:NodeKindConstraintComponent ;
  sh:value "asdasdasdas" ;
  sh:resultPath <http://schema.org/image> ;
  sh:resultSeverity sh:Violation ;
  sh:focusNode <https://smtfy.it/Skxm5Vi17> ;
  rdf:type sh:ValidationResult ;
  sh:sourceShape <http://gdb.benchmark.com/imagePath> .
```

Apache Jena. Apache Jena is a Java framework with two available versions. The basic version contains command line interface (CLI) tools for the creation and manipulation of a database. Apache Jena Fuseki offers the same tools as the basic version with additional server functionalities, including a web user interface. We used the CLI, due to the lack of SHACL support in the web interface and the fixed method of measuring time. The CLI tool allows the validation of datasets against SHACL shapes, if both inputs are available as files, but it is not possible to validate data stored in triplestores. To measure the time of validating data stored in the provided triplestore (TDB), we wrote a Java application that uses the Jena API. The documentation was lackluster [1] and only provided an example for validating datasets provided as files. We piped the output to the null device to have a more accurate time measurement. The report itself complies to the W3C standard and the extract for our example is shown in Listing 1.4.

Listing 1.4. Extract of the validation report from **Apache Jena**.

```
@prefix schema: <http://schema.org/> .
@prefix sh: <http://www.w3.org/ns/shacl#> .

sh:result    [
  a                            sh:ValidationResult ;
  sh:focusNode                 <https://smtfy.it/Skxm5Vi17> ;
  sh:resultMessage             "NodeKind[BlankNodeOrIRI] : Expected
                               BlankNodeOrIRI for \"asdasdasdas\"" ;
  sh:resultPath                schema:image ;
  sh:resultSeverity            sh:Violation ;
  sh:sourceConstraintComponent sh:NodeKindConstraintComponent ;
  sh:sourceShape               :imagePath ;
  sh:value                     "asdasdasdas"
] ;
```

```
sh:result     [
   a                                  sh:ValidationResult ;
   sh:focusNode                       <https://smtfy.it/Skxm5Vi17> ;
   sh:resultMessage                   "Or[NodeShape
                                      [4acc5427c0d3a31145d9a2b6b7c5cb74],
                                      NodeShape[24c96f02c540f8563a4b2914d2af61b4]]
                                      at focusNode \"asdasdasdas\"" ;
   sh:resultPath                      schema:image ;
   sh:resultSeverity                  sh:Violation ;
   sh:sourceConstraintComponent       sh:OrConstraintComponent ;
   sh:sourceShape                     :imagePath ;
   sh:value                           "asdasdasdas"
] ;
```

GraphDB. GraphDB is a graph database management system built upon the Java framework RDF4J. Due to this, the implementation of SHACL validation is internally equivalent to the one of RDF4J. The implementation of SHACL into GraphDB 9.1 focuses on the specific use case of validation as part of data imports. Validations of already existing repositories are not supported by the workbench. The sole available application of SHACL is restricted by file limits and has the issue that the validation process stops on a single violation and does not yield a validation report, rendering it unusable for our comparative analysis.

To circumvent this problem we tried to implement a validation for GraphDB repositories using the RDF4J API in Java. Even though this appears possible from reading the documentation, the current implementation of SHACL in RDF4J utilizes a specifically defined repository type that requires its input data in form of a local repository or RDF file. An option to utilize an existing repository as provided by GraphDB is currently not available. In contrary to our implementation of the RDF4J evaluation it is also not possible to import the raw storage of the database as a local storage, as GraphDB's file structure differs from the triplestore provided by RDF4J. The only possibility to perform the validation for an entire repository, as we need for our comparative analysis, would be to export the data from the GraphDB repository and import it again into an empty **ShaclRepository** generated by RDF4J. This was not an option for our comparative analysis, as the only relevant information extracted from it would be the export performance of GraphDB's triplestore.

Due to the problems and limitations described in this subsection we decided to not include GraphDB in our quantitative performance evaluation, as its current SHACL implementation is too limited to be meaningfully compared to the implementations of the other graph databases.

RDF4J. Similar to Apache Jena, RDF4J is a framework for processing RDF data. Therefore, many features of a complete graph database are missing. The basic RDF4J installation allows the user to store and manipulate data in the provided triplestore, which is capable of handling around 100 million triples [7]. There exists an out-of-the-box approach to validate data via SHACL with the restriction that only RDF files can be used. Even though the entirety of our dataset has to be validated, reading the data from a file instead of an indexed database could have a noticeable impact on our measurements and is therefore not an acceptable method for our evaluation.

To validate data from the provided triplestore, implementing an application that uses the RDF4J framework is required. The application connects to the triplestore, loads the SHACL shapes from a file and performs the validation. Although the described structure seems relatively simple, the outdated documentation [7] was a hurdle and required us to search through the Javadoc [8] in order to achieve the desired outcome.

If a violation of the SHACL constraints occurs, a `RepositoryException` is thrown after the entire data is checked. From this exception the validation report can be generated and written to a file. A downside of this specific implementation is the large amount of main memory necessary. These high resource demands forced us to reduce the original dataset to a subset of one million quads, since larger data exceeded our available resources. In our case 18 GB of heap memory had to be allocated for the Java Virtual Machine (JVM) to successfully generate the validation report. We were not able to determine all reasons for the large memory requirement, because even though our generated report has a size of around 1.1 GB, the used dataset consists of only 160 MB.

The validation report for RDF4J contains the most violations for our specific example. RDF4J interprets any constraint in the `sh:or` construct, and `sh:or` itself as a violation, if none of the constraints are fulfilled. This leads to a total number of four violations, which can be seen in Listing 1.5. The report complies to the W3C standard, but is missing two components. The fields `sh:value` as well as the `sh:resultMessage` are not included in the violation, which makes the identification of the cause of the violation more difficult.

Listing 1.5. Extract of the validation report from **RDF4J**.

```
@prefix sh: <http://www.w3.org/ns/shacl#> .

_:node1dvlsg0iux1660 sh:result _:node1dvlsg0iux3491406 .
_:node1dvlsg0iux3491406 sh:resultPath <http://schema.org/image>;
    sh:detail _:node1dvlsg0iux3491407 .

_:node1dvlsg0iux3491407 a sh:ValidationResult;
    sh:focusNode <https://smtfy.it/Skxm5Vi17>;
    sh:sourceConstraintComponent sh:DatatypeConstraintComponent;
    sh:sourceShape _:node1dvlsg0gqx20;
    sh:resultPath <http://schema.org/image>;
    sh:detail _:node1dvlsg0iux3491408 .

_:node1dvlsg0iux3491408 a sh:ValidationResult;
    sh:focusNode <https://smtfy.it/Skxm5Vi17>;
    sh:sourceConstraintComponent sh:PatternConstraintComponent;
    sh:sourceShape _:node1dvlsg0gqx22;
    sh:resultPath <http://schema.org/image> .

_:node1dvlsg0iux3491406 a sh:ValidationResult;
    sh:focusNode <https://smtfy.it/Skxm5Vi17>;
    sh:sourceConstraintComponent sh:OrConstraintComponent;
    sh:sourceShape <http://gdb.benchmark.com/imagePath> .

_:node1dvlsg0iux1660 sh:result _:node1dvlsg0iux3494319 .

_:node1dvlsg0iux3494319 sh:resultPath <http://schema.org/image>;
    a sh:ValidationResult;
```

```
sh:focusNode <https://smtfy.it/Skxm5Vi17>;
sh:sourceConstraintComponent sh:NodeKindConstraintComponent;
sh:sourceShape <http://gdb.benchmark.com/imagePath> .
```

Stardog. Stardog provides CLI tools for creating and interacting with the
database. There exists also an integrated development environment (IDE) called
Stardog Studio that provides a user interface and many features from the CLI
tools. It is the only graphical user interface we encountered that allows users to
create and validate SHACL shapes for a database. For our evaluation we used
the CLI tool, due to the fixed method of time measurement.

While performing the validation process using our benchmark, it is important
to increase the limit of returned validation results with the -1 flag. The default
value is 100 and Stardog will stop to validate the rest of the graph after that limit
is reached. We piped the output to the null device to have valid time measurement without additional time consumed by writing the report to the command
line or a file. The output of the report is in Turtle format and complies with the
specification made by W3C. In contrast to the other databases, Stardog generates only a single violation in the report, which still provides enough information
about violation itself. This can be seen in Listing 1.6.

Listing 1.6. Extract of the validation report from **Stardog**.

```
@prefix sh: <http://www.w3.org/ns/shacl#> .

_:bnode_2394dca2_2e9a_4242_af3d_e81fc0951ac8_6965339 a sh:ValidationResult ;
    sh:resultSeverity sh:Violation ;
    sh:sourceShape <http://gdb.benchmark.com/imagePath> ;
    sh:sourceConstraintComponent sh:NodeKindConstraintComponent ;
    sh:focusNode <https://smtfy.it/Skxm5Vi17> ;
    sh:resultPath <http://schema.org/image> ;
    sh:value "asdasdasdas" ;
    sh:resultMessage "Image is neither a schema:ImageObject nor a valid URL" .
_:bnode_2394dca2_2e9a_4242_af3d_e81fc0951ac8_3598217 sh:result
    _:bnode_2394dca2_2e9a_4242_af3d_e81fc0951ac8_6965339 .
```

4.4   Evaluation Results

The focus of our work was to evaluate the performance of the SHACL implementation from each graph database by measuring the required time to validate our
data according to the defined SHACL shapes and generate a SHACL validation
report. The obtained results are illustrated in Fig. 1 and the evaluation specifics
are summarized in Table 1.

Based on the measurements a large discrepancy between some graph
databases can be observed. Our results show that AllegroGraph requires around
11,6 times longer to validate the data and produce the validation report compared to the fastest graph database Stardog, which only took ~2 min for the
entire dataset. A noticeable difference is also visible regarding both frameworks.
RDF4J requires around 2,4 times longer than Apache Jena.

5 Discussion

The results of our performance evaluation using the benchmark suggest Stardog's implementation as the currently best performing option for SHACL validation, with Apache Jena following at a close second place. The validation in RDF4J performed significantly worse, tripling the runtime for the equivalent task in Stardog. AllegroGraph's current implementation of SHACL validation performed the worst out of the four evaluated graph databases.

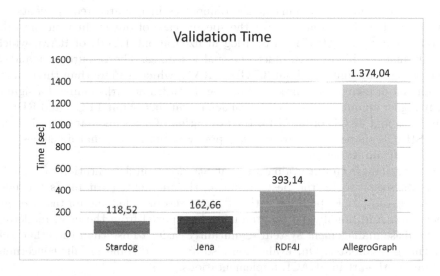

Fig. 1. Average validation time out of 8 measurements.

Table 1. Evaluation results of one million N-Quads based on the 58 SHACL shapes.

Graph database	Validation time (sec)	Number of violations	Report size	W3C compliant report	Require-ments	Limitations
Allegro Graph	1.374,04	3.567.930	1,24 GB	Yes	Validation performed by agtool	Free version supports only 5M triples
Apache Jena	162,66	3.615.753	1,82 GB	Yes	Addition application that uses Jena API was developed	Lack of documentation
RDF4J	393,14	3.676.105	1,16 GB	Yes, but no specifics on errors	Addition implementation is needed	Requires large amount of memory
Stardog	118,52	3.597.171	1,78 GB	Yes	Validation limit adjustments	Not defined

In addition to performance, we decided to include ease of use and resource demand into our evaluation. The evaluation of those factors displays a disparity between the two frameworks (RDF4J and Apache Jena) and the two complete database management systems. Concerning ease of use, the frameworks only provide out-of-the-box validation implementations for data provided as files. Validation for additional use cases like the included triplestores have to be implemented by the users of the framework, rendering the barrier of entry for the usage of those validation options higher than for the database management systems.

Another disparity between the database management systems and the frameworks can be found by looking at the differences in resource requirements for equivalent SHACL validations. For the specific case of our evaluation the validation of our data (160 MB) in Stardog utilized about 1.2 GB of RAM, which is easily manageable by even older personal machines. The resource demand of AllegroGraph amounts to about 3.7 GB of RAM, which is more than three times the amount of memory required by Stardog. Both frameworks demand a significantly higher amount of resources, with Jena requiring about 14 GB and RDF4J requiring about 18 GB of RAM for the evaluation of the same dataset using the same SHACL shapes. This exceeds the power of many personal machines and can put a strain on servers.

We conclude from our evaluation that Stardog's implementation of SHACL validation seems to be the best option at the moment, as it offers the best performing validation operation with the lowest resource demand for task like our benchmark. Additionally, no programming is required from the user, rendering the database management system significantly easier to use than the other well performing candidates. Our evaluation also uncovered some pitfalls concerning the state-of-the-art in SHACL implementations.

As SHACL can be seen as relatively new compared to other standards of the Semantic Web, only a few graph databases currently offer an implementation. For most databases that offer validation using the recommendation, the option does not seem like a focus of development. During our evaluation we encountered a significant number of lacking or inaccurate documentation. Some current implementations are unfinished, missing core functionality of the W3C standard or only adhere to specific use cases.

The large amount of violations prevents us from having a ground truth, thus we can not be sure to find all violations. Even comparing results between the different databases is difficult, because of the way some outputs are structured and messages are generated for intermediate nodes down to the node with the violation. Out of the four evaluated graph databases only AllegroGraph generated a validation report that deviated from the SHACL W3C standard, presenting the violations in a different format. This resulted in differences of information portrayed by the validation outputs, rendering them hard to compare or validate.

In addition to this problem the implementations of SHACL validation differ in their interpretation of certain shapes. An example for this behaviour is the sh:or shape, which depending on the implementation can either report all violations or ignore the other arguments after a first violation is found. Another example for inconsistencies is the treatment of subclasses, which can lead to single violations being thrown multiple times.

Due to those pitfalls we conclude that SHACL is currently still very new as a de-facto standard to perform full-scale complete performance evaluations, but our work is a first step in this direction. The still low number of graph databases offering implementations in combination with the displayed lack of adherence to the standard currently results in too many factors reducing the informative value of performance evaluations and benchmarks significantly.

6   Conclusions

As contributions for our work, we have developed a benchmark for the evaluation of the performance of the SHACL processing in graph databases and have applied it to the evaluation of four graph databases. The benchmark is published as open research data and is available for further experimentation and development.

As described in Sect. 3, our benchmark is designed to maximize utility for the current state of the art and other specific constraints (such as being restricted to the use of the free versions of the graph databases and having limited hardware capacities). While we think that it is generally applicable and yields accurate performance evaluations, other constraints or positive developments in the implementations of SHACL evaluation in graph databases may render other, more advanced approaches in the future.

One possible approach could be to provide shapes for a complete validation of a dataset, instead of just a representative subset. A benchmark evaluating the performance of complete validations would yield a more representative evaluation, but because of the substantial differences in resource demand the result would depend more on the evaluation hardware. Other approaches that could be worth trying out include handcrafted benchmark databases to be able to test specific constraints in a more controlled fashion and the expansion of the evaluation on truthfulness of the validation reports.

References

1. Apache: Jena SHACL (2019). https://jena.apache.org/documentation/shacl/index.html
2. Apache: Jena TDB (2019). https://jena.apache.org/documentation/tdb
3. Berners-Lee, T., Hendler, J., Lassila, O.: The semantic web. Sci. Am. **284**(5), 34–43 (2001)
4. Bizer, C., Schultz, A.: The Berlin SPARQL benchmark. Int. J. Semant. Web Inf. Syst. (IJSWIS) **5**(2), 1–24 (2009)
5. Capotă, M., Hegeman, T., Iosup, A., Prat-Pérez, A., Erling, O., Boncz, P.: Graphalytics: a big data benchmark for graph-processing platforms. In: Proceedings of the GRADES 2015, p. 7. ACM (2015)
6. Dominguez-Sal, D., Urbón-Bayes, P., Giménez-Vañó, A., Gómez-Villamor, S., Martínez-Bazán, N., Larriba-Pey, J.L.: Survey of graph database performance on the HPC scalable graph analysis benchmark. In: Shen, H.T., et al. (eds.) WAIM 2010. LNCS, vol. 6185, pp. 37–48. Springer, Heidelberg (2010). https://doi.org/10.1007/978-3-642-16720-1_4

7. Eclipse PMC: RDF4J (2019). https://rdf4j.org/documentation
8. Eclipse PMC: RDF4J Javadoc (2019). https://rdf4j.org/javadoc/latest/
9. Franz Inc.: AllegroGraph (2019). https://franz.com/agraph/support/documentation
10. Guha, R.V., Brickley, D., Macbeth, S.: Schema. org: evolution of structured data on the web. Commun. ACM **59**(2), 44–51 (2016)
11. International Organization for Standardization: ISO 3166 Standard for Austria (2019). https://www.iso.org/obp/ui/#iso:code:3166:AT
12. Jouili, S., Vansteenberghe, V.: An empirical comparison of graph databases. In: 2013 International Conference on Social Computing, pp. 708–715. IEEE (2013)
13. Kärle, E., Fensel, A., Toma, I., Fensel, D.: Why are there more hotels in Tyrol than in Austria? Analyzing schema.org usage in the hotel domain. In: Inversini, A., Schegg, R. (eds.) Information and Communication Technologies in Tourism 2016, pp. 99–112. Springer, Cham (2016). https://doi.org/10.1007/978-3-319-28231-2_8
14. Kärle, E., Şimşek, U., Panasiuk, O., Fensel, D.: Building an ecosystem for the Tyrolean tourism knowledge graph. In: Pautasso, C., Sánchez-Figueroa, F., Systä, K., Murillo Rodríguez, J.M. (eds.) ICWE 2018. LNCS, vol. 11153, pp. 260–267. Springer, Cham (2018). https://doi.org/10.1007/978-3-030-03056-8_25
15. Knublauch, H., Kontokostas, D.: Shapes Constraint Language (SHACL), W3C Recommendation, 20 July 2017 (2017). https://www.w3.org/TR/shacl
16. McColl, R.C., Ediger, D., Poovey, J., Campbell, D., Bader, D.A.: A performance evaluation of open source graph databases. In: Proceedings of the First Workshop on Parallel Programming For Analytics Applications, pp. 11–18. ACM (2014)
17. Ontotext: GraphDB (2019). http://graphdb.ontotext.com/documentation
18. Panasiuk, O., Kärle, E., Şimşek, U., Fensel, D.: Defining tourism domains for semantic annotation of web content. e-Rev. Tour. Res. **9** (2018). https://arxiv.org/abs/1711.03425. Research notes from the ENTER 2018 Conference on ICT in Tourism
19. Panasiuk, O., Akbar, Z., Gerrier, T., Fensel, D.: Representing GeoData for tourism with schema. org. In: GISTAM, pp. 239–246 (2018)
20. Schema Tourism Working Group: Schema tourism (2020). https://ds.sti2.org/
21. Schmidt, M., Hornung, T., Lausen, G., Pinkel, C.: SP2Bench: a SPARQL performance benchmark. In: 2009 IEEE 25th International Conference on Data Engineering, pp. 222–233. IEEE (2009)
22. Şimşek, U., Kärle, E., Holzknecht, O., Fensel, D.: Domain specific semantic validation of schema.org annotations. In: Petrenko, A.K., Voronkov, A. (eds.) PSI 2017. LNCS, vol. 10742, pp. 417–429. Springer, Cham (2018). https://doi.org/10.1007/978-3-319-74313-4_31
23. Singhal, A.: Introducing the knowledge graph: things, not strings (2012). https://googleblog.blogspot.com/2012/05/introducing-knowledge-graph-things-not.html
24. Solid IT GMBH: DB-engines ranking of graph DBMS (2020). https://db-engines.com/en/ranking/graph+dbms
25. Stardog Union Inc.: Stardog (2019). https://www.stardog.com/docs
26. Ugander, J., Karrer, B., Backstrom, L., Marlow, C.: The anatomy of the facebook social graph. CoRR abs/1111.4503 (2011). http://arxiv.org/abs/1111.4503

Dialogue Games for Explaining Medication Choices

Qurat-ul-ain Shaheen⬤, Alice Toniolo⬤, and Juliana K. F. Bowles$^{(\boxtimes)}$⬤

School of Computer Science, University of St Andrews, St Andrews KY16 9SX, UK
quratulainshaheen@gmail.com, {a.toniolo,jkfb}@st-andrews.ac.uk

Abstract. SMT solvers can be used efficiently to search for optimal paths across multiple graphs when optimising for certain resources. In the medical context, these graphs can represent treatment plans for chronic conditions where the optimal paths across all plans under consideration are the ones which minimize adverse drug interactions. The SMT solvers, however, work as a black-box model and there is a need to justify the optimal plans in a human-friendly way. We aim to fulfill this need by proposing explanatory dialogue protocols based on computational argumentation to increase the understanding and trust of humans interacting with the system. The protocols provide supporting reasons for nodes in a path and also allow counter reasons for the nodes not in the graph, highlighting any potential adverse interactions during the dialogue.

Keywords: Explanations · Dialogues games · Argumentation · SMT solvers

1 Introduction

Intelligent systems are becoming increasingly popular in today's digital world with the pervasiveness of Artificial Intelligence (AI). The focus on human-friendly integration of AI has increased in recent years with growing awareness of the need for transparency and justifiability of the black-box recommendations made by some of these systems. Limited transparency and justifiability has been shown to hamper the mainstream adoption of these systems [2].

An even more urgent need for clarity comes with critical systems, such as clinical decision support systems, and there are ongoing efforts towards eXplainable Artificial Intelligence (XAI) [2], specially for medical XAI [23]. While most of the existing approaches to XAI focus on *interpretability* of machine learning models [1], rule-based approaches can be used to *justify* decisions of non-interpretable systems by explaining why a decision is a good one rather than how it was made. We follow the later approach here.

Medical treatment plans (aka clinical guidelines) are drawn from evidence-based recommendations, and published in the UK by the National Institute for

---

This research was conducted whilst the first author was visiting the University of St Andrews.

V. Gutiérrez-Basulto et al. (Eds.): RuleML+RR 2020, LNCS 12173, pp. 97–111, 2020.
https://doi.org/10.1007/978-3-030-57977-7_7

Health and Care Excellence (NICE)[1] to document treatment practices for specific chronic diseases such as diabetes, hypertension, and so on. The plans capture a series of steps in the management of the disease, giving an indication of which advice to follow including which drugs (e.g., from a group) to prescribe at a given stage of the disease and what changes to do once the disease progresses (e.g., add a specific medication). These plans, however, fall short for patients with multiple chronic health conditions, known as *multimorbidity*, and in particular they do not account for the potential adverse drug reactions (ADRs) caused by drugs taken for different conditions [14]. Treatment plans for individual chronic conditions can essentially be regarded as graphs, and in the presence of multimorbidities we are in effect trying to search for the optimal path across several graphs which minimises ADRs as much as possible. Satisfiability Modulo Theories (SMT) solvers are popular in analysis and model checking settings because of their expressive power, arithmetic capabilities and scalability [19]. SMT solvers have been used efficiently to identify and minimise ADRs in [5–7]. There is, however, still a need to add clarity to the identified optimal path and justify why one combination of paths across different treatment plans may be preferable to another.

The use of computational argumentation has been popular in healthcare [4,15] and more recently for managing multimorbidity [9,20], because its formulation and evaluation of pros and cons can be seen as emulating human critical thinking. Recently argumentation has also generated interest for its explainability potential [12,13] because of its reasoning transparency. Artificial dialogue based on argumentation allows agents to engage in a gradual exploration of reasons for a conclusion and potential disagreement. In human argumentation, argumentation-based dialogue has shown to be effective in improving understanding of scientific topics [10]. Consequently we think argumentation is a great fit for tackling the problem of justifying optimal paths for multimorbidity treatment plans in a way that ensures human engagement.

The contribution of this paper is a novel approach for justifying recommendations of an SMT solver in an interactive way through argumentation-based dialogues. We use argumentation to augment these recommendations with explanations and propose a novel model of explanatory dialogue protocols to allow human-like engagement with the explanation model. The *explanations* model the underlying reasoning of the SMT solver while the *dialogue protocols* highlight any unresolved issues in the recommended solution.

The remaining paper is organised as follows. Section 2 summarises the background of the argumentation model underlying the explanation dialogues. Section 3 presents the dialogue protocols. Finally, Sect. 4 concludes and identifies directions for future research.

---

[1] For details see https://www.nice.org.uk.

2   Argumentation for Pharmaceutical Treatment Plans

Here we summarise the background research for the work presented in this paper and introduce relevant underlying concepts related to argumentation.

2.1   Finding Optimal Plans with SMT Solver

We base our approach on the work of Kovalov and Bowles [16] which identifies optimal treatment plans for multimorbid patients using the optimising SMT solver Z3 [18]. The authors manually convert the flowchart representations of clinical guidelines for treating specific health conditions into a compact graph which they refer to as a *Pharmaceutical Graph* (PG). A PG is a directed acyclic graph where the root node represents the diagnosed disease, and all the other nodes represent drugs or groups of drugs to be given to a patient. A maximal path in the graph represents a complete treatment plan.

Kovalov and Bowles [16] first create PGs corresponding to different health conditions for a hypothetical multimorbid patient and feed them to the SMT solver to identify the optimal paths for each of the PGs such that adverse drug reactions across all PGs are minimised. They take three types of ADRs into account: drug-drug interactions, drug-disease interactions and drug-patient interactions. Z3 is a Boolean satisfiability problem modulo theories (SMT) solver which finds the optimal assignment given by some objective function [3]. The objective function used by the authors, called *score*, is computed as a combination of medicine efficacy (positive score) and drug interaction conflict (negative score). More comprehensive extensions that incorporate side-effects, time and patient preferences have been recently developed in [7]. The approach is scalable to any number of drug alternatives.

2.2   Modelling Explanations

The resulting maximal path described above is a sequence of drugs or group of drugs for a specific health condition [16]. While PGs encode a score wrt known ADRs to extract a most effective solution, when presenting the sequence of treatments to a health professional or to a patient, the reasons for this to be indeed the most effective solution are not immediately accessible. This means that the user might have to search for additional information to better understand the solution provided. To facilitate this process, we design a multi-layer explanation model in order to have flexible interactions that can adapt to the user's need for clarification. We organise the graph into abstraction layers and explicitly mark the abstractions levels in the graph structure in terms of branches, sub-branches and nodes. We refer to the resulting graph as *PGraph*. We define four abstraction levels for the PGraph and the explanations: *Branch, Entity, Drug* and *Group*. A *Branch* is a cluster of nodes joined by an initial node and a terminating node such that initial node has only one incoming edge and the terminating node has only one outgoing edge. An *Entity* can be an atomic node representing a *Drug* or a composite node representing a group of drugs (*Group*). A *Group* is a

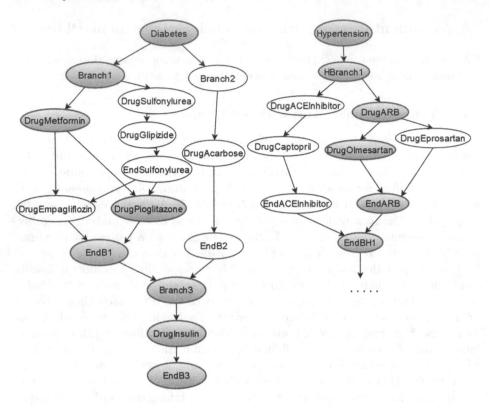

Fig. 1. PGraphs for diabetes and hypertension.

sub-branch with all member drugs related semantically. A path on a PG maps directly to a PGraph after accounting for additional marking nodes. An example PGraph is provided in Fig. 1 where the grey shaded nodes represent a path.

In addition to different levels of explanations, we also require to encode text that can be presented to a user. We base the explanation texts on the drug information provided by NICE[2] and the intuitions given in NICE pathways themselves. We manually filter out relevant information from these sources and organize it into types and levels. Types group the explanations into categories such as justification for a treatment (IP), using graph structure as a justification (PGRAPH), drug-drug conflict (DD), drug-disease conflict (CD) and drug-patient (CP) conflict, while levels correspond to the abstraction layers in the PGraph. We code these reasons with symbols R_i.

2.3   Argumentation Framework

In explaining a PGraph, our system should be able to progressively explore the solution path along PGraph identified by the SMT solver, and provide reasons

---

[2] For details see https://bnf.nice.org.uk/.

for a specific choice on request from the user. We also require the system to be able to provide reasons explaining why another path has not been taken. To this end, we have chosen to encode PGraphs as argumentation frameworks, another form of graph, where nodes represent arguments and edges represent conflicts between arguments, where an evaluation process allows the identification of alternative sets of conflict-free nodes. The requirement for our system is two-fold: the encoding of the PGraph with additional justifications in a structured logic-based framework from which we can extract arguments that justify the pathway chosen by the SMT solver; and the definition of an exploratory dialogue protocol to allow human-like engagement with the explanation model. In a separate line of work, we have formulated a structured argumentation framework that encodes the reasons directly into the framework and allows us to identify a justified solution for a treatment plan obtained via the SMT solver. In this paper, however, our focus is on the dialogue describing this justified solution, therefore we only present here an abstraction of the arguments that can be formulated about a PGraph. In order to achieve this, we make use of an abstract argumentation framework (AF) as proposed by Dung [11]. Such a framework is defined as $AF = \langle AR, att \rangle$, where AR is a set of arguments and att represents a binary relation on AR, i.e., $att \subseteq AR \times AR$.

We use the approach of reformulating preferred semantics as argument labellings by Caminada et al. [8] to generate discussions about acceptable as well as rejected arguments in explanatory dialogue games. Caminada et al. [8] propose the following definitions which are useful in this regard.

Definition 1. *For a framework* $AF = \langle AR, att \rangle$:

1. *A labelling is a total function,* $\mathcal{L}ab : AR \rightarrow \{in, out, undec\}$.
2. $\mathcal{L}ab$ *is an* admissible *labelling iff for each* $A \in AR$:
   (a) *if* $\mathcal{L}ab(A) = in$ *then* $\forall B \in AR : (B\, att\, A \supset \mathcal{L}ab(B) = out)$.
   (b) *if* $\mathcal{L}ab(A) = out$ *then* $\exists B \in AR : (B\, att\, A \wedge \mathcal{L}ab(B) = in)$.
3. $\mathcal{L}ab$ *is a* preferred *labelling iff it is an admissible labelling where* $in(\mathcal{L}ab)$ *and* $out(\mathcal{L}ab)$ *are maximal (w.r.t. set inclusion) among all admissible labellings.*
4. *A* preferred extension *is the set of in-labelled arguments of a preferred labelling.*

Here, we compute preferred extensions as above, and we then use the extensions as the basis of a dialogue game inspired by the approach of Shams et al. [22], where they use preferred semantics as the basis of a Socratic discussion. We map the optimal paths returned by the SMT solver to equivalent preferred extensions and use preferred labelling to generate discussion about in and out status of each argument representing a node on a specific path.

Internally we model three types of arguments in the AF: path arguments, explanation arguments, and prescription arguments. We assume that the conclusion of a `Path` argument is a node representing a drug or a graph structure marker such as a start branch node. An `Explain` argument for a drug is used to conclude that there is a justifications for prescribing the drug, and will include a specific reason R_i. A `Prescribe` argument concludes that if there is a justified drug, the drug can be prescribed. `Path` arguments attack all other `Path` and corresponding `Prescribe` arguments that are not on the same path. A `Path` argument can also attack `Explain` arguments of nodes not in the selected path if the latter describes an ADR for that particular `Path` argument. Consequently, each extension includes arguments prescribing a particular drug on a path in the graph along with its corresponding explanations.

3   Dialogue Games for Explanations

Formally dialogue games are interactions between two or more players according to a pre-defined set of rules [17]. The rules describe commencement conditions, permitted utterances (locutions), permitted combinations of locutions, commitments of participants, and termination conditions for the game. Dialogue game protocols have been developed for most of the primary dialogue types identified by Walton and Krabbe [24] such as Information Seeking, Inquiry, Persuasion, Negotiation, Deliberation and Eristic Dialogue.

We present two explanatory dialogue game protocols based on the Information Seeking dialogue which involves one participant seeking an answer from the other participant, who the former believes knows the answer. The objective of the dialogue game is to justify why a node is included or not included in a path.

The game has two participants: an 'Oracle' that disseminates information and a 'Seeker' who is looking for explanations. The Oracle has the AF and the extension corresponding to the recommendation by the SMT solver as part of its knowledge base. The Oracle knows the preferred labelling and shares arguments related to the treatment pathway with the Seeker at the start of the game through a *claim*. This is a list of `Path` arguments (labelled $\mathcal{L}ab(Arg) = in$ nodes) along with the `Path` arguments labelled $\mathcal{L}ab(Arg) = out$; we refer to this set as $\mathcal{S}$ where $(Arg, \mathcal{L}ab(Arg)) \in \mathcal{S}$ if $Arg \in AR$ and $\mathcal{L}ab$ is a preferred labelling.

Subsequently, the Oracle uses the explanations present in the extension to answer the questions by the Seeker. In our dialogue protocols, the Seeker corresponds to a Patient agent seeking explanations for recommended medications. We define two versions of the dialogue protocols, passive explanatory protocol and active explanatory protocol based on the role of the Seeker. In the former, the Seeker acts as a passive listener while in the latter, the Seeker plays an active role in the dialog by confirming or refuting the Oracle's assumptions about its preferences. Passive protocol covers the essential interaction and can be used in a scenario where preference information is missing such as an agent seeking information on behalf of another. Active protocol, on the other hand, provides detailed interaction which takes preferences into account and models a real world medical practice of taking patient history. The subsequent sections formalise the protocols and provide example dialogues.

Each dialogue protocol has three stages: Commencement, Progress, and Termination. The protocol specifies what speech acts can be exchanged according to what was previously exchanged in the dialogue at each phase. In our model, this is represented with a table where the right-hand side column states what speech act can be used in response to the speech act moved on the left-hand side column (see Table 1 and Table 3). In the dialogue protocol, participants have a commitment store CS which includes a set of arguments with which the participants have committed to stand by [17]. In our dialogue, the commitment store is formed by arguments exchanged and related attacks. During the dialogue, participants update the commitment store via an assertion `Assert(Arg)` such that the new commitment store results in $CS = CS \cup Arg$, assuming monotonic updates. If an argument Arg exchanged is a rejection of a previous argument, we assume that CS is updated with a new attacking argument Arg' where $Arg'\, att\, Arg$; this update is referred to as $\sim Arg$ for convenience. We provide example dialogues in Table 2 and Table 4 with the three dialogue stages marked. The tables show the locutions underlying each natural language sentence next to each sentence and highlight the corresponding explanation Types and Levels that the natural language explanation represents. The last column shows example assertions for the CS of each participant including the assertion type and argument as defined in Table 1 and Table 3.

3.1 Passive Explanatory Dialogue Game

In this dialogue, the Seeker plays a passive role and only receives updates from the Oracle. Information flow is one sided. Figure 2 shows an overview of the dialogue.

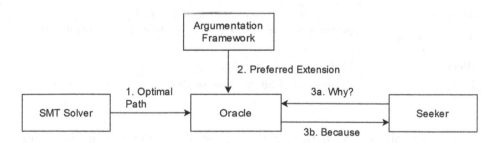

Fig. 2. Passive explanatory dialogue overview.

Commencement. The first move by Oracle (O) is a *Claim* which sets the context of the dialogue.

Progress

1. Every subsequent move by O is an explanation for the previous move of Seeker (P).
2. Each subsequent move by P is a query about an in or out label in the claim.
3. P can repeat any query until O forces it to move on by sending a *Move* locution.

Table 1. Passive explanatory dialogue protocol definition.

Request	Response
$Start_P$	$Claim_O(\mathcal{S})$
$Claim_O(\mathcal{S})$	$Why_P(query_i)$ where $query_i \in \mathcal{S}$ and query can be *in-query* or *out-query*
$Why_P(query)$	$Because_O(R_{ij})$ where R_{ij} represents all the reasons from 1 to i at abstraction level j. Different reasons at the same level can be combined using *and* or *alert* depending on the context. This response equals an assertion of one of the types defined as: *Assert(Arg)*: simple assertion where $Arg \in AR$ *Assert-Alt(Arg)*: asserting PGRAPH Type reason *Assert-CD(Arg)*: asserting a drug-disease conflict as reason *Assert-DD(Arg)*: asserting a drug-drug conflict as reason
Why_P *(in-query)*	$Alert_O(R_{ij})$ where R_{ij} as previously explained. Alert message indicates a counter reason and represents a conflict that cannot be helped
$But\text{-}Why_P(query)$	$Because_O(R_{ij-1})$ where $j-1$ is the next lower abstraction level than was used in previous $Because_O$ response for same query
$But\text{-}Why_P$ *(in-query)*	$Alert_O(R_{ij-1})$
$But\text{-}Why_P(query)$	$Move_O$ if $j-1=0$ where j equals the maximum number of levels defined
$Move_O$	$Why_P(query_k)$ where $query_k \neq query_i$ for $query_k, query_i \in \mathcal{S}$ and $query_i$ has already been dealt with
$Because_O$	End_P
$Alert_O$	End_P
End_P	No response. End dialogue session

4. O provides all the explanations at the highest abstraction level in the graph first and moves on to the next lower abstraction level for subsequent repetitions of the query until it runs out of explanations. It then uses the Move locution.
5. O provides supporting reasons (IP Type) to justify an in status or counter reasons (CD, DD Types) to explain any possible conflicts that influenced the out label assignment.

Termination

1. P can terminate the dialogue at any time by using an *End* locution.
2. O can end the dialogue when all the nodes in the claim have been justified.

3.2   An Example Dialogue

We provide an example of a passive exploratory dialogue in Table 2. Subscripts O and P represent the Oracle and Seeker respectively and identify the participant making the move. Assume that the resulting argumentation framework for a path chosen by the SMT solver on the basis of a PGraph in Fig. 1 is presented in Fig. 3.

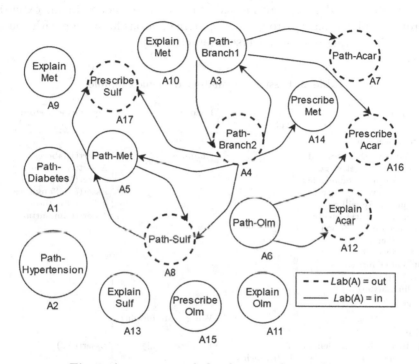

Fig. 3. Argument graph for the example in Table 2.

The AF is represented using an argument graph where the nodes represent arguments and the directed edges point towards the attacked nodes. Let arguments $A1..A8 \in AR$ represent edges in a PGraph, $A9..A13 \in AR$ represent corresponding justifications and $A14..A17 \in AR$ represent prescriptions for drugs represented by $A5..A8$. Arguments $\{A1, A2, A3, A5, A6, A9, A10, A11, A13, A14, A15\}$ represent a preferred extension which is part of the preferred labelling.

3.3   Properties of the Protocol

1. The protocol exploits the lack of path order in the extension by allowing P to query about any random node in the Claim.
2. The protocol preserves the graph abstraction levels qualitatively through abstractions of explanations.

3. O combines more than one explanations as a justification for the same query if multiple explanations exist at the same abstraction level.
4. The protocol ensures termination by preventing infinite loops using two strategies:
   (a) O cannot repeat the same answer for the same query, rather it is forced to exhaust explanations at different abstraction levels progressively.
   (b) P cannot repeat any query for which it has received a *Move* locution.
5. The protocol highlights any inconsistency between nodes in an extension through explanations by grouping supporting reasons for a node with counter reasons indicating possible adverse interactions.

Table 2. Passive explanatory dialogue example

Dialogue	Explanation type/level	Locutions	Commitment store
Commencement:			
O: You have Diabetes and Hypertension. Let us go through your recommended NICE pathways for drug treatment. We will go through each drug one by one. Suggested solution is: S= [Diabetes, in(Metformin), out(Sulfonylurea), out(Acarbose), in(Olmesartan) ...]		Claim(S)	Assert(Diabetes) Assert(Hypertension) Assert(Metformin) Assert(Sulfonylurea) Assert(Acarbose) Assert(Olmesartan) ...
Progress:			
P: Why is Metformin suggested?		Why(in-Metformin)	
O: Because it is the default treatment on the recommended pathway	Type IP/Branch Level	Because	Assert(A8)
P: But why is Metformin suggested?		But-Why(in-Metformin)	
O: Because it is initial drug for treating Diabetes	Type IP/Drug Level	Because	Assert(A9)
P: Why is Sulfonylurea not suggested?		Why(out-Sulfonylurea)	
O: Because Metformin is an alternative to Sulfonylurea	PGraph/ PGraph Level	Because	Assert-Alt (Metformin, Sulfonylurea)
P: But why is Acarbose not suggested?		But-Why(out-Acarbose)	
O: Because it adversely reacts with suggested drug Olmesartan	Type DD/Drug Level	Because	Assert-DD(Acarbose, Olmesartan)
Termination:			
P: I have now received an update on the recommended pathway.End			

3.4   Active Explanatory Dialogue Game

In this case the Seeker actively participates in the conversation and confirms or refutes the assertions of the Oracle. The protocol follows a static update approach, where Seeker's assertions do not take immediate effect. The Oracle passes the Seeker's assertions to the SMT solver to get a more customized recommendation and uses that as the basis of a new discussion. In case Seeker's assertions rule out all possible path options in the graph, the SMT solver returns the path that optimizes Seeker's preferences even if it is not possible to meet all the requirements. Figure 4 shows a schematic overview of the workflow.

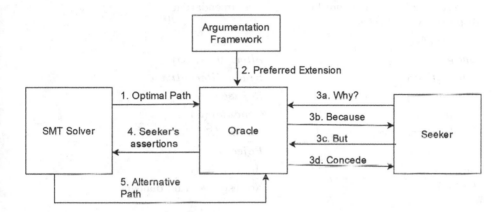

Fig. 4. Active explanatory dialogue overview.

The dialogue starts off with the Oracle going through a checklist of items with the Seeker which capture Seeker preferences such as patient intolerance of specific drugs in a medical setting. We modelled the preferences for multimorbid patients by considering drug information available online and talking to experts. We learned that the presence of three conditions need to be considered before prescribing any drug: hepatic impairment, renal impairment, and pregnancy. This information is not part of the PGraph, rather the Oracle extracts this information from the Seeker at the start and passes it to the SMT solver which takes them into account when finding the suitable path.

Commencement

1. The first move by Oracle (O) marks the start of the *Checklist* phase in which each subsequent move by O is directed towards establishing preferences of the Seeker (P).
2. Each move by P in this phase confirms or refutes the assertion made by O in previous move.
3. O ends *Checklist* phase by send a *Claim* locution which proceeds as before.

Table 3. Active explanatory dialogue protocol definition.

Request	Response
$Checklist_O$	$Ready\text{-}Checklist_P$
$Assert\text{-}Item_O(Arg_i)$	$Assert\text{-}Item_P(Arg_i)$ where $Arg_i \in AR$ is the ith item on the check list and can equal $\sim Arg_i$ to show rejection of the assumption by the Seeker
$Because_O(R_{ij})$ with a simple assertion, $Assert_O(Arg)$ as only this assertion type is defeasible. The rest represent facts which cannot be disputed by the Seeker	$Assert_P(Arg)$ where $Arg \in AR$. A positive Arg shows approval by Seeker whereas $\sim Arg$ represents rejection of the recommendation
$Assert_P(Arg)$	$Concede_O$
End_P	$Alternative_O(\mathcal{S})$
$Alternative_O$	$Ready\text{-}Alternative_P$
$Alternative_O$	$Refuse_P$
$Accept_O(\mathcal{S})$	$Concede_P(\mathcal{S})$
$Ready\text{-}Alternative_P$	$Claim_O(\mathcal{S})$
$Accept_O(\mathcal{S})$	$Reject_P$
$Reject_P$	$Alternative_O$
$Refuse_P$	No response. End dialogue

Progress

1. The progress rules for passive dialogue hold. Additionally each explanation for a query about an *in* labelled argument requires P to state its preference for the argument $Arg \in AR$ mentioned in the explanation by either confirming or refuting the assumption of O regarding Arg.
2. O can propose an alternative claim after all the labels in the first claim have been discussed. The dialogue then proceeds with the alternative claim as before.

Termination

1. P can end the dialogue at any time by using an *End* locution as before.
2. P accepts the proposed solution.
3. P refuses the offer of O to discuss an alternative claim.

Active Explanatory Dialogue Protocol extends Passive Dialogue Protocol with additional responses given in Table 3. Table 4 provides an example of how this dialogue starts.

3.5   Properties of the Protocol

1. O can use the assertions of P regarding its preferences as justifications when discussing the alternative claim.

2. Since the same query can be repeated, P must repeat the assertions. This could lead to an inconsistency if P changes the truth value for its assertion. This can be resolved in two ways:
   (a) By preventing P from changing the truth value for the same query.
   (b) By allowing P to change truth values and letting the last truth value hold. This last value can then be passed to the SMT solver.
3. O can use an estimate of how much P's assertions contradict its world view and use a threshold value to proceed with finding an alternative claim. O could resolve minor objections by itself if the estimate is less than the threshold value.

Table 4. Active explanatory dialogue game example.

Dialogue	Explanation type/level	Locution	Commitment store
Commencement:			
O: Let's go through your basic health check list		Checklist	
P: OK. I am ready		Ready	
O: Do you suffer from Hepatic Impairment?	Type CP/Drug Level	Assert-Item	Assert(C2)
P: No, I do not suffer from Hepatic Impairment		Assert-Item	Assert($\sim$C2)
O: Do you suffer from Renal Impairment?	Type CP/Drug Level	Assert-Item	Assert(C3)
P: No, I do not suffer from Renal Impairment		Assert-Item	Assert($\sim$C3)

4 Conclusion and Future Work

Explanations are an important tool to increase the trust we have on the recommendations of AI systems. Because of their critical importance, numerous approaches have been developed for clinical decision support such as expert systems [21], SMT solvers [5,6], and argumentation [9,15]. Here we use argumentation in an explanatory role to explain the decisions of the SMT solver.

We show how the recommendations of a black-box model like the SMT solver, can be justified through argumentation-based explanatory dialogue games. We describe how the dialogue games can provide explanations for the underlying reasoning of the SMT solver in calculating optimal paths which minimize ADRs. We also show that the games protocol is flexible and can highlight possible ADRs qualitatively. The approach allows engaging with the justifications behind the recommendations at various abstraction levels, resulting in a dialogue model which adapts to specific needs of the user. It also allows additional information such as preferences to be introduced without overwhelming the user. The argument formulation is very expressive and allows both supporting reasons for selecting a node to be modelled as well as counter reasons expressed as a negative relationship between entities. The reasons themselves form part of the premise of the arguments, and are represented as propositions which are mapped to natural language representation during the dialogue. This approach can be used for interactive explanatory dialogues to explain similar sequence graphs in different domains when the underpinning justification model is provided.

In the future, we plan to divide the Oracle between multiple agent specialists as it will enable a more modular approach. Another possible direction is to explore the changes in the dialogue protocol if the Seeker's assertions have immediate effect. The current protocol takes the credibility of the agents for granted. It will be interesting to see how adding a credibility function can affect the dependability of the dialogue game. Most importantly, we plan to evaluate the approach through user studies involving health practitioners and patients alike and how they engage with our explanatory dialogue games. This will not only give us a mechanism to validate our approach, but also explore further arguments such as whether in some cases the optimal solution computed by an SMT solver is not in fact the preferred one.

References

1. Adadi, A., Berrada, M.: Peeking inside the black-box: a survey on explainable artificial intelligence (XAI). IEEE Access **6**, 52138–52160 (2018)
2. Biran, O., Cotton, C.: Explanation and justification in machine learning: a survey. In: IJCAI-17 Workshop on Explainable AI (XAI), vol. 8 (2017)
3. Bjørner, N., Phan, A.-D., Fleckenstein, L.: νZ- an optimizing SMT solver. In: Baier, C., Tinelli, C. (eds.) TACAS 2015. LNCS, vol. 9035, pp. 194–199. Springer, Heidelberg (2015). https://doi.org/10.1007/978-3-662-46681-0_14
4. Black, E., Atkinson, K.: Dialogues that account for different perspectives in collaborative argumentation. In: Proceedings of the 8th International Conference on Autonomous Agents and Multiagent Systems, pp. 867–874 (2009)
5. Bowles, J., Caminati, M.B.: An integrated approach to a combinatorial optimisation problem. In: Ahrendt, W., Tapia Tarifa, S.L. (eds.) IFM 2019. LNCS, vol. 11918, pp. 284–302. Springer, Cham (2019). https://doi.org/10.1007/978-3-030-34968-4_16
6. Bowles, J., Caminati, M., Cha, S., Mendoza, J.: A framework for automated conflict detection and resolution in medical guidelines. Sci. Comput. Program. **182**, 42–63 (2019). https://doi.org/10.1016/j.scico.2019.07.002
7. Bowles, J.K.F., Caminati, M.B.: Balancing prescriptions with constraint solvers. In: Liò, P., Zuliani, P. (eds.) Automated Reasoning for Systems Biology and Medicine. CB, vol. 30, pp. 243–267. Springer, Cham (2019). https://doi.org/10.1007/978-3-030-17297-8_9
8. Caminada, M.W.A., Dvoák, W., Vesic, S.: Preferred semantics as socratic discussion. J. Log. Comput. **26**(4), 1257–1292 (2014). https://doi.org/10.1093/logcom/exu005
9. Čyras, K., Oliveira, T.: Resolving conflicts in clinical guidelines using argumentation. In: Proceedings of the International Joint Conference on Autonomous Agents and Multiagent Systems, AAMAS, vol. 3, pp. 1731–1739, February 2019

10. De Vries, E., Lund, K., Baker, M.: Computer-mediated epistemic dialogue: explanation and argumentation as vehicles for understanding scientific notions. J. Learn. Sci. **11**(1), 63–103 (2002)
11. Dung, P.M.: On the acceptability of arguments and its fundamental role in nonmonotonic reasoning, logic programming and n-person games. Artif. Intell. **77**(2), 321–357 (1995)
12. Fan, X., Toni, F.: On computing explanations in argumentation. In: Proceedings of the Twenty-Ninth AAAI Conference on Artificial Intelligence (AAAI 2015), pp. 1496–1492. AAAI Press (2015)
13. García, A.J., Chesañvar, C.I., Rotstein, N.D., Simari, G.R.: Formalizing dialectical explanation support for argument-based reasoning in knowledge-based systems. Expert. Syst. Appl. **40**(8), 3233–3247 (2013). https://doi.org/10.1016/j.eswa.2012.12.036
14. Hughes, L.D., McMurdo, M.E.T., Guthrie, B.: Guidelines for people not for diseases: the challenges of applying UK clinical guidelines to people with multimorbidity. Age Ageing **42**(1), 62–69 (2012)
15. Hunter, A., Williams, M.: Aggregating evidence about the positive and negative effects of treatments. Artif. Intell. Med. **56**(3), 173–190 (2012). https://doi.org/10.1016/j.artmed.2012.09.004
16. Kovalov, A., Bowles, J.K.F.: Avoiding medication conflicts for patients with multimorbidities. In: Ábrahám, E., Huisman, M. (eds.) IFM 2016. LNCS, vol. 9681, pp. 376–390. Springer, Cham (2016). https://doi.org/10.1007/978-3-319-33693-0_24
17. McBurney, P., Parsons, S.: Dialogue game protocols. In: Huget, M. P. (ed.) Communication in Multiagent Systems. LNCS (LNAI), vol. 2650, pp. 269–283. Springer, Heidelberg (2003). https://doi.org/10.1007/978-3-540-44972-0_15
18. de Moura, L., Bjørner, N.: Z3: an efficient SMT solver. In: Ramakrishnan, C.R., Rehof, J. (eds.) TACAS 2008. LNCS, vol. 4963, pp. 337–340. Springer, Heidelberg (2008). https://doi.org/10.1007/978-3-540-78800-3_24
19. de Moura, L., Bjørner, N.: Satisfiability modulo theories: introduction and applications. Commun. ACM **54**(9), 69–77 (2011). https://doi.org/10.1145/1995376.1995394
20. Oliveira, T., Dauphin, J., Satoh, K., Tsumoto, S., Novais, P.: Argumentation with goals for clinical decision support in multimorbidity. In: Proceedings of the 17th International Conference on Autonomous Agents and MultiAgent Systems (AAMAS 2018), pp. 2031–2033 (2018)
21. Rivas Echeverría, F., Rivas Echeverría, C.: Application of expert systems in medicine. In: Proceedings of the 2006 Conference on Artificial Intelligence Research and Development, p. 3–4. IOS Press, NLD (2006)
22. Shams, Z., De Vos, M., Oren, N., Padget, J.: Normative practical reasoning via argumentation and dialogue. In: Proceedings of the Twenty-Fifth International Joint Conference on Artificial Intelligence, pp. 1244–1250. AAAI Press (2016)
23. Tjoa, E., Guan, C.: A survey on explainable artificial intelligence (XAI): towards medical XAI (2019)
24. Walton, D., Krabbe, E.: Commitment in Dialogue: Basic Concepts of Interpersonal Reasoning. State University of New York Press, New York (1995)

Invertible Bidirectional Metalogical Translation Between Prolog and RuleML for Knowledge Representation and Querying

Mark Thom[1]([⊠])(iD), Harold Boley[2]([⊠])(iD), and Theodoros Mitsikas[3]([⊠])(iD)

[1] RuleML, Lethbridge, AB, Canada
markjordanthom@gmail.com
[2] University of New Brunswick, Fredericton, NB, Canada
harold.boley@unb.ca
[3] National Technical University of Athens, Athens, Greece
mitsikas@central.ntua.gr

Abstract. The paper presents BiMetaTrans(Prolog, RuleML), an invertible bidirectional metalogical translator across subsets of ISO Prolog and RuleML/XML 1.02 on the level of Negation-as-failure Horn logic with Equality. BiMetaTrans, itself written in Prolog, introduces a tighter integration between RuleML and Prolog, which enables the reuse of, e.g., RuleML Knowledge Bases (KBs) and query engines. A Prolog/`'$V'` encoding is defined as the BiMetaTrans translation source-and-target counterpart to RuleML/XML. This metalogical encoding, along with the introduction of the split translation pattern, allows BiMetaTrans to build upon the abstraction of Definite Clause Grammars (DCGs), supporting invertible bi-translation. The BiMetaTrans DCG is explored and an invertibility proof is outlined. BiMetaTrans is exemplified for knowledge representation and querying applied to an Air Traffic Control KB.

1 Introduction

In decentralized systems such as peer-to-peer [1] or multi-agent [2] architectures, peers or agents should be equipped with invertible translators for information exchange so that they can send/receive data and knowledge to/from other peers or agents, on-the-fly, in a round-trippable manner. This paper presents a RuleML-Prolog translator and outlines its invertibility proof.

In Logic Programming (LP) [3], multidirectional algorithms such as the one for `append` have often been used to exemplify the declarative advantages of specifying multiple functions as a single predicate. While most of LP's multidirectional predicates constitute "programming-in-the-small", few Knowledge Bases (KBs) of predicate definitions exist for multidirectional "programming-in-the-large." This paper contributes to filling the gap by presenting an (extensible) 'mid-size' invertible bidirectional translation algorithm, BiMetaTrans(Prolog,

© Springer Nature Switzerland AG 2020
V. Gutiérrez-Basulto et al. (Eds.): RuleML+RR 2020, LNCS 12173, pp. 112–128, 2020.
https://doi.org/10.1007/978-3-030-57977-7_8

RuleML), applicable to (extensible) subsets of ISO Prolog and RuleML. The source of BiMetaTrans is available[1], consisting of about 1200 lines of code including comprehensive documentation, and can be easily downloaded and run in any ISO Prolog system. The source directory also includes a test suite featuring an ISO Prolog variant of an Air Traffic Control (ATC) KB [4–6] as a use case.

A common sublanguage of RuleML 1.02 (particularly, of NafFologEq, one of its anchor languages)[2] and of ISO Prolog is proposed to become an anchor language, *Negation-as-failure (Naf) Horn logic with Equality (**NafHornlogEq**),* which is motivated by combining the following:

- A practical LP language – often restricted to NafHornlog (and further to NafDatalog) or to HornlogEq – with many implementations and applications.
- A target language for a Naf extension of the graph-relational PSOATransRun [7].
- The interchange language for BiMetaTrans(Prolog/'$V', RuleML/XML) of this paper, where the Eq component is restricted to syntactic equality.

Made bidirectionally translatable between RuleML – a KB-interoperation hub [8] – and Prolog – an actively refined and expanded ISO standard [9] – NafHornlogEq can become the de facto standard for its expressivity level of knowledge representation. For the current NafHornlogEq subset, BiMetaTrans already provides ISO Prolog with the XML format of RuleML, and RuleML/XML with the common presentation syntax of Prolog. This enables the reuse of, e.g., KB libraries, query engines, analysis tools, editors/IDEs, APIs, and composed translators. Subsequently, for increasing subsets, bidirectional, semantics-preserving translations between the two languages will facilitate further interoperation and reuse.

Regarding the metalogical aspect, BiMetaTrans(Prolog, RuleML) is itself written entirely in Prolog, and translates RuleML/XML from and to equivalent Prolog *compounds* (tree-shaped Prolog terms with a *function symbol*, at their root). BiMetaTrans uses a specialized Prolog encoding, Prolog/'$V', a shorthand for "Metalogic Prolog with variable-as-'$V'-compound-reification," which is described in Sect. 3. Its purpose is to permit processing of KBs and queries as ground terms. A rigorous exploration of the concept of metalogical encoding and its applications is found in Sect. 1.2 of [10].

Once the encoding and the mapping between it and RuleML/XML are given, we will restrict our attention to their bi-translation. This approach sacrifices no expressivity, as programs written in pure Prolog (or more accurately, Hornlog) can be encoded as Prolog/'$V' (and vice versa) by replacing variable names with a Prolog compound (resp. the inverse) headed by the function symbol '$V',

---

[1] https://github.com/mthom/scryer-prolog/blob/master/src/examples/bimetatrans/.

[2] See penultimate row of http://deliberation.ruleml.org/1.02/relaxng/#anchor table. Also note row for NafNegHornlogEq on the sublanguage path to NafFologEq. Our initial version of BiMetaTrans – like Prolog – assumes ordered conjunctions, disjunctions, and rulebases, although the corresponding RuleML/XML `formula` edges with `index="1"`, `index="2"`, ... attributes (http://wiki.ruleml.org/index.php/Glossary_of_Deliberation_RuleML_1.02#.40index) are omitted for simplicity.

whose only subterm is the text of the variable name rendered as a symbol (see the translation table of Sect. 3.1 for details).

On the RuleML/XML side, BiMetaTrans targets: (1) the *ifthen-compact form*[3], using `<then>` and `<if>` edges – in this Prolog-aligned order – on `<Implies>` nodes as shown in Fig. 1a; (2) the *mapClosure form*[4], omitting – for Prolog alignment – `<Forall>` and `<Exists>` wrappers; (3) a *minified (xmL) rendering* where the XML is stripped of extraneous whitespace, which is not a limitation since RuleML/XML can be rendered as RuleML/xmL without content loss.

The rest of this paper is organized thus: We begin with a primer on Definite Clause Grammars (DCGs), a domain-specific language for context-free parsing and generation in Prolog. Next we explain our Prolog/`'$V'` encoding and its correspondence to various elements of RuleML/XML, restricted to NafHornlogEq. An outline of a formalized proof of the translator's bidirectionality and termination properties under appropriate term groundedness assumptions follows. We then give an overview of the specification of BiMetaTrans(Prolog, RuleML) as a DCG, with examples of bi-translating parts of a core ATC KB, and descriptions of the interoperation achieved. The conclusions also discuss future work.

2 DCGs and Bidirectional Translation

BiMetaTrans is written almost entirely in the domain-specific language of DCGs [11]. To convey how BiMetaTrans achieves its bidirectionality, we describe how DCGs work by detailing how they might be implemented in raw Prolog. Because of their modular compositionality, DCGs can capture entire grammars, groups of their productions, as well as their individual productions.

Prolog source code shares the same internal representation as Prolog data, allowing abstract syntax trees to be directly manipulated at compile time using specially designated Prolog predicates known as *term expansions*. Many Prolog systems support term expansion and often implement DCGs using it.[5] Here is an example of a DCG of BiMetaTrans, before and after term expansion:

Before DCG Expansion	After DCG Expansion
`sign('-') --> "-".`	`sign('-',_A,_B) :- _A = ['-'|_B].`
`sign('+') --> "+".`	`sign('+',_A,_B) :- _A = ['+'|_B].`

Note how the variables `_A` and `_B` only appear in the expanded DCG. They are component to a specialized Prolog data structure commonly known as the "difference list" [3]. Difference lists are lists with uninstantiated tails. By keeping

---

[3] http://wiki.ruleml.org/index.php/Specification_of_Deliberation_RuleML_1.02# XSLT-Based_Compactifiers.

[4] https://wiki.ruleml.org/index.php/Glossary_of_Deliberation_RuleML_1.02#.40 mapClosure.

[5] https://www.metalevel.at/prolog/dcg#implementation.

track of a logical variable bound to the uninstantiated tail, it becomes possible to concatenate terms to difference lists in constant time.

DCGs maintain an underlying difference list of grammar items through two additional arguments in the heads of grammar clauses: one to the head, and one to the as-yet uninstantiated tail. The variable _A is bound to the difference list starting with the character '-' and terminating at the tail variable _B.

To see how tail variables are threaded across multiple lists, we turn to the more elaborate example:

Before DCG Expansion	After DCG Expansion
`conditions([I | Is]) -->`	`conditions([I | Is], _A, _B) :-`
`    condition(I),`	`    condition(I, _A, _C),`
`    conditions(Is).`	`    conditions(Is, _C, _B).`

In the post-expansion body of `conditions`, `condition` and `conditions` are both expanded as calls to the named grammar rules. The variable _C is bound to the tail of the difference list created by `condition` and to the head of the difference list next created by `conditions`. The tail of the caller is always that of its final called grammar, here named _B. If the DCG succeeds, _B will be bound to either [] or the head of another difference list.

The underlying list passed among the DCGs of BiMetaTrans is always a RuleML/XML string that is either parsed or generated, depending on the translation direction. The bi-translatability of Prolog/'$V' terms is addressed via the *split translation pattern*, a technique of reflecting a parsing strategy across translation boundaries. The reflected strategy is expected to perform the inverse translation of the counterpart element. Small changes to the reflected strategy are sometimes needed, but in general, the pattern is highly effective.

The pattern is applied by first writing a uni-translation of a RuleML/XML element, after checking that Item is unbound. Here, we give the first half of the `ruleml_atom` DCG production, before applying split translation, with an 'if' part to the left of "->" and a 'then' part in the lines below it:

```
ruleml_atom(Item) -->
    (   { var(Item) } ->
        list_ws("<Atom>"),
        list_ws("<Rel>"),
        prolog_symbol(Name),
        list_ws("</Rel>"),
        ruleml_items(Args),
        list_ws("</Atom>"),
        { Item =.. [Name | Args] }
    ;   . . .
    ).
```

The variable `Item` stands for a Prolog/'$V' term, since it is specified as an explicit grammar argument. `var(Item)` succeeds when `Item` is a free variable, which BiMetaTrans takes as proof that it is translating from RuleML/XML to Prolog/'$V'. The atom's name and arguments are bound to the variables

`Name` and `Args`. The extraction of those data from the implicit XML string will be explained in later sections. Central to the split translation pattern is the observation that the predicate "=..", as with many other ISO Prolog built-ins, is itself bidirectional. It presupposes that one of its arguments contains enough information to determine the other. In one direction, the list has the function symbol of the compound at its head, followed by a list of its arguments at its tail: the `Name` and `Args` of the structure, in this context. Conversely, if `Name` and `Args` are specified, as they are in the first half of `ruleml_atom`, the Prolog compound just described is bound to `Item` on the left-hand side.

Therefore, to apply the pattern in the second half, we reflect the translation of the 'then' part from the first half across the boundary of translation, here (and everywhere in BiMetaTrans) signified by a ";" for the 'else' part:

```
ruleml_atom(Item) -->
    (     . . .
    ;   { Item =.. [Name | Args] },
        list("<Atom>"),
        list("<Rel>"),
        prolog_symbol(Name),
        list("</Rel>"),
        ruleml_items(Args),
        list("</Atom>")
    ).
```

In the above reflected (inverse) direction of translation, `Name` and `Args` are extracted from the specified Prolog/`'$V'` term `Item`, and control is threaded to the bidirectional DCG productions `prolog_symbol` and `ruleml_items`. Some small differences are present in the reflected translation: `list_ws` is replaced by `list`, which doesn't match (or, for that matter, generate) trailing whitespace as `list_ws` does. Also, the order of the XML element matching was not changed in the reflected translation.

3   The Prolog/`'$V'` Bidirectional Metalogical Translation

Prolog/`'$V'` KBs are encoded according to a convention that reifies RuleML variables by name. Initially, it may seem simpler to translate RuleML variables directly, to and from Prolog variables, but we soon discover a problem. In many popular Prolog implementations, including those in which BiMeta-Trans was tested, the variable names are never stored. In fact, once variables have been rendered to the Prolog heap, their textual, source-level names are promptly discarded and forgotten by the Prolog engine.

Therefore, if we want fully invertible translation, we must store variable names in terms, so they can be recovered by an inverse translation, thus completing a round-trip. As detailed in a row of the translation table of Sect. 3.1, BiMetaTrans *reifies* RuleML variable names to Prolog symbols wrapping them each in a Prolog compound with the function symbol `'$V'`. The leading "$" was so chosen because atoms with leading "$"'s are seldom used by Prolog programmers, making `'$V'` an unlikely source of name clash.

3.1   The BiMetaTrans Translation Table and Syntax Graph

We define the mapping $\chi_{'\$V'}$ as translating from Prolog/'$V' to the equivalent RuleML/XML elements and the mapping π_{xmL} as translating in the inverse direction. The aim of this section is to outline a proof showing that $\chi_{'\$V'} \circ \pi_{xmL} = id_{xmL}$ and $\pi_{xmL} \circ \chi_{'\$V'} = id_{'\$V'}$; in words, both compositions yield the identity function.

The recursive definition of $\chi_{'\$V'}$ is given in the table below, similar in style to the tables in [12]. We should stress that, while the translator uses minified XML (or xmL, as in the mapping subscripts), the second column of the table uses indented XML for readability (see Sect. 1 for a definition of minified XML).

Prolog/'$V' Syntax	RuleML/xmL

`[`
    $assertitem_1$
`,` . . .
`,` $assertitem_n$
`]`
	`<Assert mapClosure="universal">`
	    $\chi_{'\$V'}(assertitem_1)$
	    . . .
	    $\chi_{'\$V'}(assertitem_n)$
	`</Assert>`

`?-` $queryitem$	`<Query mapClosure="existential">`
	    $\chi_{'\$V'}(queryitem)$
	`</Query>`

`(`
    $conjunct_1$
`,` . . .
`,` $conjunct_n$
`)`
	`<And>`
	    $\chi_{'\$V'}(conjunct_1)$
	    . . .
	    $\chi_{'\$V'}(conjunct_n)$
	`</And>`

`(`
    $disjunct_1$
`;` . . .
`;` $disjunct_n$
`)`
	`<Or>`
	    $\chi_{'\$V'}(disjunct_1)$
	    . . .
	    $\chi_{'\$V'}(disjunct_n)$
	`</Or>`

$consequent$ `:-` $antecedent$	`<Implies>`
	    `<then>`$\chi_{'\$V'}(consequent)$`</then>`
	    `<if>`$\chi_{'\$V'}(antecedent)$`</if>`
	`</Implies>`

$pred$ `(`
    $argument_1,$
    . . .
    $argument_n$
        `)`
	`<Atom>`
	    `<Rel>`$\chi_{'\$V'}(pred)$`</Rel>`
	    $\chi_{'\$V'}(argument_1)$
	    . . .
	    $\chi_{'\$V'}(argument_n)$
	`</Atom>`

continued on next page

continued from previous page	

func (
  $argument_1$,
  . . .
  $argument_n$
)
	`<Expr>`
	  `<Fun>`$\chi_{'\$V'}(func)$`</Fun>`
	  $\chi_{'\$V'}(argument_1)$
	  . . .
	  $\chi_{'\$V'}(argument_n)$
	`</Expr>`

$left = right$	`<Equal>`
	  $\chi_{'\$V'}(left)$
	  $\chi_{'\$V'}(right)$
	`</Equal>`

\+ form	`<Naf>`
	  $\chi_{'\$V'}(form)$
	`</Naf>`

"prologstring"	`<Data` `iso:type="string">`prologstring`</Data>`
prolognumber	`<Data` `iso:type="number">`prolognumber`</Data>`
prologcharseries	`<Data` `iso:type="symbol">`prologcharseries`</Data>`
'capitalizedprologcharseries'	`<Ind>`capitalizedprologcharseries`</Ind>`
'\$V'(prologcharseries)	`<Var>`prologcharseries`</Var>`

[$argument_1$, ..., $argument_n$]	`<Plex>`
	  $\chi_{'\$V'}(argument_1)$
	  . . .
	  $\chi_{'\$V'}(argument_n)$
	`</Plex>`

[$argument_1$, ..., $argument_n$ |
repo]
	`<Plex>`
	  $\chi_{'\$V'}(argument_1)$
	  . . .
	  $\chi_{'\$V'}(argument_n)$
	  `<repo>`
	    $\chi_{'\$V'}(repo)$
	  `</repo>`
	`</Plex>`

prolognumber and *prologstring* are expected to conform to the lexical grammar of numbers and strings as defined in the ISO Prolog standard [9]. As such, $\chi_{'\$V'}$ is not applied to them. A similar constraint applies to *prologcharseries*, which is assumed to start with a lower case letter followed by a sequence of alphanumeric characters. *capitalizedprologcharseries* differs only in that the first letter must be upper case. As shown in the table, Prolog's convention of distinguishing variables from symbols by capitalizing the former, in BiMetaTrans becomes a convention of RuleML distinguishing Individuals from `<Data>`[6]. A *capitalizedprologcharseries* may also represent a symbol, in which case it is printed between single quotes so as not to be mistaken for a variable.

---

[6] Complementing RuleML's `xsi:type`, we introduce `iso:type` for ISO Prolog types.

Most elements of RuleML/XML below the root element `<RuleML>`[7] are constrained to appear as children of certain container elements. The two top-most container elements are the performatives `<Assert>` and `<Query>`. `<Assert>` issues new facts and rules to the underlying RuleML KB while `<Query>` posts queries to its query engine. `<Assert>` makes an implicit `<Rulebase>` assumption, containing `<Assert>`'s children.

To indicate the main RuleML/XML elements' parent-child relations, and as an overview of how the translator DCG is built up from smaller DCGs, we present the grammar of the NafHornlogEq dialect of RuleML/XML as a syntax graph in Fig. 1a. The supplemental syntax graph in Fig. 1b elaborates Fig. 1a's Term box. Taken together, they comprise a single graph describing the grammar as a whole.

In each graph, boxes labeled by XML elements map one-to-one to the rows of the translation table. Solid arrows visualize the choice operator in DCGs and EBNF, indicating that an origin box chooses any of its destination boxes. Dashed arrows originate from boxes with angular bracketed text, which are always XML elements; consequently, their destination boxes are the children of their origin box's parent XML element. The children are said to be sequenced if they are meant to appear in a prescribed left-to-right order. Sequencing is denoted in the syntax graphs by sequencers, horizontal arrows with rectangular heads overlaying each of the dashed arrows fanning out from an origin.

Other boxes are labeled by intermediate nonterminals. In Fig. 1a, a solid (choice) arrow points from the intermediate Condition box to the intermediate Conclusion box. It entails that the `<Atom>` and `<Equal>` elements, the children of the Conclusion box, are also admissible as conditions in the grammar.

Choice arrowheads are in some cases marked by a "?" or "*" modifier, meaning that the corresponding XML parent can have, respectively, an optional child or zero or more occurrences of its destination as children. Sequenced arrows may also be marked by the "?" or "*" modifiers.

Lastly, there are two cases of labeled choice arrows in the composite syntax graph. In RuleML/XML, the consequent and antecedent children of `<Implies>` must be wrapped by `<then>` and `<if>` elements, in that order. The ordering reflects the Prolog convention for writing implications/inference rules using the infix operator " :- ", which places the consequent on its left-hand side and the antecedent on the right.

3.2   An Invertibility Proof Outline

We now consider the invertibility property: $\pi_{\mathrm{xmL}} \circ \chi_{{}'\$\mathrm{V}'} = id_{{}'\$\mathrm{V}'} \wedge \chi_{{}'\$\mathrm{V}'} \circ \pi_{\mathrm{xmL}} = id_{\mathrm{xmL}}$ ("$\circ$" denotes function composition and id_X the identity function on set X).

---

[7] The `<RuleML>` root is assumed by BiMetaTrans(Prolog/`'$V'`, RuleML/XML), thus simplifying its various (KB-only, query-only, KB&query) translation uses.

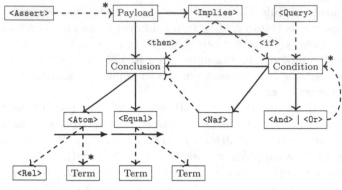

(a) The top-level of the syntax graph.

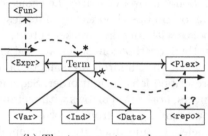

(b) The term syntax subgraph.

Fig. 1. RuleML/XML elements and their children.

The following definitions will be needed. Let $\mathcal{R} = \{=, :\text{-}, \backslash+, \text{'\$V'}, \text{'.'}\}$ be the set of *reserved symbols* and $\mathcal{S} \supset \mathcal{R}$ the set of *ISO Prolog symbols*. A RuleML/XML document is $\mathcal{R}$-*valid* if its atoms never contain a member of $\mathcal{R}$ in their `<Rel>` elements. Note that $\mathcal{R}$-validity applies to all document parts, e.g. to RuleML/XML KBs (rooted in `<Assert>`) and queries (rooted in `<Query>`).

With these definitions in place, we outline the invertibility proof, having established the translation table and syntax graph to help us present the proof as a case analysis. We will partly show that $\pi_{\text{xmL}} \circ \chi_{\text{'\$V'}} = id_{\text{'\$V'}}$, leading to the analysis of an exemplary case.

A valid RuleML/XML KB or query can be viewed as a traversal tree of the syntax graph, all of whose leaves correspond to grammar terminals. The traversal tree must have either the `<Assert>` or `<Query>` box as its root. $\chi_{\text{'\$V'}}$ is defined on the set of subtrees of all valid traversal trees, and so, we outline an inductive proof on the height of a given traversal tree. Since each traversal tree is finite, the proof will implicitly show that BiMetaTrans terminates on valid inputs.

$\mathcal{R}$-validity requires that RuleML/XML atoms named under the `<Rel>` elements of `<Atom>` elements are not members of $\mathcal{R}$. This constraint is vital to the invertibility of BiMetaTrans. For example, suppose we naïvely translated this (minified) RuleML/xmL atom:

`<Atom><Rel>=</Rel><Var>x</Var><Var>y</Var></Atom>`

BiMetaTrans would represent the atom as the Prolog compound specifiable in Prolog under the equivalent ($\sim$) prefix and infix forms:

$$\texttt{'='('\$V'(x), '\$V'(y))} \sim \texttt{'\$V'(x) = '\$V'(y)}$$

Following the translation table in the opposite direction, it would produce

`<Equal><Var>x</Var><Var>y</Var></Equal>`

which is not the original XML. The mistranslation occurs because plain Prolog compounds are the targets of both the `Atom` and `Equal` elements, leaving $\chi_{\texttt{'\$V'}}$ unable to tell which of the two was the source. Therefore, we see that disallowing RuleML atoms with a `Rel` element value of "=" is necessary to avoid ambiguity. In effect, the Prolog symbol "`'='`" can only be used for the translation of `Equal` elements.[8]

The leaves `<Var>`, `<Ind>`, and `<Data>` are the subjects of the induction basis. We have already seen an example translation sending `<Var>` to a "`'\$V'`" compound and back. Since `'\$V'` $\in \mathcal{R}$, this can be done at no information loss. `<Ind>` is more subtle in that on the RuleML/XML side, we suppose that all Individuals are capitalized strings. We can represent capitalized strings as Prolog symbols under the requirement that they be printed in single quotes to avoid confusion with variable names, which are always unquoted, capitalized strings. Similarly, the contents of `<Data>` are recognized on both translation sides by unique lexical characteristics that need no special effort to be distinguished from other forms.

For the induction hypothesis (IH), we assume that invertibility holds for all trees of height bounded by some $h \geq 1$. BiMetaTrans uses two recursive patterns based on the outgoing arrow types of the tree's root box. We outline the IH by demonstrating the invertibility of a single instance of each.

We focus on the `<Implies>` element of the case analysis. `<Implies>` has two outgoing sequenced arrows to its child edge elements `<then>` and `<if>`. Referring to the translation table, we see that `<Implies>` elements are translated as Prolog compounds headed by `:-` $\in \mathcal{R}$. First, we want to show this equation:

$$\pi_{\texttt{xmL}} \circ \chi_{\texttt{'\$V'}}(\boldsymbol{then} \texttt{:-} \boldsymbol{if}) = \pi_{\texttt{xmL}} \circ \chi_{\texttt{'\$V'}}(\boldsymbol{then}) \texttt{:-} \pi_{\texttt{xmL}} \circ \chi_{\texttt{'\$V'}}(\boldsymbol{if}) \qquad (1)$$

Consulting the translation table, we find a row permitting this rewrite:

$$\chi_{\texttt{'\$V'}}(\boldsymbol{then} \texttt{:-} \boldsymbol{if}) \rightsquigarrow \texttt{<Implies>}$$
$$\texttt{<then>}\chi_{\texttt{'\$V'}}(\boldsymbol{then})\texttt{</then>}$$
$$\texttt{<if>}\chi_{\texttt{'\$V'}}(\boldsymbol{if})\texttt{</if>}$$
$$\texttt{</Implies>}$$

---

[8] A conclusion compound with function symbol `'='` is not permissible in an ISO Prolog KB, but we are concerned only with Prolog/`'\$V'` encodings as ground terms.

Then, π_{xmL} performs the inverse transformation, establishing Eq. (1). The IH entails

$$\pi_{\text{xmL}} \circ \chi_{\text{'}\$\text{V'}}(\textit{then}) = \textit{then}$$

and similarly by swapping *if* for *then*, completing the argument for this case.

For recursion based on arrows of the second type, we consider the case of the Condition box. The Condition box in Fig. 1a does not directly pertain to a RuleML/XML element, but chooses one among <Atom>, <Equal>, and <Naf>. Any of the three descends into a subtree of height $< h$, so we use the IH.

Proofs of the invertibility of other elements can be similarly obtained, with some modifications for variable numbers of children or an optional child, completing the $\pi_{\text{xmL}} \circ \chi_{\text{'}\$\text{V'}}$ direction. The proof of $\chi_{\text{'}\$\text{V'}} \circ \pi_{\text{xmL}} = id_{\text{xmL}}$ is symmetric.

4 A Guided Tour of BiMetaTrans via ATC KB Examples

In this section we walk through the implementation of BiMetaTrans as a Prolog DCG. We will follow the exposition with examples of translating an ISO Prolog variant[9] of a POSL ATC KB to RuleML/XML.

The sole public predicate of BiMetaTrans is `parse_ruleml/3`. Its first two arguments are Prolog-content lists; the third is a string containing a RuleML/XML serialization (parsed by BiMetaTrans as RuleML/xmL 'on-the-fly') consisting of an (optional) assertion followed by (optional) queries. It has these modes:

```
parse_ruleml(+AssertItems, +QueryItems, ?XML)    % Realizes χ'$V' of Sect. 3
parse_ruleml(?AssertItems, ?QueryItems, +XML)    % Realizes πxmL of Sect. 3
```

The modes constrain the inputs to fit one of two patterns, each describing a translation direction. The first, where `AssertItems` and `QueryItems` are instantiated and `XML` is possibly a free variable, describes translation from Prolog/'`$V`' to RuleML/xmL. The other direction is captured by the second mode, where the (un)instantiation conditions are swapped: a RuleML/xmL string is assigned to `XML` while `AssertItems` and `QueryItems` may be unbound. A third assumption of `parse_ruleml` not expressed by its modes is that its inputs, when instantiated, are ground, meaning they do not contain free variables. These assumptions help ensure that BiMetaTrans is deterministic and will terminate on all valid inputs.

---

[9] http://users.ntua.gr/mitsikas/ATC_KB/ATC_KB_ISO_PL.pl.

The possible children of `<Assert>` elements are disjunctively connected by

```
ruleml_assert_item(Item) -->
   ruleml_implies(Item) | ruleml_equal(Item) | ruleml_atom(Item).
```

using the "|" operator, which realizes the *choice operator* in the EBNF meta-syntax: In DCGs, "|" causes its operands to be backtracked over from left to right until one succeeds. Thus, the `<Implies>`, `<Equal>`, and `<Atom>` elements are valid children of the `<Assert>` element, as seen in the translation table.

The remaining boxes of the syntax graph/rows of the translation table are similarly represented by other DCGs. For container elements with one or more children, the "*"s of the syntax graph, we have – for the greedy consumption of children – patterns such as the following:

```
ruleml_assert_items([Item | Items]) -->
   ruleml_assert_item(Item),
   ruleml_assert_items(Items).
ruleml_assert_items([]) --> [].
```

Here, children of an `<Assert>` fill the argument list until an `</Assert>` is met.

We now turn to the NafHornlogEq ATC KB (see Footnote 9), which we have translated into Prolog/'$V' (see the end of this section). Its purpose is to help determine the separation minima of pairs of aircraft according to various ATC regulations.

The first clause is a ground fact describing aircraft Characteristics, from left to right – type, weight (kilograms), wingspan (feet), and approach speed (knots):

```
aircraftChar(['B763', 186880.06, 156.08, 140.0]).
```

BiMetaTrans renders the fact as an atom because its head `aircraftChar` $\notin \mathcal{R}$:

```
<Atom>
    <Rel>aircraftChar</Rel>
    <Plex>
        <Ind>B763</Ind>
        <Data iso:type="number">186880.06</Data>
        <Data iso:type="number">156.08</Data>
        <Data iso:type="number">140.0</Data>
    </Plex>
</Atom>
```

The aircraft Char's are collected in a single `<Plex>`, specialized to a RuleML/XML counterpart for Prolog's list data type. Each `<Data>` element is matched by the `ruleml_data` DCG. The contents of `<Data>` elements are matched and generated by the following `ruleml_data_contents` grammar with three disjoint cases:

```
ruleml_data_contents(number, Cs) -->
   ruleml_number(Cs).
ruleml_data_contents(symbol, Cs) -->
   ruleml_symbol(Cs).
ruleml_data_contents(string, Cs) -->
   ruleml_string(Cs).
```

The `ruleml_data_contents` DCG notably breaks from the "|" convention of other choice-driven DCGs: the first argument is used to pass or receive type information to/from the caller, which is (resp.) generated as the "`iso:type`" attribute or used to index the clauses of `ruleml_data_contents`, depending on the translation direction.

The preceding grammars match disjoint character sequences. Consequently, numbers, strings, and symbols are inlined into Prolog/`'$V'` compounds without annotation. "`'B763'`" is a *capitalizedprologcharseries* that is not wrapped in a "$V", and so is considered an `Individual`.

A more advanced example is found in a rule for categorizing an aircraft in its wake turbulence category, according to regulations set by the International Civil Aviation Organization (ICAO). The original NafHornlogEq rule in ISO Prolog is given on the left, and the encoded Prolog/`'$V'` source is on the right:[10]

ISO Prolog	Prolog/'$V'
`icaoCategory(Aircraft, heavy) :-` `    aircraftChar([Aircraft, Kg | Rest]),` `    greaterThanOrEqual(Kg, 136000.0),` `    \+ icaoCategory(Aircraft, super).`	`icaoCategory('$V'(aircraft), heavy) :-` `    aircraftChar(['$V'(aircraft), '$V'(kg)` `	'$V'(rest)]),` ` greaterThanOrEqual('$V'(kg), 136000.0),` ` \+ icaoCategory('$V'(aircraft), super).`

In the following "co-alignment" and "DCG" tables, circle superscripts co-reference between the children of `Naf` ("1") and `Var` ("2") as well as the source ("black") and target ("white"). While in the co-alignment table, the source is on the right of the target, in the DCG table, the source is below the target.

For the co-alignment table, recalling the `<Implies>` box in the syntax graph of Fig. 1a, we see that `<then>` precedes `<if>`. The child of `<if>` is an `<And>` containing, as its first child, an `aircraftChar` `<Atom>` with a single `<Plex>` argument. This example's use of `<Plex>` contains an optional (EBNF's "?") child `<repo>` (Prolog's "|"). A `<repo>` must be either a `<Var>` or another `<Plex>`. This distinction is realized by a structural check. The second `<And>` child is a `greaterThanOrEqual` atom. The third conjunct is a Naf that contains an `icaoCategory` atom.

For the DCG table, notice that the `<Naf>` and `<Var>` elements each contain one element, albeit with different children.

---

[10] In the Emacs text editor, the reification can be done by the interactive command `M-x` `query-replace-regexp` with basically `\([A-Z][a-z]*\)` as the matching expression and `'$V'(\,(downcase \1))` as the transform. Such a command could also be named as an Emacs Lisp function.

The targeted RuleML/XML is on the left while the Prolog/`'$V'` rule has been co-aligned on the right, where its tree structure is made more explicit:

RuleML/XML	Prolog/'$V'

```<Implies>```
 ```<then>```
  ```<Atom>```
   ```<Rel>icaoCategory</Rel>```
   ```<Var>aircraft```[2]```</Var>```
   ```<Data iso:type="symbol">heavy</Data>```
  ```</Atom>```
 ```</then>```
 ```<if>```
  ```<And>```
   ```<Atom>```
    ```<Rel>aircraftChar</Rel>```
    ```<Plex>```
     ```<Var>aircraft```[2]```</Var>```
     ```<Var>kg```[2]```</Var>```
     ```<repo>```
      ```<Var>rest```[2]```</Var>```
     ```</repo>```
    ```</Plex>```
   ```</Atom>```
   ```<Atom>```
    ```<Rel>greaterThanOrEqual</Rel>```
    ```<Var>kg```[2]```</Var>```
    ```<Data iso:type="number">136000.0</Data>```
   ```</Atom>```
   ```<Naf>```
    ```<Atom>```[1]
     ```<Rel>icaoCategory</Rel>```
     ```<Var>aircraft```[2]```</Var>```
     ```<Data iso:type="symbol">super</Data>```
    ```</Atom>```
   ```</Naf>```
  ```</And>```
 ```</if>```
```</Implies>```
	```icaoCategory(```
	 ```'$V'(```
	  ```aircraft```[2]
	 ```),```
	 ```heavy```
	```) :- aircraftChar([```
	 ```'$V'(```
	  ```aircraft```[2]
	 ```),```
	 ```'$V'(```
	  ```kg```[2]
	 ```)```
	 ```|```
	 ```'$V'(```
	  ```rest```[2]
	 ```)]),```
	```greaterThanOrEqual(```
	 ```'$V'(```
	  ```kg```[2]
	 ```),```
	 ```136000.0,```
	 ```),```
	```\+ icaoCategory(```[1]
	 ```'$V'(```
	  ```aircraft```[2]
	 ```),```
	 ```super```
	```).```

For the DCGs, circle-superscripted parts of `ruleml_naf` and `ruleml_var` translate the circle-superscripted data of the co-alignment table:

DCG production for Naf	DCG production for Var

```ruleml_naf(I) -->```
 ```({ var(I) } ->```
  ```list_ws("<Naf>"),```
  ```ruleml_condition(NI)```[1]```,```
  ```{ Item = (\+ NI) },```
  ```list_ws("</Naf>")```
 ```; "<Naf>",```
  ```{ Item = (\+ NI) },```
  ```ruleml_condition(NI)```[1]```,```
  ```"</Naf>"```
 ```).```
	```ruleml_var(V) -->```
	 ```({ var(V) } ->```
	  ```list_ws("<Var>"),```
	  ```ruleml_var_contents(VCs)```[2]```,```
	  ```{ atom_chars(VN, VCs) },```
	  ```{ V = '$V'(VN) },```
	  ```list_ws("</Var>")```
	 ```; "<Var>",```
	  ```{ V = '$V'(VN) },```
	  ```{ atom_chars(VN, VCs) },```
	  ```ruleml_var_contents(VCs)```[2]```,```
	  ```"</Var>"```
	 ```).```

As a final example, we consider a query against the ATC KB in ISO Prolog (see Footnote 9). Here is its presentation syntax before and after reifying (see Footnote 10) to Prolog/'$V':

ISO Prolog	Prolog/'$V'
`?- icaoCategory('B763', Wtc).`	`?- icaoCategory('B763','$V'(wtc)).`

This is the translation of the second column to (minified) RuleML/xmL:

`<Query><Atom><Rel>icaoCategory</Rel><Ind>B763</Ind><Var>wtc</Var></Atom></Query>`

The only new element introduced by this case is `<Query>`. Note that, unlike the `<Assert>` performative, `<Query>` does not implicitly contain a `<Rulebase>`.

When posed to either a RuleML/XML or ISO Prolog engine with a KB of just the sample fact and rule, this query will succeed, binding its variable `<Var>wtc</Var>` or `Wtc` to the symbol **heavy**.

5   Conclusions

This paper presents BiMetaTrans, an invertible bidirectional metalogical translator between RuleML/XML and Prolog/'$V'. The latter is an encoding used to represent the complete contents of RuleML/XML KBs/queries as Prolog terms.

The case for writing invertible translators in DCGs is bolstered by comparing the simplicity and compactness of BiMetaTrans to recent approaches of the functional programming community in this area [13–15]. DCGs natively harness the declarativity of Prolog, making them at once simple, efficient, and effective.

The grammar of the NafHornlogEq RuleML language, and its translation to Prolog/'$V', were explained in a syntax graph and translation table, respectively. We gave a proof outline of BiMetaTrans' invertibility, focusing on the $\pi_{xmL} \circ \chi_{'$V'}$ direction, and examined its operation on a NafHornlogEq ATC KB.

Future work includes extending the RuleML/XML use of `<Equal>` from Prolog's "=" for syntactic unification to its **is** primitive for (arithmetic) functional built-ins, e.g. as in PSOATransRun's Prolog conversion. BiMetaTrans could also be extended to NafHornlogEq RuleML superlanguages, e.g. adding strong Negation for the anchor NafNegHornlogEq and Disjunctive conclusions for a NafDisHornlogEq. Moreover, we intend to explore ways of automating the reflection step of the split translation pattern.

BiMetaTrans was created and is being developed in Scryer Prolog[11], an ISO Prolog system under development by the first author. Its unique features include "partial strings"[12], which provide a 24-fold reduction in memory usage over how strings are typically represented in Prolog systems. Partial strings pack characters in UTF-8 format, but act as difference lists of characters. This allows their

---

[11] https://github.com/mthom/scryer-prolog.

[12] https://github.com/mthom/scryer-prolog#strings-and-partial-strings.

use in DCGs, which, combined with their compact representation, makes them well-suited to generating/parsing large (RuleML/)XML KBs/queries as strings.

BiMetaTrans could be composed with the PSOA RuleML API [16], creating a translation chain from ISO Prolog via RuleML/XML to PSOA RuleML presentation syntax (for subsets of each).

References

1. Iamnitchi, A., Trunfio, P., Ledlie, J., Schintke, F.: Peer-to-peer computing. In: D'Ambra, P., Guarracino, M., Talia, D. (eds.) Euro-Par 2010. LNCS, vol. 6271, pp. 444–445. Springer, Heidelberg (2010). https://doi.org/10.1007/978-3-642-15277-1_42
2. Kravari, K., Bassiliades, N., Boley, H.: Cross-community interoperation between knowledge-based multi-agent systems: a study on EMERALD and Rule Responder. Expert Syst. Appl **39**(10), 9571–9587 (2012)
3. Sterling, L., Shapiro, E.Y.: The Art of Prolog: Advanced Programming Techniques. MIT Press, Cambridge (1994)
4. Mitsikas, T., Stefaneas, P., Ouranos, I.: A rule-based approach for air traffic control in the vicinity of the airport. In: Lambropoulou, S., Theodorou, D., Stefaneas, P., Kauffman, L.H. (eds.) AlModTopCom 2015. SPMS, vol. 219, pp. 423–438. Springer, Cham (2017). https://doi.org/10.1007/978-3-319-68103-0_20
5. Mitsikas, T., Almpani, S., Stefaneas, P., Frangos, P., Ouranos, I.: Formalizing air traffic control regulations in PSOA RuleML. In: Proceedings of the Doctoral Consortium and Challenge@ RuleML+ RR 2018 hosted by 2nd International Joint Conference on Rules and Reasoning, vol. 2204, CEUR Workshop Proceedings (2018)
6. Deryck, M., et al.: Aligning, interoperating, and co-executing air traffic control rules across PSOA RuleML and IDP. In: Fodor, P., Montali, M., Calvanese, D., Roman, D. (eds.) RuleML+RR 2019. LNCS, vol. 11784, pp. 52–66. Springer, Cham (2019). https://doi.org/10.1007/978-3-030-31095-0_4
7. Boley, H., Zou, G.: Perspectival knowledge in PSOA RuleML: representation, model theory, and translation. CoRR abs/1712.02869, v3 (2019)
8. Boley, H.: The RuleML knowledge-interoperation hub. In: Alferes, J.J.J., Bertossi, L., Governatori, G., Fodor, P., Roman, D. (eds.) RuleML 2016. LNCS, vol. 9718, pp. 19–33. Springer, Cham (2016). https://doi.org/10.1007/978-3-319-42019-6_2
9. ISO: ISO/IEC 13211–1:1995: Information technology – programming languages – prolog – part 1: general core (1995)
10. Basin, D.A., Constable, R.L.: Metalogical frameworks. In: Proceedings of the Second Annual Workshop on Logical Frameworks, Edinburgh, UK, June 1991
11. Pereira, F., Warren, D.H.D.: Definite clause grammars for language analysis - a survey of the formalism and a comparison with augmented transition networks. Artif. Intell. **13**, 231–278 (1980)
12. Boley, H.: RIF RuleML Rosetta Ring: round-tripping the Dlex subset of Datalog RuleML and RIF-Core. In: Governatori, G., Hall, J., Paschke, A. (eds.) RuleML 2009. LNCS, vol. 5858, pp. 29–42. Springer, Heidelberg (2009). https://doi.org/10.1007/978-3-642-04985-9_6
13. Rendel, T., Ostermann, K.: Invertible syntax descriptions: unifying parsing and pretty printing. SIGPLAN Not. **45**(11), 1–12 (2010)

14. Duregård, J., Jansson, P.: Embedded parser generators. ACM SIGPLAN Not. **46**(12), 107–117 (2011)
15. Matsuda, K., Wang, M.: FliPpr: a prettier invertible printing system. In: Felleisen, M., Gardner, P. (eds.) ESOP 2013. LNCS, vol. 7792, pp. 101–120. Springer, Heidelberg (2013). https://doi.org/10.1007/978-3-642-37036-6_6
16. Al Manir, M.S., Riazanov, A., Boley, H., Baker, C.J.O.: PSOA RuleML API: a tool for processing abstract and concrete syntaxes. In: Bikakis, A., Giurca, A. (eds.) RuleML 2012. LNCS, vol. 7438, pp. 280–288. Springer, Heidelberg (2012). https://doi.org/10.1007/978-3-642-32689-9_23

Technical Communication Papers

Reasoning Under Uncertainty in Knowledge Graphs

Luigi Bellomarini[1(✉)], Eleonora Laurenza[1], Emanuel Sallinger[2,3], and Evgeny Sherkhonov[3]

[1] Banca d'Italia, Rome, Italy
bellomarini@yahoo.it
[2] TU Wien, Vienna, Austria
[3] University of Oxford, Oxford, UK

Abstract. We provide a framework for probabilistic reasoning in Vadalog-based Knowledge Graphs (KGs), able to satisfy the requirements of ontological reasoning: full recursion, powerful existential quantification, and the ability to express inductive definitions. Vadalog is based on Warded Datalog $+/-$, an existential rule language that strikes a good balance between computational complexity: with tractable reasoning in data complexity, and expressive power covering SPARQL under set semantics and the entailment regime for OWL 2 QL. Vadalog and its logical core Warded Datalog$+/-$ are not covered by existing probabilistic programming and statistical relational models for many reasons including weak support for existentials, recursion and the impossibility to express inductive definitions. We introduce Soft Vadalog, a probabilistic extension to Vadalog satisfying these desiderata. It defines a probability distribution over the nodes of a chase network, a structure induced by the grounding of a Soft Vadalog program with the chase procedure.

Keywords: Knowledge Graphs · Reasoning · Markov Logic Networks

1 Introduction

Knowledge Representation and Reasoning (KRR) languages adopted in Knowledge Graphs (KGs) systems should support a number of desiderata, including: a predilection for a rule-based fully explainable approach having simple syntax, high expressive power, low complexity, probabilistic reasoning and, importantly, explainability [2]. VADALOG is a state-of-the-art logic-based KRR language based on Warded Datalog$^\pm$ [3], a member of the Datalog$^\pm$ family [4]. Datalog$^\pm$ languages are also known as *existential rules* or *tuple-generating dependencies*, which generalize Datalog rules with existential quantifiers in heads. Warded Datalog$^\pm$ supports recursion and existential quantification, while introducing syntactic restrictions to guarantee decidability and data tractability [2].

© Springer Nature Switzerland AG 2020
V. Gutiérrez-Basulto et al. (Eds.): RuleML+RR 2020, LNCS 12173, pp. 131–139, 2020.
https://doi.org/10.1007/978-3-030-57977-7_9

Example 1. Consider a Knowledge Graph G, with facts describing semantics relationships between constants a, b, c, l, m, n:

$$\{\text{Triple}(a, b, c), \text{Inverse}(b, l), \text{Restriction}(m, l), \text{Subclass}(m, n)\}$$

Let us extend G with the following existential rules, encoding the membership part of the OWL 2 semantics entailment regime for OWL 2 QL (see [2,10]):

$$0.9 :: \text{Type}(x, y), \text{Restriction}(y, z) \rightarrow \exists v \, \text{Triple}(x, z, v) \tag{1}$$

$$0.8 :: \text{Type}(x, y), \text{SubClass}(y, z) \rightarrow \text{Type}(x, z) \tag{2}$$

$$0.7 :: \text{Triple}(x, y, z), \text{Inverse}(y, w) \rightarrow \text{Triple}(z, w, x) \tag{3}$$

$$\text{Triple}(x, y, z), \text{Restriction}(w, y) \rightarrow \text{Type}(x, w). \tag{4}$$

Ignoring what precedes the :: symbols, intuitively, Rule (1) encodes that if x is of type y (as expressed by the atom Type*) and is involved in a binary relation z (expressed by the atom* Restriction*), then there exists some value v s.t. the tuple (x, v) occurs in some instance of z (as specified by the atom* Triple*). Similarly, Rules (2–4) encode usual notions of subclass, inverse, and type restriction.* ∎

An example of (ontological) reasoning task over G is the query: *"What are all the entailed* Triples*?"*. We see such triples are $\text{Triple}(c, l, a)$ and $\text{Triple}(c, l, v_0)$, where v_0 is a fresh arbitrary value (a *labeled null*). Let us now consider a modified version Example 1, where Rules (1–3) are not definitive but hold with a certain probability. We prefix them with a weight proportional to such bias (indicated by the number before the :: symbol). A probabilistic reasoning task would then consist in answering, over such uncertain logic programs, queries like: *"What is the probability for each* Triple *to be entailed?"*. We wish to compute the marginal probability of entailed facts, so, e.g., of $\text{Triple}(c, l, a)$ and $\text{Triple}(c, l, v_0)$.

To enable such scenarios, we need KRR languages able to perform probabilistic reasoning and, at the same time, satisfy the requirements for ontological reasoning: (i) adoption of *well-founded semantics* [6], (ii) powerful existential quantification, supporting the quantification of SPARQL and OWL 2 QL, (iii) full recursion, (iv) ability to express non-ground inductive definitions (e.g., transitive closure) [7,16]. While probabilistic reasoning is of interest to three research areas, *probabilistic logic programming* (e.g., ProbLog) [1,5,19,21–23,25], *probabilistic programming languages* (e.g., BLOG) [8,14,17,18] and *statistical relational learning* (e.g., Markov Logic Networks) [13,16,20], none of the approaches fits our requirements as they fail either in providing simultaneous support for recursion and existential quantification or do not allow inductive definitions.

Contribution. In this short paper we propose the following contributions:

– We introduce SOFT VADALOG, a probabilistic extension to VADALOG. It allows reasoning on Probabilistic Knowledge Graphs (PKGs) while guaranteeing the desiderata for ontological reasoning. A SOFT VADALOG program defines a probability distribution over the nodes of a *chase network*, a structure obtained via grounding of the program with a *chase-based* procedure.

- We propose the *MCMC-chase* algorithm, an approximate technique for marginal inference combining a Markov Chain Monte Carlo method (specifically the Metropolis-Hastings algorithm) with a *chase-based* procedure. Chase procedures are used in databases to enforce logic rules by generating entailed facts. Here, the chase application is guided by MCMC and marginal inference is performed in the process.

Overview. In Sect. 2 we provide motivation for our approach and analyze the related work. In Sect. 3, we introduce PKGs and SOFT VADALOG. In Sect. 4 we present the MCMC-chase algorithm. Section 5 concludes the paper.

2   Motivation and Related Work

Let us briefly recap the three main related research areas to argue why extending Vadalog-based KGs with probabilistic reasoning needs a tailored approach.

Probabilistic Logic Programming (PLP) approaches [5] adopt the well-known distribution semantics [22]. For the task at hand here, it offers insufficient support in handling recursion and existentials together in a single decidable fragment. In fact, apart from some PLP languages which simply forbid recursion, most of others (e.g., ICL [19], PRISM [23], LPAD [21,25] ProbLog [5], cPlint [1]) do not allow non-ground probabilistic rules involving the creation of new values; others do not disclose details about how recursion is handled (e.g., cProbLog [15]).

These limitations are self-evident going back to Example 1 and trying to answer the query *"What are all the entailed Triples?"* over G. Existing PLP techniques fail to conclude Triple(c, l, v_0), because they abort when running into a probabilistic recursive rule that involves the creation of new values.

Probabilistic Programming Languages (PPL) systems, such as BLOG [17], BLP [14], Church [8], Figaro [18], are typically based on an underlying Bayesian network model and forbid recursion or existential quantification.

In *Statistical Relational Learning* (SRL) approaches, FO formulas are a template for the definition of graphical models, and inference then consists of construction of the network (grounding) and probabilistic inference on it. Examples are *Relational Bayesian Networks* [13] and *Markov Logic Networks (MLN)* [20]. Yet, as it is well known that FO logic can only express that a given relation is transitive, but cannot in general specify its closure [12], any FO logic theory expressed via MLNs cannot enforce marginal probability zero for models with facts not in the range of the transitive closure, making MLN unsuitable for reasoning over KGs. In Example 1, with FO logic semantics, one can make arbitrary conclusions leading to incorrect results. For example, as $\{\text{Triple}(a, b, c), \text{Inverse}(b, n)\}$ falsifies the premise of Rule (3), we can incorrectly conclude Triple(c, b, a).

This is one example of a broader area, studied more deeply by [7] and [16], that refer to the "ability to express (non-ground) inductive definitions", such as a graph path in terms of its edges. LP^{MLN} [16] is also relevant in SRL: it combines logic programming and the log-linear semantics of MLNs. Yet, it is unsuitable for reasoning on KGs, as it adopts stable model semantics instead of well-founded semantics, the standard option for nonmonotonic normal programs in the database context and very promising for ontological reasoning [11].

3   Probabilistic Knowledge Graphs

Our approach consists of the following steps: (i) first we define a Probabilistic Knowledge Graph as the ensemble of an input database D and a set Σ of uncertain first-order rules, (ii) then, given a query Q, i.e., an n-ary predicate appearing in Σ, we construct a structure, called *chase network*, that comprises all possible databases that can be obtained from D by applying rules in Σ. This structure is already enough to compute marginal probabilities. However, we need to mitigate two issues: logical inference in the presence of general FO rules is undecidable or intractable; computing exact marginal probabilities is intractable as well (#P-hard). For the first issue, we leverage the language VADALOG, for which logical inference can be done in polynomial time in input data size. For the second, we compute *approximate* marginal probability. Thus, (iii) we introduce an MCMC method that simultaneously performs logical and marginal inference and allows to efficiently answer queries over large PKGs.

Datalog$^\pm$ and VADALOG. SOFT VADALOG is an extension of VADALOG, a language in the Datalog$^\pm$ family [9]. We first introduce needed concepts.

Datalog$^\pm$ generalizes Datalog, with existential quantification in the rule conclusion. A *rule* is a first-order sentence of the form $\forall \bar{x} \forall \bar{y} (\varphi(\bar{x}, \bar{y}) \rightarrow \exists \bar{z}\, \psi(\bar{x}, \bar{z}))$, where φ (the *body*) and ψ (the *head*) are conjunctions of atoms (for brevity we will omit universal quantifiers and use comma to denote conjunctions). The semantics of a set of existential rules Σ over an instance D, denoted $\Sigma(D)$, is defined via the *chase procedure*. This procedure adds new facts to D (possibly involving generation of new labeled nulls used to satisfy the existentially quantified variables) until the final result $\Sigma(D)$ satisfies all the existential rules of Σ. More formally, initially $\Sigma(D) = D$. By a *unifier* we mean a mapping from variables to constants or labeled nulls. We say $\rho = \varphi(\bar{x}, \bar{y}) \rightarrow \exists \bar{z}\, \psi(\bar{x}, \bar{z})$ is *applicable* to $\Sigma(D)$ if there is a unifier θ_ρ such that $\varphi(\bar{x}\theta_\rho, \bar{y}\theta_\rho) \subseteq \Sigma(D)$ and θ_ρ has not been used to generate new facts in $\Sigma(D)$ via ρ. If ρ is applicable to $\Sigma(D)$ with a unifier θ_ρ, then it performs a *chase step*, i.e., it *generates* new facts $\psi(\bar{x}\theta'_\rho, \bar{z}\theta'_\rho)$ that are added to $\Sigma(D)$, where $\bar{x}\theta_\rho = \bar{x}\theta'_\rho$ and $z_i\theta'_\rho$, for each $z_i \in \bar{z}$, is a fresh labeled null that does not occur in $\Sigma(D)$. The chase step easily generalizes to a set of rules. The chase procedure performs chase steps until no rule in Σ is applicable. $\Sigma(D)$ is in principle potentially infinite because of the generation of infinite labeled nulls. However, for the purpose of this work, we will consider the chase up to isomorphism of facts, which is sufficient for our logical reasoning task in Warded Datalog$^\pm$ and is finite [3], as we shall see.

Given a *query* $Q = (\Sigma, \text{Ans})$ and an instance D, called an *extensional database* (EDB), where Σ is a set of rules and Ans an n-ary predicate, a tuple $\bar{t} \in dom(D)^n$ is an *answer* to Q over D if $\text{Ans}(\bar{t}) \in \Sigma(D)$. Since $\Sigma(D)$ is potentially infinite, the number of answers to a query could be infinite as well. For this, we are interested in finding a representative set of answers, called *universal answer set*, that can be embedded into any other answer set with a renaming of labeled nulls. In our setting, a *logical reasoning task* is computing a universal answer set.

A VADALOG program is a set of facts and rules that obey specific restrictions on the syntax of the rules (namely, *wardedness* [10]) which ensure that the reasoning task is decidable and scalable [4], i.e., there is a finite subset $\Sigma'(D) \subset \Sigma(D)$ s.t. the universal answer sets for a query Q over D calculated via $\Sigma(D)$ and $\Sigma'(D)$ are isomorphic. Thanks to this property, in VADALOG, a solution to the reasoning task can be obtained by executing just a finite number of chase steps. In particular, given two isomorphic facts h and h' (i.e., having same terms up to renaming of the labeled nulls), one needs to explore only h and so never perform chase steps starting from h'. As a consequence, for the purpose of this work, we will consider chase up to isomorphism of facts. By a *warded chase step* we refer to a chase step limited to those unifiers allowed by such criterion.

Syntax of SOFT VADALOG. We extend VADALOG to SOFT VADALOG with soft rules. A *soft* VADALOG *rule* is a pair (ρ, w), where ρ is a (usual) VADALOG rule and $w \in \mathbb{R} \cup \{+\infty, -\infty\}$, a real number, is a *weight*, reflecting how strong a constraint is and so the absolute bias for a model to respect it (or not to respect it, in the case of negative weights). A soft rule $(\rho, +\infty)$ is called a *hard* rule.

By abuse of notation, ρ denotes a soft rule and $w(\rho)$ its weight. A SOFT VADALOG *program* is a set of soft VADALOG rules.

Semantics of SOFT VADALOG. A SOFT VADALOG program specifies a probability distribution over the facts generated by any application of the chase procedure over a given database instance (*chase network*). To define this distribution, let us start from Probabilistic Knowledge Graphs.

A Probabilistic Knowledge Graph *is a pair* $\langle D, \Sigma \rangle$, *where D is a database instance and Σ is a* SOFT VADALOG *program.* A PKG can be viewed as a template for constructing *chase networks*. Given a PKG $\mathcal{G} = \langle D, \Sigma \rangle$ and a set of database instances $\mathbf{D}$, each closed under the hard rules of Σ and with relation symbols from $D \cup \Sigma$, a *chase network* $\Gamma(\mathcal{G})$ is a tuple $\langle \mathbf{W}, \mathbf{T}, \lambda, W_0 \rangle$, where:

1. $\mathbf{W}$ is a set of nodes and $\mathbf{T}$ is a set of edges.
2. $\lambda : \mathbf{W} \to \mathbf{D}$ *is a total injective labeling function associating nodes W of $\mathbf{W}$ to database instances $\lambda(W)$.*
3. $W_0 \in \mathbf{W}$ *is a source node, s.t.* $\lambda(W_0) = cl_\Sigma(D)$, *i.e., W_0 is associated to the closure of D w.r.t. the hard rules of Σ.*
4. *There is an edge $t_s \in \mathbf{T}$ from W to W' iff $\lambda(W')$ can be obtained from $\lambda(W)$ by one transition step. A transition step s from $\lambda(W)$ to $\lambda(W')$ consists of a warded chase step of at least one applicable soft rule with one unifier followed by the closure w.r.t. the hard rules of Σ. Edge t_s is then labeled by $\sum_{\rho \in \sigma} w(\rho)$, where σ is the set of soft rules applied.*

Note that since a transition step always adds new facts, there are no (directed) cycles in the chase network; also, as, λ is injective, all the paths in the chase network leading to the same database instance will converge into the same terminal node; moreover, two nodes W and W' can be connected by multiple edges (the chase network has a *multigraph* structure), one for each possible transition step from $\lambda(W)$ to $\lambda(W')$. Furthermore, the chase network is finite by wardedness, as we consider the chase up to isomorphism, as discussed earlier. Apart from the technical side, this is intuitively justified by the fact that such isomorphic space should not be considered at all because its facts are semantically irrelevant for query answering and so should be for marginal probability.

We define the *weight* $w(W)$ of a node W in $\Gamma(\mathcal{G})$ as the sum of the edge labels on all the paths from W_0 to W. The chase network induces the following probability distribution over its nodes: $P(W) = \frac{1}{Z} \exp w(W)$, where Z is a normalization constant (a *partition function*), to make $P(W)$ a proper distribution, defined as $Z = \sum_W \exp w(W)$. For a given fact f, its *marginal probability* $P(f)$ can be calculated as $\sum_{W_i : f \in \lambda(W_i)} P(W_i)$.

Figure 1 summarizes the chase network for Example 1. Nodes are facts f in database instances $\lambda(W_i)$, where W_i is a node of the chase network. Facts f are annotated with a set $\{W_0, \ldots, W_n\}$ of nodes of the chase network s.t. for each W_i in the set, $f \in \lambda(W_i)$. Solid edges are warded chase steps applying hard rules; dashed edges are for soft rules, with weight γ.

Let us now compute the marginal probability of Triples. We have $w(W_0) = 0$. Then it follows $w(W_1) = 0.7$ and $w(W_2) = 0.7 + 0.8 = 1.5$, $w(W_3) = 0.7 + 0.9 = 1.6$, and $w(W_4) = 0.7 + (0.8 + 0.9) \times 2 = 4.3$. So we can calculate marginal probability for $Triple(c, l, a)$. This fact appears for W_1, W_2, W_3, W_4, so we have: $(e^{0.7} + e^{1.5} + e^{1.6} + e^{4.3})/Z = 0.98$, with $Z = 1 + e^{0.7} + e^{1.5} + e^{1.6} + e^{4.3}$. Similarly, for $Triple(c, l, v_0)$, we have: $(e^{1.6} + e^{4.3})/Z = 0.91$.

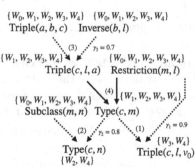

Fig. 1. Chase network for Example 1.

Probabilistic Reasoning. Given an instance D and a query $Q = (\Sigma, \text{Ans})$, the *probabilistic reasoning task* consists in computing the set $\{\langle \bar{t}, P(\bar{t}) \rangle\}$, where $\text{Ans}(\bar{t}) \in \mathbf{D}$, with $\mathbf{D}$ being the instances associated to nodes in $\Gamma(\mathcal{G})$, defined on the PKG $\mathcal{G} = \langle D, \Sigma \rangle$, and $P(\bar{t})$ is the marginal probability of $\text{Ans}(\bar{t})$.

Reasoning on PKGs is a computationally hard problem. For marginal inference, an exploration of the full chase network is needed and thus an exponential number of chase executions, each with polynomial complexity in the size of D. This makes it NP-hard. By adapting the proof for #P-hardness of query answering over probabilistic databases [24], it can be shown that marginal inference in SOFT VADALOG is #P-hard, where the program is assumed to be fixed.

4 The MCMC-Chase Algorithm

MCMC-chase is an independence sampling MCMC where the chase is seen as a Markov process over the nodes of the chase network. Given a PKG $\mathcal{G} = \langle D, \Sigma \rangle$, the MCMC-chase satisfies soft rules of Σ, applied to D, with a probability that is proportional to the rule weight and generates nodes of $\Gamma(\mathcal{G})$. The algorithm keeps track of the weight of the current node. A node is accepted or rolled back according to an *acceptance probability*, in a Metropolis-Hastings style.

Algorithm 1 gives pseudo-code for the MCMC-chase. It takes as input a PKG $\mathcal{G}$ and returns samples from the distribution $P(W) = \frac{1}{Z} \exp w(W)$ over the nodes $\mathbf{W}$ of the chase network $\Gamma(\mathcal{G})$. The algorithm performs N iterations, each consisting of S steps, with S extracted from a Poisson (*jump*) distribution (line 5). In each step, forward or backward depending on a value δ uniformly chosen, the algorithm selects subsets $\mathbf{R_a}$ and $\mathbf{R_u}$ of rules from Σ with a probability proportional to $w(\rho)$ (lines 10–11) of applicable or undoable (that generated leaf facts) rules. *Forward steps* (line 12) try to apply a transition step with the selected rules $\mathbf{R_a}$ to the current node $\mathcal{T}$ of the chase network. *Backward steps* (line 13) try to undo a transition step with rules in $\mathbf{R_u}$.

Algorithm 1. MCMC-chase

1: **function** MCMC-CHASE($\mathcal{G} = \langle D, \Sigma \rangle, N$)
2: $\quad \mathbf{W}_S = \emptyset$ $\qquad\qquad$ ▷ samples from the distribution over the nodes $\mathbf{W}$ of $\Gamma(\mathcal{G})$
3: $\quad \mathcal{D}^0 = D$
4: $\quad$ **for** $n \leftarrow 1$ to N **do** $\qquad\qquad\qquad\qquad\qquad$ ▷ N: # of iterations
5: $\qquad$ Sample $S \sim \mathcal{P}(\lambda)$ $\qquad\qquad\qquad$ ▷ # of steps, from a Poisson distr.
6: $\qquad \mathcal{T} \leftarrow \mathcal{D}^{n-1}$
7: $\qquad w(\mathcal{T}) \leftarrow w(\mathcal{D}^{n-1})$
8: $\qquad$ **for** $s \leftarrow 1$ to S **do**
9: $\qquad\qquad$ Sample $\delta \sim \mathcal{U}(0,1)$; Sample $\mu \sim \mathcal{U}(0,1)$
10: $\qquad\qquad \mathbf{R_f} \leftarrow$ all applicable ρ in Σ s.t. $\mu < 1 - e^{-w(\rho)}$
11: $\qquad\qquad \mathbf{R_u} \leftarrow$ all undoable ρ in Σ s.t. $\mu < 1 - e^{-w(\rho)}$
12: $\qquad\qquad$ **if** $\delta < 0.5$ **then** TRANSITION_STEP($\mathcal{T}, \mathbf{R_a}$)
13: $\qquad\qquad\qquad$ **else** UNDO_TRANSITION_STEP($\mathcal{T}, \mathbf{R_u}$)
14: $\qquad \alpha \leftarrow f(\mathcal{T})/f(\mathcal{D}^{n-1})$ $\qquad\qquad\qquad$ ▷ acceptance probability
15: $\qquad$ With prob. $\min(1, \alpha)$ add $\langle \mathcal{T}, w(\mathcal{T}) \rangle$ to $\mathbf{W}_S$
16: $\qquad$ **if** accepted **then** $\mathcal{D}^n \leftarrow \mathcal{T}$ **else** $\mathcal{D}^n \leftarrow \mathcal{D}^{n-1}$ $\qquad$ ▷ accept or rollback
$\quad$ **return** $\mathbf{W}_S$

In forward (resp. backward) steps, applicable (resp. undoable) hard rules are used to add (resp. remove) facts from the closure of $\mathcal{T}$; applicable (resp. undoable) soft rules are applied and their weight is summed to (resp. subtracted from) the total weight of $\mathcal{T}$. When applicable, hard rules are in $\mathbf{R_a}$ and $\mathbf{R_u}$ (lines 10–11) and therefore applied or undone, without affecting the total weight. After S steps, an *acceptance function* $f(\mathbf{Y}) = \exp w(\mathbf{Y})$ evaluates the acceptability of the current node. Finally, all accepted nodes and their weights are returned.

Observe that the stochastic process underlying MCMC-chase is *memoryless* (i.e., it satisfies the *Markov property*) by construction, since a future process status—a candidate node of the chase network—only depends on the present one: a candidate node inherits all the facts only from one previously generated node, and some facts are added to or removed from it by the applicable rules.

5 Conclusion

Motivated by the fact that a probabilistic extension of Warded Datalog$^{\pm}$ is not covered by existing approaches, we introduced the SOFT VADALOG language and discussed its semantics. It features soft rules in the presence of full recursion, existential quantification, and inductive definitions. Given the hardness of the probabilistic reasoning task, we contributed an MCMC algorithm for approximate marginal inference with SOFT VADALOG.

Acknowledgements. The work on this paper was supported by EPSRC programme grant EP/M025268/1, the EU H2020 grant 809965, and the Vienna Science and Technology (WWTF) grant VRG18-013.

References

1. Alberti, M., Bellodi, E., Cota, G., Riguzzi, F., Zese, R.: cplint on SWISH: probabilistic logical inference with a web browser. IA **11**(1), 47–64 (2017)
2. Bellomarini, L., Gottlob, G., Pieris, A., Sallinger, E.: Swift logic for big data and knowledge graphs. In: Tjoa, A.M., Bellatreche, L., Biffl, S., van Leeuwen, J., Wiedermann, J. (eds.) SOFSEM 2018. LNCS, vol. 10706, pp. 3–16. Springer, Cham (2018). https://doi.org/10.1007/978-3-319-73117-9_1
3. Bellomarini, L., Sallinger, E., Gottlob, G.: The vadalog system: datalog-based reasoning for knowledge graphs. In: VLDB (2018)
4. Calì, A., Gottlob, G., Pieris, A.: Towards more expressive ontology languages: the query answering problem. Artif. Intell. **193**, 87–128 (2012)
5. De Raedt, L., Kimmig, A.: Probabilistic (logic) programming concepts. Mach. Learn. **100**(1), 5–47 (2015). https://doi.org/10.1007/s10994-015-5494-z
6. Denecker, M., Bruynooghe, M., Marek, V.W.: Logic programming revisited: logic programs as inductive definitions. ACM Trans. Comput. Log. **2**(4), 623–654 (2001)
7. Fierens, D., et al.: Inference and learning in probabilistic logic programs using weighted boolean formulas. TPLP **15**, 358–401 (2015)
8. Goodman, N.D., Mansinghka, V.K., Roy, D.M., Bonawitz, K., Tenenbaum, J.B.: Church: a language for generative models. In: UAI (2008)
9. Gottlob, G., Lukasiewicz, T., Pieris, A.: Datalog+/−: questions and answers. In: KR (2014)
10. Gottlob, G., Pieris, A.: Beyond SPARQL under OWL 2 QL entailment regime: rules to the rescue. In: IJCAI, pp. 2999–3007 (2015)
11. Hernich, A., Kupke, C., Lukasiewicz, T., Gottlob, G.: Well-founded semantics for extended datalog and ontological reasoning. In: PODS (2013)
12. Huth, M., Ryan, M.D.: Logic in Computer Science - Modelling and Reasoning about Systems, 2nd edn. Cambridge University Press, Cambridge (2004)

13. Jaeger, M.: Probabilistic logic and relational models. In: Alhajj, R., Rokne, J. (eds.) Encyclopedia of Social Network Analysis and Mining, 2nd edn. Springer, New York (2018). https://doi.org/10.1007/978-1-4614-6170-8_157

14. Kersting, K., De Raedt, L.: Basic principles of learning Bayesian logic programs. In: De Raedt, L., Frasconi, P., Kersting, K., Muggleton, S. (eds.) Probabilistic Inductive Logic Programming. LNCS (LNAI), vol. 4911, pp. 189–221. Springer, Heidelberg (2008). https://doi.org/10.1007/978-3-540-78652-8_7

15. Latour, A.L.D., Babaki, B., Dries, A., Kimmig, A., Van den Broeck, G., Nijssen, S.: Combining stochastic constraint optimization and probabilistic programming. In: Beck, J.C. (ed.) CP 2017. LNCS, vol. 10416, pp. 495–511. Springer, Cham (2017). https://doi.org/10.1007/978-3-319-66158-2_32

16. Lee, J., Wang, Y.: Weighted rules under the stable model semantics. In: KR, pp. 145–154. AAAI Press (2016)

17. Milch, B., Marthi, B., Russell, S.J., Sontag, D., Ong, D.L., Kolobov, A.: BLOG: probabilistic models with unknown objects. In: IJCAI (2005)

18. Pfeffer, A.: Figaro: an object-oriented probabilistic programming language, Charles River Analytics (2009)

19. Poole, D.: The independent choice logic and beyond. In: De Raedt, L., Frasconi, P., Kersting, K., Muggleton, S. (eds.) Probabilistic Inductive Logic Programming. LNCS (LNAI), vol. 4911, pp. 222–243. Springer, Heidelberg (2008). https://doi.org/10.1007/978-3-540-78652-8_8

20. Richardson, M., Domingos, P.M.: Markov logic networks. Mach. Learn. **62**(1–2), 107–136 (2006). https://doi.org/10.1007/s10994-006-5833-1

21. Riguzzi, F.: A top down interpreter for LPAD and CP-logic. In: Basili, R., Pazienza, M.T. (eds.) AI*IA 2007. LNCS (LNAI), vol. 4733, pp. 109–120. Springer, Heidelberg (2007). https://doi.org/10.1007/978-3-540-74782-6_11

22. Sato, T.: A statistical learning method for logic programs with distribution semantics. In: ICLP, pp. 715–729. MIT Press (1995)

23. Sato, T., Kameya, Y.: PRISM: a language for symbolic-statistical modeling. In: IJCAI, pp. 1330–1339 (1997)

24. Suciu, D., Olteanu, D., Ré, C., Koch, C.: Probabilistic Databases. Synthesis Lectures on Data Management. Morgan & Claypool Publishers, San Rafael (2011)

25. Vennekens, J., Verbaeten, S., Bruynooghe, M.: Logic programs with annotated disjunctions. In: Demoen, B., Lifschitz, V. (eds.) ICLP 2004. LNCS, vol. 3132, pp. 431–445. Springer, Heidelberg (2004). https://doi.org/10.1007/978-3-540-27775-0_30

Distributed Reasoning for Restricted Weakly-Linear Disjunctive Tuple-Generating Dependencies

Arash Karimi[✉] and Jia-Huai You

University of Alberta, Edmonton, AB, Canada
akarimi@ualberta.ca

Abstract. We study the problem of distributed reasoning over connected database components with a class of ontologies based on disjunctive tuple-generating dependencies, called restricted weakly-linear disjunctive tuple-generating dependencies. This language extends linear tuple-generating dependencies as well as linear disjunctive Datalog. We provide the first distributability results on these queries and report experimental results on real-world ontology benchmark suites.

1 Introduction

Ontology-mediated queries (OMQs) [7] provide key formalisms for effective access to heterogeneous and incomplete data with a unified conceptual view of various data sources and paves the way for enriching user queries with domain knowledge. A major challenge of OMQ answering is provisioning of coordination-free reasoning, which has been tackled in recent years by *query distribution over components* [2]. The question is: given an OMQ Q, whether the answer to Q for any database D, denoted $Q(D)$, coincides with $\bigcup_{1 \leq i \leq n} Q(D_i)$, where $D_1, \ldots, D_n$ are the (maximally connected) components of D.

The problem of checking whether an OMQ is distributable is in general undecidable even for ontology-mediated queries based on Datalog [2]. However, for some fragments of existential rule languages, such as *linear*, *guarded*, and *sticky*, this problem is known to be decidable for conjunctive queries [6]. Despite this, the scope of current decidability results is limited due to the lack of support to represent even simple constructs such as *disjunctive* axioms. In particular, disjunction, with which one can model classification, is a useful property in the biology domain among many others for which the importance of coordination-free query answering is most apparent.

Consider, for instance, an ontology in the domain of biological sciences which is specified by the following set of disjunctive existential rules, which describes different types of organisms in terms of their effect on their victim. In particular,

V. Gutiérrez-Basulto et al. (Eds.): RuleML+RR 2020, LNCS 12173, pp. 140–149, 2020.
https://doi.org/10.1007/978-3-030-57977-7_10

if an organism x with a weak immune system (WeakImmune(x)) hosts a parasitic prokaryote (Parasitic(y)), it gets sick by it (GetsSickBy(x, y)). If x gets sick by y, then y harms x and y is parasitic. The rest of the rules are self-explanatory.

$$\sigma_1 : \text{Organism}(x) \rightarrow \text{Eukaryote}(x) \vee \text{Prokaryote}(x)$$
$$\sigma_2 : \text{Prokaryote}(x) \rightarrow \text{Bacteria}(x) \vee \text{Archaea}(x)$$
$$\sigma_3 : \text{Parasitic}(x) \rightarrow \exists y \, \text{Hosts}(y, x), \text{Harms}(x, y)$$
$$\sigma_4 : \text{Hosts}(x, y) \rightarrow \text{Organism}(x), \text{DependsOn}(y, x)$$
$$\sigma_5 : \text{Parasitic}(y), \text{Hosts}(x, y), \text{WeakImmune}(x) \rightarrow \text{GetsSickBy}(x, y)$$
$$\sigma_6 : \text{GetsSickBy}(x, y) \rightarrow \text{Parasitic}(y), \text{Harms}(y, x)$$
$$\sigma_7 : \text{Bacteria}(x), \text{Harms}(x, y) \rightarrow \text{Infectious}(x), \text{Victim}(y)$$

In this paper, we study the problem of distribution over components for ontology-mediated queries constructed from what we call *restricted weakly-linear tuple-generating dependencies* and a subset we introduce as *bidirectionally-guarded* queries, and additionally, for the first time, we conduct experiments to evaluate the performance of distributed reasoning on real-world ontology benchmarks.

2   Preliminaries

Let C and V be pairwise disjoint countably infinite sets of *constants* and *variables*. A *schema* is a finite set $\mathbf{S}$ of predicate symbols where each symbol $R \in \mathbf{S}$ has an *arity*, denoted $arity(R)$. *Terms* are elements in C $\cup$ V. An *atom* over $\mathbf{S}$ is an expression of the form $R(\mathbf{t})$, where $R \in \mathbf{S}$ and $\mathbf{t} \in (\text{C} \cup \text{V})^{arity(R)}$. An *instance* over a schema $\mathbf{S}$ is a set of atoms. A *database* over $\mathbf{S}$ is a finite instance over $\mathbf{S}$ that contains only constants. The *active domain* of an instance I, denoted $adom(I)$, is the set of all terms occurring in I.

Given two instances I and J (over the same schema), a *homomorphism* $h : I \rightarrow J$ is a substitution on terms that is identity on constants and for every atom $R(\mathbf{t})$ of I we have that $R(h(\mathbf{t})) \in J$ which may be alternatively written as $h(R(\mathbf{t})))$ is an atom of J. A *conjunctive query* (CQ) over $\mathbf{S}$ is a formula of the form $\exists \mathbf{y} \, \phi(\mathbf{x}, \mathbf{y})$, where $\mathbf{x}$ and $\mathbf{y}$ are tuples of variables in V and $\phi(\mathbf{x}, \mathbf{y})$ is a conjunction of atoms over $\mathbf{S}$ and $\mathbf{x} \cup \mathbf{y}$. A CQ is *answer-guarded* if it has an atom that contains $\mathbf{x}$, and it is *acyclic* if its hypergraph is α-acyclic (cf. [10]). Furthermore, it is quantifier-free if $\mathbf{y} = \emptyset$. The *evaluation* of a CQ q over an instance I, denoted $q(I)$, is defined as the set of all tuples $h(\mathbf{t})$ of constants such that h is a homomorphism from q to I. A *union of conjunctive queries* (UCQ) is a disjunction of CQs that share the same free variables. Given two queries q and q' over $\mathbf{S}$, $q \subseteq q'$ if for every $\mathbf{S}$-database D, $q(D) \subseteq q'(D)$. Two queries q and q' over $\mathbf{S}$ are *equivalent*, denoted $q \equiv q'$, if $q \subseteq q'$ and $q' \subseteq q$. A query language $\mathcal{Q}'$ is at least as expressive as another query language $\mathcal{Q}$, denoted $\mathcal{Q} \preceq \mathcal{Q}'$, if for every $\mathbf{S}$-query $q \in \mathcal{Q}$, there is an $\mathbf{S}$-query $q' \in \mathcal{Q}'$ such that $q \equiv q'$. $\mathcal{Q}$ and $\mathcal{Q}'$ are *equi-expressive*, denoted $\mathcal{Q} = \mathcal{Q}'$, if $\mathcal{Q} \preceq \mathcal{Q}'$ and $\mathcal{Q}' \preceq \mathcal{Q}$. With CQ (resp. UCQ), we denote the class of all queries definable by some CQ (resp. UCQ).

A *disjunctive tuple-generating dependency* (DTGD, also called a *rule*) σ is a first-order formula $\forall \mathbf{x}(\phi(\mathbf{x}) \rightarrow \bigvee_{i=1}^{n} \exists \mathbf{y}_i \, \psi_i(\mathbf{x}_i, \mathbf{y}_i))$, where ϕ and ψ_i $(1 \le i \le n)$ are conjunctions of atoms. The formula ϕ (resp. $\bigvee_{i=1}^{n} \psi_i$) is called the *body* of σ, denoted $body(\sigma)$ (resp. the *head* of σ, denoted $head(\sigma)$). The set of predicates appearing in Σ is called the *schema* of Σ, denoted $sch(\Sigma)$.

A DTGD without disjunction is called a *tuple-generating dependency* (TGD). We denote by TGD the class of all finite sets of TGDs. A *Datalog rule* is a TGD without existential variables. A finite set of Datalog rules is called a *Datalog program*. A *disjunctive Datalog rule* is a DTGD without existential variables. A finite set of disjunctive Datalog rules is called a *disjunctive Datalog program*.

We say a TGD set Σ' is a *rewriting* of a CQ q w.r.t. a set of DTGDs Σ if there exists a predicate P_q such that for each database D over the schema of Σ, and for each tuple of constants $\mathbf{a}$, we have $D \cup \Sigma \models q(\mathbf{a})$ if and only if $D \cup \Sigma' \models P_q(\mathbf{a})$. A set Σ' of TGDs is a rewriting of Σ if it is a rewriting of every atomic query over $sch(\Sigma)$. A rule σ is *linear* if it has at most one body atom. A rule set Σ is *linear* if all rules of Σ are linear.

An *ontology-mediated query* (OMQ) over $\mathbf{S}$ is a triple $Q = (\mathbf{S}, \Sigma, q)$ in which $\mathbf{S}$ is called the *data schema*, Σ is a finite set of DTGDs, and q is a CQ over $\mathbf{S} \cup sch(\Sigma)$. Given an OMQ $Q = (\mathbf{S}, \Sigma, q)$ and a database D where $arity(q) = n$, we define the *certain answer* to Q over D as: $\mathsf{ans}(D, \Sigma, q) = \{\mathbf{a} \in \mathbf{C}^n \mid D \cup \Sigma \models q(\mathbf{a})\}$, and semantically interpret Q by assigning $Q(D) = \mathsf{ans}(D, \Sigma, q)$ for all databases D. For an OMQ $Q = (\mathbf{S}, \Sigma, q)$, if Σ belongs to a class $\mathcal{C}$, we then say that Q belongs to $\mathcal{C}$.

Connectedness is a key notion to characterize the distributable fragments of TGDs [2,6]. A finite instance I is called *connected* if for all $x, y \in adom(I)$, there exists a sequence $\beta_1, \ldots, \beta_n$ of atoms in I such that a) $x \in adom(\beta_1)$ and $y \in adom(\beta_n)$, and b) for each $1 \le i < n$, $adom(\beta_i) \cap adom(\beta_{i+1}) \ne \emptyset$. Furthermore, $I' \subseteq I$ is called a *component* of I if I' is connected and for every $\alpha \in I \setminus I'$, $I' \cup \{\alpha\}$ is not connected. The set of all components of such an instance I is denoted $co(I)$.

A TGD is *connected* if so is its body, and a TGD set Σ is *connected* if every TGD in Σ has this property. For each class $\mathcal{Q}$ of query languages, we denote by $con\mathcal{Q}$ the class of all OMQs that belong to $\mathcal{Q}$ and are connected (i.e., their rule sets as well queries are connected).

Given a database D over schema $\mathbf{S}$, an OMQ $Q = (\mathbf{S}, \Sigma, q)$ is said to *distribute over components* if $Q(D) = \bigcup_{D' \in co(D)} Q(D')$. We will simply call such a query *distributable*.

3   Bidirectionally-Guarded Queries

Let us first introduce a subclass of DTGDs which we call *restricted weakly-linear*.

Definition 1. *The labelled dependency graph* $G_\Sigma = (N, E, \mu)$ *of a DTGD set* Σ *is the smallest labelled digraph such that:*

1. *N contains all predicates that occur in Σ;*
2. *for two nodes $P, Q \in N$, and a rule $\sigma \in \Sigma$ if P and Q occur in body(σ) and head(σ), respectively, then $\sigma \in \mu(P, Q)$; and*
3. *$(P, Q) \in E$ whenever $\mu(P, Q)$ is non-empty.*

A predicate Q depends on a rule $\sigma \in \Sigma$ if G_Σ has a path which ends in Q and involves an edge labelled with σ. A predicate Q is called non-disjunctive *if it only depends on non-disjunctive rules, and otherwise it is* disjunctive. *An atom is* disjunctive *if its predicate is, and otherwise it is called* non-disjunctive. *A rule set Σ is restricted weakly-linear (RWL) if (i) each rule in Σ has at most one occurrence of a disjunctive predicate in the body, and (ii) for each rule $\sigma \in \Sigma$ of the form $\chi \wedge Q(\mathbf{t}) \rightarrow \bigvee_{i=1}^{n} P_i(\mathbf{x}_i)$, in which χ is a conjunction of non-disjunctive atoms and $Q(\mathbf{t})$ is a disjunctive atom, the set of all variables which occur in Q but neither in χ nor in the head of σ is $\emptyset$. The class of all finite sets of restricted weakly-linear DTGDs is denoted by* RWL.

The class of all finite sets of disjunctive Datalog rules that are also RWL is a subclass of *weakly-linear* (WL) rules, introduced in [13], where condition (ii) in Definition 1 is relaxed. It was shown that any WL disjunctive Datalog program can be rewritten to a set of non-disjunctive Datalog rules in polynomial time. We use this transformation for a proper subclass, RWL disjunctive Datalog, with a slight modification to make it suitable for establishing our distribution results. In the sequel, when we make a reference to Ξ, we are talking about this particular Datalog rewriting.[1]

To establish our distribution results, we need some conditions/assumptions. First, we assume that the given DTGDs are under a restricted syntax known as *normal form*. These DTGDs are composed of rules of the form (1) $B \rightarrow \exists \mathbf{z} \, H$, or (2) $\phi \rightarrow \psi$, where B and H are atoms, ϕ is a conjunction of atoms, and ψ is a disjunction of atoms. Let us denote the set of rules of the form (1) (resp. (2)) by $\Sigma_\exists$ (resp. $\Sigma_\forall$). This assumption is based on a result in [1] (cf. Prop. 2) that any DTGD set can be rewritten to the normal form while preserving certain answers for acyclic or quantifier-free CQs. From now on, a given rule set is $\Sigma = \Sigma_\exists \cup \Sigma_\forall$.

Second, we will focus on a syntactically-restricted fragment of RWL rules that are guarded. A rule set Σ is called *guarded* (G) if for each rule $\sigma \in \Sigma$, body(σ) contains an atom α such that $adom(\alpha) = adom(body(\sigma))$. We denote the set of all G rules by G.

Then, we consider the class of OMQs where a query q involves at most one disjunctive atom from the underlying $\Sigma_\forall$. Let us denote this class by (RWL ∩ G, Q), where Q is the class of queries definable by answer-guarded CQs that are either acyclic or quantifier-free. In general, it is unknown whether the problem of distribution over components for this class of OMQs is decidable. In this paper, we show that we can characterize and decide the problem of distribution over components for a subclass which we call *bidirectionally-guarded.*

---

[1] Our version of transformation Ξ is slightly different from that of [13] to make it work for our problem of deciding distribution over components. The details can be found in the full report of this work.

Definition 2. *Let* $Q = (\mathbf{S}, \Sigma = \Sigma_\forall \cup \Sigma_\exists, q) \in (\mathsf{RWL} \cap \mathsf{G}, \mathsf{Q})$ *in which* $q = \exists \mathbf{y}\phi(\mathbf{x}, \mathbf{y}) \in \mathsf{Q}$. *$Q$ is called* bidirectionally-guarded *if the output of the Ξ transformation on $\Sigma_\forall$ is guarded, or equivalently if it satisfies the following conditions:*
(1) for each rule $\chi \wedge Q(\mathbf{t}) \rightarrow \bigvee_{i=1}^{n} P_i(\mathbf{x}_i) \in \Sigma$, *we have: (i)* $var(\chi) \subseteq \bigcup_{i=1}^{n} \mathbf{x}_i$, *and*
(ii) $\exists i$ *s.t.,* $var(P_i(\mathbf{x}_i)) = var(\bigwedge_{i=1}^{n} P_i(\mathbf{x}_i))$; *(2) for each rule* $\chi \rightarrow \bigvee_{i=1}^{n} P_i(\mathbf{x}_i) \in \Sigma$,
we have: (a) $var(\chi) = \bigcup_{i=1}^{n} \mathbf{x}_i$, *and (b)* $\exists i$ *s.t.,* $var(P_i(\mathbf{x}_i)) = var(\bigwedge_{i=1}^{n} P_i(\mathbf{x}_i))$; *and*
(3) The maximum arity of all disjunctive predicates occurring in Σ is 1. We denote the set of bidirectionally-guarded queries by BG.

Note that the restriction imposed on the arity of disjunctive predicates is to ensure that the output of Ξ on $\Sigma_\forall$ is guarded. Moreover, the requirement that the rule sets in BG queries are guarded guarantee that the certain answers are preserved.[2] This condition is needed in establishing the main results of this paper.

Example 1. *Consider the rule set Σ in Introduction. It can be verified that any query* $Q = (\mathbf{S}, \Sigma, q) \in (\mathsf{RWL} \cap \mathsf{G}, \mathsf{Q})$, *where* $\Sigma = \{\sigma_1, \ldots, \sigma_7\}$, *is bidirectionally-guarded.*

Definition 2 is formulated with the goal that $\mathsf{BG} \preceq (\mathsf{RWL} \cap \mathsf{G}, \mathsf{Q})$ holds rather directly. Let DIST be the class of queries that distribute over components. We can show

Theorem 1. $\mathsf{BG} \cap \mathsf{DIST} = \mathsf{conBG}$.

4   Deciding Distributability via Rewriting

Since BG rules are by definition guarded, the complexity of checking Theorem 1 is upper bounded by that of equivalence checking of guarded fragment which is known to be in 2ExpTime [5]. In this section we show that this complexity can be reduced for a subset which we call BG^S queries, to single exponential time. A query $Q = (\mathbf{S}, \Sigma = \Sigma_\forall \cup \Sigma_\exists, q) \in \mathsf{BG}$ is in BG^S, called *singly bidirectionally-guarded* if $\Sigma_\forall$ is restricted to linear rules. This is relevant to our experiments since the ontologies we used turn out to be linear rules.

Example 2. *Let* $\Sigma_1 = \{\sigma_1, \sigma_2, \sigma_3, \sigma_4\}$ *be the first four rules of the rule set in Introduction. Then, each query* $Q = (\mathbf{S}, \Sigma_1, q) \in (\mathsf{RWL} \cap \mathsf{G}, \mathsf{Q})$ *belongs to* BG^S.

Note that as a corollary to Theorem 1, we have $\mathsf{BG}^S \cap \mathsf{DIST} = \mathsf{conBG}^S$.

For BG^S queries, we utilize UCQ-rewritability of OMQs composed of linear DTGDs with CQs [8], to realize distribution over components for BG^S queries. Our rewriting-based checking mechanism to decide $\mathsf{Dist}(Q)$ is presented in Algorithm 1, which takes as input a query $Q \in \mathsf{BG}^S$ that consists of a rule set Σ

---

[2] Guardedness here refers to the given DTGDs.

and an answer-guarded CQ q, and returns true if Q is distributable and false, otherwise. It computes a UCQ-rewriting Q' of Q. It is clear that $Q \in$ DIST if and only if $Q' \in$ DIST. In the rest of the algorithm, a mechanism to decide Dist(Q') is presented.

Algorithm 1. Checking membership of $Q \in \mathsf{BG}^S$ in DIST

Input: An OMQ $Q \in \mathcal{Q} = \mathsf{BG}^S$;
Output: Boolean value IsDistributable;

1: **procedure** Dist(Q), WHERE $Q \in \mathcal{Q}$
2: IsDistributable $\leftarrow true$; $Temp \leftarrow false$;
3: Construct the UCQ-rewriting $Q'(\mathbf{x})$ of Q;
4: **for each** $CQ\ q' = \exists \mathbf{y}(\bigwedge_{i=1}^{n} R_i(\mathbf{x}, \mathbf{y}))) \in Q'(\mathbf{x})$
5:     **for each** $D' \in co(D[q'])$, where $D[q'] = \bigwedge_{i=1}^{n} R_i(\langle \mathbf{x}, * \rangle, \langle \mathbf{y}, * \rangle)$, and $\langle v, * \rangle$ is a fresh constant;
6:         **if** $\langle \mathbf{x}, * \rangle \in Q(D')$
7:             $Temp \leftarrow true$; **break**;
8:     **if** $Temp == false$
9:         IsDistributable $\leftarrow false$; **break**;
10: **return** IsDistributable

The procedure Dist(Q) always terminates for any given $Q \in \mathcal{Q}$, since for all the given OMQs the size of rewritten UCQ is always finite [8]. Moreover, the complexity of UCQ-rewriting of linear disjunctive TGDs, which is known to be in ExpTime [11], provides an upper bound for this algorithm.

5 Experiments on OMQs Based on Linear Disjunctive TGDs

We conducted two experiments on three ontology benchmarks. The first experiment concerns the evaluation of our distributability checking algorithm and in the second, we evaluate the performance of forward chaining for distributed vs. centralized schemes. All experiments were done on a private cluster and on the Amazon EC2 platform. For this purpose, we utilized EC2 instances of type a1.2xlarge. The physical cluster is managed with VMware Fusion version 11.5.3 and a virtual cluster of 8 Virtual Machines (VMs) is provisioned to run the experiments. Each VM is located on a separate physical host and configured with 4 vCPUs, 8 GB of RAM and 128 GB of local disk. The software on each VM is 64-bit macOS Catalina.

A master-slave architecture was adopted where each slave machine runs a chase engine (for the second experiment) and the partial query results are aggregated back in the master machine to answer the query posed by any client (the first experiment). For the second experiment, we compared different statistics derived from our distributed approach, using chase engines RDFox [17] and Graal [4], against centralized approaches for query processing.

Experimented Ontologies: The first benchmark in our experiments is LUBM$_{20}^{\exists}$ [15], for which we generated instances with 100K, 500K, and 1M facts with the data generator and singled out axioms that correspond to linear rules. All manually curated queries are CQs in SPARQL 1.0 syntax. We added 30 more handcrafted queries to the available query pool. Thus, forming 50 overall OMQs up for evaluation. The second benchmark concerns linear rules from Open Biomedical Ontology (OBO) corpus [18]. For this benchmark, we ended up with 50 terminating linear ontologies for which we handcrafted acyclic CQs and created an initial database for each. The last benchmark is MOWLCorp corpus [16], which was selected for evaluations on linear disjunctive rules. For the last two corpora, our selected ontologies were those for which the number of their existential axioms was 10. This gives us 41 and 73 linear ontologies from a total of 125 and 132 ontologies from OBO and MOWLCorp corpora, respectively.

For each considered ontology, we perform standard transformation to extract the corresponding DTGDs.[3] For each OMQ $Q = (\mathbf{S}, \Sigma, q)$ as constructed above and targeted query q, we perform the following tasks: (i) acyclicity checking of Σ and q; (ii) membership checking about whether it belongs to BG^S, (iii) checking whether it is distributable, and (iv) distributed reasoning with it.

For testing the acyclicity conditions for the rule sets, following [8], we replace all occurrences of $\vee$ with $\wedge$, and check rules for membership in WA [9] and aGRD [3].

To check whether Q belongs to BG^S (for the MOWLCorp corpus), we first find the normalized form for the given rule set. Then, we apply our implementation of transformation Ξ on the resulting rule set. Finally we check the conditions for BG^S, manually, on the transformed OMQ. We implemented a module to track dependencies of Σ to output disjunctive atoms. Also, while ensuring all CQs involve at most one occurrence of these atoms, we check acyclicity of CQs manually or handcraft them to be acyclic.

For (iii), we perform UCQ-rewriting of $\Xi(\Sigma)$. We then apply Algorithm 1 on Q as a decision module for distributability checking on the master machine for both BG^S queries as well as those consisting of only linear TGDs. We use *pure* [14] for UCQ-rewriting of both query types as above. For (iv), for each distributable query $Q = (\mathbf{S}, \Sigma, q)$ from step (iii), we perform chase experiments on $\Xi(\Sigma)$, as depicted in Table 2.

After preprocessing and acyclicity checking, for the collection of ontologies from the MOWLCorp, 10 were found to be terminating under tested acyclicity conditions, for each of which we handcrafted 10 acyclic CQs and an initial database for each OMQ was considered. Thus, overall, 100 OMQs were tested from the last corpus.

Table 1 shows statistics on distributability checking of the considered corpora. Overall, 50 linear OMQs from the LUBM$_{20}^{\exists}$ benchmark suite have been tested for distributability and 37 (74%) of them satisfied distributability condition of Algorithm 1 and the other 13 did not. For the OBO ontology benchmark, the same number were considered for distributability checking and 42 (84%) satisfied

---

[3] We refer to [12] for details on this standard normalization procedure. Our normalized forms follow their Table 1, but with an additional form $A_1 \sqcap \cdots \sqcap A_n \sqsubseteq B_1 \sqcup \cdots \sqcup B_m$.

Table 1. Statistical results for distributability membership checking

Ontology	# Total OMQs	# Dist. OMQs	Avg. dist. checking time (s)	Avg. query rewriting time (s)
$LUBM_{20}^{\exists}$	50	37	31.5	25.3
OBO	50	42	56.6	43.3
MOWLCorp	100	40	63.2	29.9

this condition. Furthermore, among 100 OMQs considered from the MOWLCorp corpus, we found 60 (60%) that belong to BG^S. Of these OMQs, 40 (67%) passed the distributability test of Algorithm 1 which form 40% of the total number of considered OMQs for this corpus.

The second experiment is conducted over distributable queries. Given a database D which is the result of transforming the input RDF store, the number of components of D for each $Q \in DIST$ gives us the number of cluster machines needed for evaluation. At each node i, we deployed Graal and RDFox chase engines to compute the chase of the ith component of D and rules in parallel, using the skolem and the restricted variants of chase respectively. All the results of local computations are sent and aggregated at the master node. Table 2 gives the statistics related to this operation (including comparisons of the chase performance for centralized and distributed schemes as described above) for these two chase engines regarding the evaluation time on the master node for the considered OMQs.

Table 2. Statistics of distributed vs. centralized chase schemes

Ontologies	Centr. (s)				Distr. (s)				Avg. # components
	RDFox		Graal		RDFox		Graal		
	Restr.	Sk.	Restr.	Sk.	Restr.	Sk.	Restr.	Sk.	
$LUBM_{20}^{\exists}$	65.2	72.3	2375.8	2450.2	24.9	26.7	338.0	343.1	8
OBO	261.4	264.3	4223.0	4264.4	75.1	77.8	904.9	903.4	5
MOWLCorp	342.4	351.6	4237.0	4243.9	58.2	63.7	631.5	640.0	4

6   Conclusion

In this paper we studied distributed reasoning for a class of disjunctive TGDs we introduced as restricted weakly-linear disjunctive TGDs. We discovered sufficient conditions for OMQs based on these dependencies to be distributable over connected database components. We showed experimentally that query answering using state-of-the-art chase engines can be significantly improved in selected ontology benchmarks for distributable ontology-mediated queries. The results of this paper can benefit chase-based and rewriting-based query answering approaches alike.

References

1. Ahmetaj, S., Ortiz, M., Simkus, M.: Rewriting guarded existential rules into small datalog programs. In: Proceedings of the ICDT-18 (2018)
2. Ameloot, T.J., Ketsman, B., Neven, F., Zinn, D.: Datalog queries distributing over components. ACM Trans. Comput. Logic (TOCL) $18(1)$, 5 (2017)
3. Baget, J.-F.: Improving the forward chaining algorithm for conceptual graphs rules. In: Proceedings of the KR-04, vol. 4, pp. 407–414 (2004)
4. Baget, J.-F., Leclère, M., Mugnier, M.-L., Rocher, S., Sipieter, C.: Graal: a toolkit for query answering with existential rules. In: Bassiliades, N., Gottlob, G., Sadri, F., Paschke, A., Roman, D. (eds.) RuleML 2015. LNCS, vol. 9202, pp. 328–344. Springer, Cham (2015). https://doi.org/10.1007/978-3-319-21542-6_21
5. Bárány, V., Ten Cate, B., Segoufin, L.: Guarded negation. J. ACM $62(3)$, 22 (2015)
6. Berger, G., Pieris, A.: Ontology-mediated queries distributing over components. In: Proceedings of the IJCAI 2016, pp. 943–949 (2016)
7. Bienvenu, M., Ten Cate, B., Lutz, C., Wolter, F.: Ontology-based data access: a study through disjunctive datalog, CSP, and MMSNP. ACM TODS $39(4)$, 33 (2014)
8. Bourhis, P., Manna, M., Morak, M., Pieris, A.: Guarded-based disjunctive tuple-generating dependencies. ACM TODS $41(4)$, 27 (2016)
9. Fagin, R., Kolaitis, P.G., Miller, R.J., Popa, L.: Data exchange: semantics and query answering. In: Calvanese, D., Lenzerini, M., Motwani, R. (eds.) ICDT 2003. LNCS, vol. 2572, pp. 207–224. Springer, Heidelberg (2003). https://doi.org/10.1007/3-540-36285-1_14
10. Gottlob, G., Leone, N., Scarcello, F.: The complexity of acyclic conjunctive queries. J. ACM $48(3)$, 431–498 (2001)
11. Gottlob, G., Manna, M., Morak, M., Pieris, A.: On the complexity of ontological reasoning under disjunctive existential rules. In: Rovan, B., Sassone, V., Widmayer, P. (eds.) MFCS 2012. LNCS, vol. 7464, pp. 1–18. Springer, Heidelberg (2012). https://doi.org/10.1007/978-3-642-32589-2_1
12. Grau, B.C., Motik, B., Stoilos, G., Horrocks, I.: Computing datalog rewritings beyond horn ontologies. In: Proceedings of the AAAI 2013 (2013)
13. Kaminski, M., Nenov, Y., Grau, B.C.: Datalog rewritability of disjunctive datalog programs and its applications to ontology reasoning. In: Proceedings of the AAAI 2014 (2014)
14. König, M., Leclère, M., Mugnier, M.-L., Thomazo, M.: Sound, complete and minimal UCQ-rewriting for existential rules. Semant. Web $6(5)$, 451–475 (2015)
15. Lutz, C., Seylan, İ., Toman, D., Wolter, F.: The combined approach to OBDA: taming role hierarchies using filters. In: Alani, H., et al. (eds.) ISWC 2013. LNCS, vol. 8218, pp. 314–330. Springer, Heidelberg (2013). https://doi.org/10.1007/978-3-642-41335-3_20
16. Matentzoglu, N., Parsia, B.: The Manchester OWL Corpus (MOWLCorp), original serialisation, July 2014

17. Motik, B., Nenov, Y., Piro, R., Horrocks, I., Olteanu, D.: Parallel materialisation of datalog programs in centralised, main-memory RDF systems. In: AAAI 2014 (2014)
18. Smith, B., et al.: The OBO foundry: coordinated evolution of ontologies to support biomedical data integration. Nat. Biotechnol. **25**(11), 1251 (2007)

Symbolic Similarity Relations for Tuning Fully Integrated Fuzzy Logic Programs

Ginés Moreno[✉] and José A. Riaza

Department of Computing Systems, UCLM, 02071 Albacete, Spain
{Gines.Moreno,JoseAntonio.Riaza}@uclm.es

Abstract. Inspired by our previous experiences in the design of fuzzy logic languages not dealing yet with similarity relations, in this work we introduce a symbolic extension of FASILL (acronym of "Fuzzy Aggregators and Similarity Into a Logic Language"). Since one of the most difficult tasks when specifying a fuzzy logic program is determining the right weights/connectives used in the rules and the similarity relation of FASILL programs, our technique is able to symbolically execute them with unknown parameters, so that the user can guess the impact of their possible values in further developments. Then, it is possible to automatically tune such programs by appropriately substituting (with the concrete values that best satisfy the user's preferences) the symbolic constants appearing in their program rules and similarity relations.

Keywords: Fuzzy logic programs · Similarity · Symbolic execution · Tuning

1 Introduction

In essence, Bousi∼Prolog [3] and MALP [5] represent two different ways for introducing fuzzy constructs in the logic language Prolog by embedding similarity relations or using fuzzy connectives for dealing with truth degrees beyond {*true*, *false*}, respectively. We have recently combined both approaches in the design of FASILL [1] (acronym of "*Fuzzy Aggregators and Similarity Into a Logic Language*"), whose symbolic extension, called sFASILL and inspired by our initial experiences with MALP described in [6,7][1], constitutes the kernel of this paper. Once defined both the syntax and the operational semantics of sFASILL, it is possible to apply our empowered tuning technique (coping now with similarity relations) that we are developing at https://dectau.uclm.es/fasill/sandbox.

---

[1] Although there exist other approaches somehow connected with our preliminary works [6,7], in the sense that they are also able to *tune* fuzzy operators [10–12], none of them manage similarity relations as our current work does.

This work has been partially supported by the EU (FEDER), the State Research Agency (AEI) and the Spanish *Ministerio de Economía y Competitividad* under grants TIN2016-76843-C4-2-R and PID2019-104735RB-C42 (AEI/FEDER, UE).

© Springer Nature Switzerland AG 2020
V. Gutiérrez-Basulto et al. (Eds.): RuleML+RR 2020, LNCS 12173, pp. 150–158, 2020.
https://doi.org/10.1007/978-3-030-57977-7_11

In this work, given a complete lattice L, we consider a first order language $\mathcal{L}_L$ built upon a signature Σ_L, that contains the elements of a countably infinite set of variables $\mathcal{V}$, function and predicate symbols (denoted by $\mathcal{F}$ and Π, respectively) with an associated arity—usually expressed as pairs f/n or p/n, respectively, where n represents its arity—, and the truth degree literals Σ_L^T and connectives Σ_L^C from L. Therefore, a well-formed formula in $\mathcal{L}_L$ can be either:

- A *value* $v \in \Sigma_L^T$, which will be interpreted as itself, i.e., as the truth degree $v \in L$.
- $p(t_1, \ldots, t_n)$, if $t_1, \ldots, t_n$ are terms over $\mathcal{V} \cup \mathcal{F}$ and p/n is an n-ary predicate. This formula is called *atomic* (atom, for short).
- $\varsigma(e_1, \ldots, e_n)$, if $e_1, \ldots, e_n$ are well-formed formulas and ς is an n-ary connective with truth function $[\![\varsigma]\!] : L^n \mapsto L$.

Definition 1 (Complete Lattice). *A complete lattice is a partially ordered set $(L, \leq)$ such that every subset S of L has infimum and supremum elements. Then, it is a bounded lattice, i.e., it has bottom and top elements, denoted by $\bot$ and $\top$, respectively.*

Example 1. In this paper we use the lattice $([0,1], \leq)$, where $\leq$ is the usual ordering relation on real numbers, and three sets of conjunctions/disjunctions corresponding to the fuzzy logics of Gödel, Łukasiewicz and Product (with different capabilities for modelling *pessimistic*, *optimistic* and *realistic scenarios*). It is possible to include also other fuzzy connectives (aggregators) like the arithmetical average $@_{\mathtt{aver}}(x, y) \triangleq (x + y)/2$ or the linguistic modifier $@_{\mathtt{very}}(x) \triangleq x^2$.

As usual, a *substitution* σ is a mapping from variables from $\mathcal{V}$ to terms over $\mathcal{V} \cup \mathcal{F}$ such that $Dom(\sigma) = \{x \in \mathcal{V} \mid x \neq \sigma(x)\}$ is its domain. Substitutions are usually denoted by sets of mappings like, $\{x_1/t_1, \ldots, x_n/t_n\}$, being $id = \{\}$ the identity substitution. Substitutions are extended to morphisms from terms to terms in a natural way. The composition of substitutions is denoted by juxtaposition, i.e., $\sigma\theta$ denotes a substitution δ such that $\delta(x) = \theta(\sigma(x))$ for all $x \in \mathcal{V}$.

Definition 2 (Similarity Relation). *Given a domain $\mathcal{U}$ and a lattice L with a fixed t-norm $\wedge$, a similarity relation $\mathcal{R}$ is a fuzzy binary relation on $\mathcal{U}$, that is, a fuzzy subset on $\mathcal{U} \times \mathcal{U}$ (namely, a mapping $\mathcal{R} : \mathcal{U} \times \mathcal{U} \to L$) fulfilling the following properties: reflexive $\forall x \in \mathcal{U}, \mathcal{R}(x, x) = \top$, symmetric $\forall x, y \in \mathcal{U}, \mathcal{R}(x, y) = \mathcal{R}(y, x)$, and transitive $\forall x, y, z \in \mathcal{U}, \mathcal{R}(x, z) \geq \mathcal{R}(x, y) \wedge \mathcal{R}(y, z)$.*

The structure of this paper is as follows. The mathematical concepts introduced so far will be used in Sect. 2 for describing the FASILL language and presenting its symbolic extension. Next, in Sect. 3 we adapt the original operational semantics to the symbolic language sFASILL for running and tuning programs. Finally, in Sect. 4 we conclude and propose some future work.

2 The FASILL Language and Its Symbolic Extension

The fuzzy logic language FASILL relies on complete lattices and similarity relations [1]. We are now ready for summarizing its *symbolic* extension where, in essence, we allow some undefined values (truth degrees) and connectives in program rules as well as in the associated similarity relation, so that these elements can be systematically computed afterwards. The symbolic extension of FASILL defined in this paper is called sFASILL.

Here, given a complete lattice L, we consider an augmented signature $\Sigma_L^\#$ producing an augmented language $\mathcal{L}_L^\# \supseteq \mathcal{L}_L$ which may also include a number of symbolic values and symbolic connectives which do not belong to L. Symbolic objects are usually denoted as $o^\#$ with a superscript $\#$ and, in our tool, their identifiers always start with $\#$. An $L^\#$-*expression* is now a well-formed formula of $\mathcal{L}_L^\#$ which is composed by values and connectives from L as well as by symbolic values and connectives. We let $\exp_L^\#$ denote the set of all $L^\#$-expressions in $\mathcal{L}_L^\#$.

Given a $L^\#$-expression E, $[\![E]\!] = E'$ refers to the new $L^\#$-expression obtained after evaluating as much as possible the connectives in E. Particularly, if E does not contain any symbolic value or connective, then $[\![E]\!] = v \in L$. In order to simplify the resulting $L^\#$-expressions, we can take advantage of some properties of the connectives of L like $\top \& x = x \& \top = x$, $\bot \mid x = x \mid \bot = x$ or $\sup\{x, \bot\} = \sup\{\bot, x\} = x$, for all $x \in L$.

In the following we consider *symbolic substitutions* that are mappings from symbolic values and connectives to expressions over $\Sigma_L^T \cup \Sigma_L^C$. We let $\mathsf{sym}(o^\#)$ denote the symbolic values and connectives in $o^\#$. Given a symbolic substitution Θ for $\mathsf{sym}(o^\#)$, we denote by $o^\#\Theta$ the object that results from $o^\#$ by replacing every symbolic symbol $e^\#$ by $e^\#\Theta$.

Definition 3 (Symbolic Similarity Relation). *Given a domain $\mathcal{U}$ and a lattice L with a fixed—possibly symbolic—t-norm $\wedge$, a symbolic similarity relation is a mapping $\mathcal{R}^\# : \mathcal{U} \times \mathcal{U} \to \exp_L^\#$ such that, for any symbolic substitution Θ for $\mathsf{sym}(\mathcal{R}^\#)$, the result of fully evaluating all L-expressions in $\mathcal{R}^\#\Theta$, say $[\![\mathcal{R}^\#\Theta]\!]$, is a similarity relation.*

Definition 4 (Symbolic Rule and Symbolic Program). *Let L be a complete lattice. A symbolic rule over L is a formula $A \leftarrow \mathcal{B}$, where the following conditions hold:*

- *A is an atomic formula of $\mathcal{L}_L$ (the head of the rule);*
- *$\leftarrow$ is an implication from L or a symbolic implication;*
- *$\mathcal{B}$ (the body of the rule) is a symbolic goal, i.e., a well-formed formula of $\mathcal{L}_L^\#$;*

A sFASILL program is a tuple $\mathcal{P}^\# = \langle \Pi^\#, \mathcal{R}^\#, L \rangle$ where $\Pi^\#$ is a set of symbolic rules, $\mathcal{R}^\#$ is a symbolic similarity relation between the elements of the signature Σ of $\Pi^\#$, and L is a complete lattice.

Example 2. Consider a symbolic sFASILL program $\mathcal{P}^\# = \langle \Pi^\#, \mathcal{R}^\#, L \rangle$ based on lattice $L = ([0, 1], \leq)$, and the following set of symbolic rules $\Pi^\#$ and symbolic similarity relation $\mathcal{R}^\#$ (expressed as a graph –or a matrix – on $\mathcal{U} = \{vanguardist, elegant, modern, metro, taxi, bus\}$):

$$\Pi^{\#} = \begin{cases} R_1 : vanguardist(rizt) & \leftarrow 0.9 \\ R_2 : elegant(hydropolis) & \leftarrow s_3^{\#} \\ R_3 : close(hydropolis, taxi) \leftarrow 0.7 \\ R_4 : good\_hotel(x) & \leftarrow @_{s4}^{\#}(elegant(x), @_{very}(close(x, metro))) \end{cases}$$

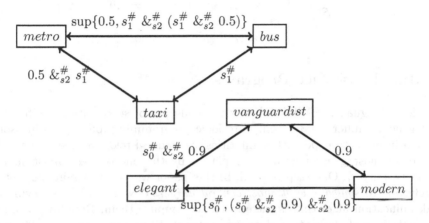

where $\&_{s2}^{\#}$ is a symbolic t-norm for the symbolic similarity relation $\mathcal{R}^{\#}$.

Given that Definition 3 seems to be quite demanding in order to design valid symbolic similarity relations, we present a method for achieving this goal in a simple and safe way, starting from an initial set of *symbolic similarity equations*.

Definition 5 (Symbolic Similarity Scheme). *Given a domain $\mathcal{U}$ and a lattice L, a symbolic similarity scheme $\mathcal{S}^{\#}$ is a set of equations $x \sim y = v$, where $x, y \in \mathcal{U}$ and v is an $L^{\#}$-expression.*

The closure of a symbolic similarity scheme is performed by the following algorithm inspired by [2,4,9] which, in essence, is an adaptation of the classical Warshall's algorithm for computing transitive closures.

Definition 6 (Algorithm for closure of a symbolic similarity scheme).
Input: *a domain $\mathcal{U}$, a lattice L with a fixed t-norm $\wedge$, and a symbolic similarity scheme $\mathcal{S}^{\#}$.*
Output: *a symbolic similarity relation $\mathcal{R}^{\#} : \mathcal{U} \times \mathcal{U} \to L$.*

1. *Start with a symbolic relation* $\mathcal{R}^{\#}(x, y) = \begin{cases} \top & if \ x = y \\ v & if \ (x \sim y = v) \in \mathcal{S}^{\#} \ ; \\ \bot & otherwise \end{cases}$
2. *For each $x, y \in \mathcal{U}$, set $\mathcal{R}^{\#}(x, y) = \llbracket \sup \{\mathcal{R}^{\#}(x, y), \mathcal{R}^{\#}(y, x)\} \rrbracket$;*
3. *Then, for each $x, y \in \mathcal{U}$, set $\mathcal{R}^{\#}(x, y) = \llbracket \sup_{\forall z \in \mathcal{U}} \{\mathcal{R}^{\#}(x, z) \wedge \mathcal{R}^{\#}(z, y)\} \rrbracket$;*
4. *Finally, return the symbolic similarity relation $\mathcal{R}^{\#}$.*

Example 3. Consider the symbolic similarity relation $\mathcal{R}^{\#}$ of Example 2 on $\mathcal{U} = \{vanguardist, elegant, modern, metro, taxi, bus\}$. The closure of the following symbolic similarity scheme $\mathcal{S}^{\#}$ with a symbolic t-norm $\&_{s2}^{\#}$ produces the symbolic similarity relation $\mathcal{R}^{\#}$:

$$\mathcal{S}^{\#} = \begin{cases} elegant \sim modern & = s_0^{\#} \\ modern \sim vanguardist & = 0.9 \\ metro \sim bus & = 0.5 \\ bus \sim taxi & = s_1^{\#} \end{cases}$$

3   Running sFASILL Programs

As a logic language, sFASILL inherits the concepts of substitution, unifier and most general unifier (*mgu*) from pure logic programming, but extending some of them in order to cope with similarities, as Bousi~Prolog [3] does, where the concept of most general unifier is replaced by the one of *weak most general unifier* (w.m.g.u.). One step beyond, in this paper we extend again this notion by referring to *symbolic weak most general unifiers* (s.w.m.g.u.) and a symbolic weak unification algorithm is introduced to compute them. Roughly speaking, the *symbolic weak unification algorithm* states that two *expressions* (i.e, terms or atomic formulas) $f(t_1, \ldots, t_n)$ and $g(s_1, \ldots, s_n)$ weakly unify if the root symbols f and g are close with a certain—possibly symbolic—degree (i.e. $\mathcal{R}^{\#}(f, g) = r \neq \perp$) and each of their arguments t_i and s_i weakly unify.

More technically, the symbolic weak unification algorithm we are going to use, can be seen as an reformulation/extension of the ones appearing in [13] (since now we manage arbitrary complete lattices) and [1,3] (because now we deal with symbolic similarity relations). We formalize it as a transition system supported by a symbolic similarity-based unification relation "⇒". The unification of the expressions $\mathcal{E}_1$ and $\mathcal{E}_2$ is obtained by a state transformation sequence starting from an initial state $\langle G \equiv \{\mathcal{E}_1 \approx \mathcal{E}_2\}, id, \alpha_0 \rangle$, where id is the identity substitution and $\alpha_0 = \top$ is the supreme of $(L, \leq)$: $\langle G, id, \alpha_0 \rangle \Rightarrow \langle G_1, \theta_1, \alpha_1 \rangle \Rightarrow \cdots \Rightarrow \langle G_n, \theta_n, \alpha_n \rangle$. When the final state $\langle G_n, \theta_n, \alpha_n \rangle$, with $G_n = \emptyset$, is reached (i.e., the equations in the initial state have been solved), the expressions $\mathcal{E}_1$ and $\mathcal{E}_2$ are unifiable by symbolic similarity with s.w.m.g.u. θ_n and *symbolic unification degree* α_n, where α_n is a $\mathcal{L}^{\#}$-expression (instead of a value, in contrast to [1,3,13]). Therefore, the final state $\langle \emptyset, \theta_n, \alpha_n \rangle$ signals out the unification success. On the other hand, when expressions $\mathcal{E}_1$ and $\mathcal{E}_2$ are not unifiable, the state transformation sequence ends with failure (i.e., $G_n = Fail$).

The *symbolic similarity-based unification relation*, "⇒", is defined as the smallest relation derived by the following set of transition rules (where $Var(t)$ denotes the set of variables of a given term t).

$$\frac{\langle\{f(t_1,\ldots,t_n)\approx g(s_1,\ldots,s_n)\}\cup E,\theta,r_1\rangle \qquad \mathcal{R}^{\#}(f,g)=r_2\neq\bot}{\langle\{t_1\approx s_1,\ldots,t_n\approx s_n\}\cup E,\theta,r_1\wedge r_2\rangle}\ 1$$

$$\frac{\langle\{X\approx X\}\cup E,\theta,r_1\rangle}{\langle E,\theta,r_1\rangle}\ 2 \qquad \frac{\langle\{X\approx t\}\cup E,\theta,r_1\rangle \quad X\notin Var(t)}{\langle(E)\{X/t\},\theta\{X/t\},r_1\rangle}\ 3$$

$$\frac{\langle\{t\approx X\}\cup E,\theta,r_1\rangle}{\langle\{X\approx t\}\cup E,\theta,r_1\rangle}\ 4 \qquad \frac{\langle\{X\approx t\}\cup E,\theta,r_1\rangle \quad X\in Var(t)}{\langle Fail,\theta,r_1\rangle}\ 5$$

$$\frac{\langle\{f(t_1,\ldots,t_n)\approx g(s_1,\ldots,s_n)\}\cup E,\theta,r_1\rangle \qquad \mathcal{R}^{\#}(f,g)=\bot}{\langle Fail,\theta,r_1\rangle}\ 6$$

Rule 1 decomposes two expressions and annotates the relation between the function (or predicate) symbols at their root. The second rule eliminates spurious information and the fourth rule interchanges the position of the symbols to be handled by other rules. The third and fifth rules perform an occur check of variable X in a term t. In case of success, it generates a substitution $\{X/t\}$; otherwise the algorithm ends with failure. It can also end with failure if the relation between function (or predicate) symbols in $\mathcal{R}^{\#}$ is $\bot$, as stated by Rule 6.

Usually, given two expressions $\mathcal{E}_1$ and $\mathcal{E}_2$, if there is a successful transition sequence, $\langle\{\mathcal{E}_1\approx\mathcal{E}_2\},id,\top\rangle\Rightarrow^{\star}\langle\emptyset,\theta,E\rangle$, then we write that $wmgu^{\#}(\mathcal{E}_1,\mathcal{E}_2)=\langle\theta,E\rangle$, being θ the *symbolic weak most general unifier* of $\mathcal{E}_1$ and $\mathcal{E}_2$, and E is their *symbolic unification degree*.

Example 4. Given the complete lattice $L=([0,1],\leq)$ of Example 1 and the symbolic similarity relation $\mathcal{R}^{\#}$ of Example 2, two different symbolic weak unification processes, using a symbolic t-norm $\&_{s2}^{\#}$, are:

$$\langle\{modern(taxi)\approx vanguardist(bus)\},id,1\rangle \overset{\text{Rule }1}{\Longrightarrow} \langle\{taxi\approx bus\},id,0.9\rangle$$
$$\overset{\text{Rule }1}{\Longrightarrow} \langle\{\},id,0.9\ \&_{s2}^{\#}\ s_1^{\#}\rangle$$

$$\langle\{close\_to(X,taxi)\approx close\_to(ritz,busbus)\},id,1\rangle \overset{\text{Rule }1}{\Longrightarrow} \langle\{X\approx ritz,taxi\approx bus\},id,1\rangle$$
$$\overset{\text{Rule }3}{\Longrightarrow} \langle\{taxi\approx bus\},\{X/ritz\},1\rangle \overset{\text{Rule }1}{\Longrightarrow} \langle\{\},\{X/ritz\},s_1^{\#}\rangle$$

In order to describe the procedural semantics of the sFASILL language, in the following we denote by $\mathcal{C}[A]$ a formula where A is a sub-expression (usually an atom) which occurs in the –possibly empty– context $\mathcal{C}[]$ whereas $\mathcal{C}[A/A']$ means the replacement of A by A' in the context $\mathcal{C}[]$. Moreover, $Var(s)$ denotes the set of distinct variables occurring in the syntactic object s and $\theta[Var(s)]$ refers to the substitution obtained from θ by restricting its domain to $Var(s)$. In the next definition, we always consider that A is the selected atom in a goal $\mathcal{Q}$, L is the complete lattice associated to $\Pi^{\#}$ and, as usual, rules are renamed apart:

Definition 7 (Computational Step). *Let $\mathcal{Q}$ be a goal and σ a substitution. The pair $\langle\mathcal{Q};\sigma\rangle$ is a state. Given a symbolic program $\langle\Pi^{\#},\mathcal{R}^{\#},L\rangle$ and a (possibly symbolic) t-norm $\wedge$ in L, a computation is formalized as a state transition* *system, whose transition relation $\leadsto$ is the smallest relation satisfying these rules*

1) Successful step *(denoted as $\overset{SS}{\leadsto}$):*

$$\frac{\langle \mathcal{Q}[A], \sigma \rangle \qquad A' \leftarrow \mathcal{B} \in \Pi^{\#} \qquad wmgu^{\#}(A, A') = \langle \theta, E \rangle \qquad E \neq \bot}{\langle \mathcal{Q}[A/E \wedge \mathcal{B}]\theta, \sigma\theta \rangle} \; \text{SS}$$

2) Failure step *(denoted as $\overset{FS}{\leadsto}$):*

$$\frac{\langle \mathcal{Q}[A], \sigma \rangle \qquad \nexists A' \leftarrow \mathcal{B} \in \Pi^{\#} : wmgu^{\#}(A, A') = \langle \theta, E \rangle}{\langle \mathcal{Q}[A/\bot], \sigma \rangle} \; \text{FS}$$

3) Interpretive step *(denoted as $\overset{IS}{\leadsto}$):*

$$\frac{\langle \mathcal{Q}; \sigma \rangle \text{ where } \mathcal{Q} \text{ is a } L^{\#}\text{-expression}}{\langle [\![\mathcal{Q}]\!]; \sigma \rangle} \; \text{IS}$$

Definition 8 (Derivation and Symbolic Fuzzy Computed Answer). *A derivation is a sequence of arbitrary length $\langle \mathcal{Q}; id \rangle \leadsto^* \langle \mathcal{Q}'; \sigma \rangle$. When $\mathcal{Q}'$ is an $L^{\#}$-expression that cannot be further reduced, $\langle \mathcal{Q}'; \sigma' \rangle$, where $\sigma' = \sigma[Var(Q)]$, is called a symbolic fuzzy computed answer (sfca). Also, if $\mathcal{Q}'$ is a concrete value of L, we say that $\langle \mathcal{Q}'; \sigma' \rangle$ is a fuzzy computed answer (fca).*

The following example illustrates the operational semantics of sFASILL.

Example 5. Let $\mathcal{P}^{\#} = \langle \Pi^{\#}, \mathcal{R}^{\#}, L \rangle$ be the program from Example 2. It is possible to perform this derivation with sfca $\langle \mathcal{Q}_1; \sigma_1 \rangle = \langle @_{s3}^{\#}(0.6 \;\&_{s2}^{\#}\; s_2^{\#}, 0), \{x/ritz\}\rangle$ for $\mathcal{P}^{\#}$ and goal $\mathcal{Q} = good\_hotel(x)$:

$$
\begin{aligned}
&\langle good\_hotel(x), id \rangle && \overset{SS}{\leadsto}{}^{R4} \\
&\langle @_{s4}^{\#}(elegant(x_1), @_{very}(close(x_1, metro))), \{x/x_1\}\rangle && \overset{SS}{\leadsto}{}^{R2} \\
&\langle @_{s4}^{\#}(s_3^{\#}, @_{very}(close(ritz, metro))), \{x/ritz\}\rangle && \overset{FS}{\leadsto} \\
&\langle @_{s4}^{\#}(s_3^{\#}, @_{very}(0)), \{x/ritz\}\rangle && \overset{IS}{\leadsto} \\
&\langle @_{s4}^{\#}(s_3^{\#}, 0), \{x/ritz\}\rangle
\end{aligned}
$$

Apart from this derivation, there exists a second one ending with the alternative sfca $\langle \mathcal{Q}_2; \sigma_2 \rangle = \langle @_{s4}^{\#}((s_0^{\#} \;\&_{s2}^{\#}\; 0.9) \;\&_{godel}\; 0.9, @_{very}((0.5 \;\&_{s2}^{\#}\; s_1^{\#}) \;\&_{godel}\; 0.7)),$ $\{x/hydropolis\}\rangle$ associated to the same goal (observe the presence of symbolic constants coming from the symbolic similarity relation, which were not allowed in our precedent works [6,7]):

$$\langle good\_hotel(x), id \rangle \qquad\qquad \underset{\rightsquigarrow}{\text{SS}}\ ^{R4}$$

$$\langle @_{s4}^{\#}(elegant(x_1), @_{very}(close(x_1, metro))), \{x/x_1\} \rangle \qquad \underset{\rightsquigarrow}{\text{SS}}\ ^{R1}$$

$$\langle @_{s4}^{\#}((s_0^{\#} \ \&_{s2}^{\#}\ 0.9)\ \&_{godel}\ 0.9, @_{very}(close(hydropolis, metro))), \{x/hydro...\} \rangle \quad \underset{\rightsquigarrow}{\text{SS}}\ ^{R3}$$

$$\langle @_{s4}^{\#}((s_0^{\#} \ \&_{s2}^{\#}\ 0.9)\ \&_{godel}\ 0.9, @_{very}((0.5\ \&_{s2}^{\#}\ s_1^{\#})\ \&_{godel}\ 0.7)), \{x/hydro...\} \rangle$$

Now, let $\Theta = \{s_0^{\#}/0.8, s_1^{\#}/0.8, \&_{s2}^{\#}/\&_{luka}, s_3^{\#}/1.0, @_{s4}^{\#}/@_{aver}\}$ be a symbolic substitution that can be used for instantiating the previous sFASILL program in order to obtain a non-symbolic, fully executable FASILL program. This substitution can be obtained by our tuning tool after introducing a couple of test cases (namely, $0.4->$ good_hotel(hydropolis) and $0.6->$ good_hotel(ritz)) representing the desired degrees for two goals, according the user preferences.

4   Conclusions and Future Work

The symbolic extension of the FASILL language designed in this paper is based on symbolic similarity relations useful for designing tuning techniques (beyond our preliminary versions dealing with MALP programs presented in [6,7]) intended to substitute symbolic values/connectives that best fit a set of test cases provided by users a priori.

In the future we plan to improve the efficiency of our approach by using the thresholded operational semantics defined in [1] as well as SAT/SMT solvers in the line of [8].

References

1. Julián Iranzo, P., Moreno, G., Penabad, J.: Thresholded semantic framework for a fully integrated fuzzy logic language. J. Log. Algebr. Meth. Program. **93**, 42–67 (2017)
2. Julián-Iranzo, P.: A procedure for the construction of a similarity relation. In: Proceedings of the 12th International Conference on Information Processing and Management of Uncertainty in Knoledge-based Systems (IPMU 2008), 22–27 June, Torremolinos (Málaga), Spain, pp. 489–496. U. Málaga (ISBN 978-84-612-3061-7) (2008)
3. Julián-Iranzo, P., Rubio-Manzano, C.: A declarative semantics for bousi~prolog. In: Proceedings of 11th International ACM SIGPLAN Conference on Principles and Practice of Declarative Programming, PPDP 2009, Coimbra, Portugal, pp. 149–160. ACM (2009)
4. Kandel, A., Yelowitz, L.: Fuzzy chains. IEEE Trans. Syst. Man Cybern. SMC **4**(5), 472–475 (1974)
5. Medina, J., Ojeda-Aciego, M., Vojtáš, P.: Similarity-based Unification: a multiadjoint approach. Fuzzy Sets Syst. **146**, 43–62 (2004)
6. Moreno, G., Penabad, J., Riaza, J.A., Vidal, G.: Symbolic execution and thresholding for efficiently tuning fuzzy logic programs. In: Hermenegildo, M.V., Lopez-Garcia, P. (eds.) LOPSTR 2016. LNCS, vol. 10184, pp. 131–147. Springer, Cham (2017). https://doi.org/10.1007/978-3-319-63139-4_8

7. Moreno, G., Riaza, J.A.: An online tool for tuning fuzzy logic programs. In: Costantini, S., Franconi, E., Van Woensel, W., Kontchakov, R., Sadri, F., Roman, D. (eds.) RuleML+RR 2017. LNCS, vol. 10364, pp. 184–198. Springer, Cham (2017). https://doi.org/10.1007/978-3-319-61252-2_13

8. Moreno, G., Riaza, J.A.: Using SAT/SMT solvers for efficiently tuning fuzzy logic programs. In: 2020 IEEE International Conference on Fuzzy Systems, FUZZ-IEEE 2020, Glasgow, UK, pp. 1–8. IEEE (2020). (in press)

9. Naessens, H., De Meyer, H., De Baets, B.: Algorithms for the computation of t-transitive closures. IEEE Trans. Fuzzy Syst. **10**(4), 541–551 (2002)

10. De Raedt, L., Kimmig, A.: Probabilistic (logic) programming concepts. Mach. Learn. **100**(1), 5–47 (2015). https://doi.org/10.1007/s10994-015-5494-z

11. Riguzzi, F., Swift, T.: The PITA system: tabling and answer subsumption for reasoning under uncertainty. Theory Pract. Log. Program. **11**(4–5), 433–449 (2011)

12. Sagonas, K.F., Swift, T., Warren, D.S.: XSB as an efficient deductive database engine. In: Proceedings of ACM SIGMOD International Conference on Management of Data, pp. 442–453. ACM Press (1994)

13. Sessa, M.I.: Approximate reasoning by similarity-based SLD resolution. Theoret. Comput. Sci. **275**(1–2), 389–426 (2002)

Contestable Black Boxes

Andrea Aler Tubella[1]([⊠])[iD], Andreas Theodorou[1][iD], Virginia Dignum[1][iD],
and Loizos Michael[2,3]

[1] Umeå University, Umeå, Sweden
{andrea.aler,andreas.theodorou,virginia.dignum}@umu.se
[2] Open University of Cyprus, Latsia, Cyprus
loizos@ouc.ac.cy
[3] Research Center on Interactive Media, Smart Systems, and Emerging Technologies,
Nicosia, Cyprus

Abstract. The right to contest a decision with consequences on individuals or the society is a well-established democratic right. Despite this right also being explicitly included in GDPR in reference to automated decision-making, its study seems to have received much less attention in the AI literature compared, for example, to the right for explanation. This paper investigates the type of assurances that are needed in the contesting process when algorithmic black boxes are involved, opening new questions about the interplay of contestability and explainability. We argue that specialised complementary methodologies to evaluate automated decision-making in the case of a particular decision being contested need to be developed. Further, we propose a combination of well-established software engineering and rule-based approaches as a possible socio-technical solution to the issue of contestability, one of the new democratic challenges posed by the automation of decision making.

Keywords: Right to contest · AI ethics · Explainable AI

1 Introduction

Searching for efficiency and cheaper solutions, governments and organisations are increasingly investing in automated solutions for a variety of decisions and activities, ranging from deciding on benefit claims to assessing the risk of recidivism in felons. With such life-changing determinations being treated automatically, the *right to contest* a decision must be ensured for all automated decision applications. Precisely outlining this necessity, Article 22 of the European Union's General Data Protection Regulations (GDPR) stipulates that whenever a decision which legally or significantly affects an individual relies solely on automated processing, then the right to contest the decision must be guaranteed. Similarly, although this right is not as explicitly phrased in the American law, we have already seen legal cases where the plaintiffs sued governmental organisations using algorithmic decision systems looking for accountability.

© Springer Nature Switzerland AG 2020
V. Gutiérrez-Basulto et al. (Eds.): RuleML+RR 2020, LNCS 12173, pp. 159–167, 2020.
https://doi.org/10.1007/978-3-030-57977-7_12

Complementing the current attention in the literature on *fairness, transparency, explainability* and *accountability* for automated decision-making systems, in this work we focus on *the right to contest decisions*, an aspect that has received considerably less research focus. This paper investigates the type of assurances that are needed in the contesting process when algorithmic black boxes are involved, opening new questions about the interplay of contestability and explainability. Further, we propose a combination of well-established software engineering and rule-based approaches as a possible socio-technical solution to the issue of contestability, one of the new democratic challenges posed by the automation of decision making.

2   A Right in Its Own Right

The right to contest a decision that strongly impacts an individual takes many forms. It encompasses the right of appeal allowing to ask for a court's decision to be changed and even the right to challenge the outcome of an election. Appealing is the democratic mechanism enacted to correct errors and allow for reparation. In the case of automated decision-making, this right is equally acknowledged. For example, Article 22 of GDPR explicitly states the right to contest significant decisions resulting relying solely on automated processing. Likewise, due process is a right recognised in the Anglo-American legal system, and it has been argued that individuals affected by decisions based on predictive algorithms should have similar rights to those in the legal system with respect to how their personal data is used in such adjudications, including the right to challenge them [6].

The ability to guarantee the right to contest is inextricably tied to the fundamental principles of *responsible AI* [8]: transparency, explainability and accountability. Transparency plays a crucial role in ensuring that stakeholders are aware that they are being subjected to automated decision making and that they have the right to challenge it [5]. Further, to be able to understand a decision and assess if they believe that a contest needs to be raised, stakeholders need to be given a good explanation on how that decision was reached [17]. However, general provisions for explainability and transparency are not sufficient to guarantee the right of contest: whereas explanation and transparency methodologies focus on exposing the internal logic behind an algorithm or on describing how or why a specific decision was taken [14], they do not specifically reveal whether relevant rules and regulations have been adhered to or violated and why. To base this determination on an explanation requires a thorough examination of the explanation itself in light of the legal framework, which may be open to interpretation depending on its accuracy and level of detail. In contrast, the focus of a contesting procedure is expressly to ascertain *post hoc* whether relevant rules and regulations were followed for a particular decision. Contesting therefore goes beyond the scope of explanation: it is not only the decision itself, but also the socio-legal context in which it was taken that need to be accounted for.

To effectively address the right to contest a decision, policies should openly specify the regulations and adequacy determinations for specific applications [12]. Further, if a decision is challenged and mistakes are discovered a proper attribution of accountability and effective methods of compensation are needed. For this, AI governance is necessary to ensure that any *moral responsibility* or *legal accountability* is properly appropriated by the relevant stakeholders, together with the processes that support the redressing, mitigation, and evaluation of potential harm, alongside with the means to monitor and intervene on the system's operation. These should be accompanied with pre-established procedures for when a decision is contested, allowing to determine whether the relevant stipulations were followed in a way that is not open to interpretation. Thus, we argue that specialised complementary methodologies to evaluate automated decision-making in the case of a decision being contested need to be developed.

For this reason, in the remainder of this paper we put forward a socio-technical approach to establishing a contesting procedure for automated decisions, combining well-established software engineering practices and rule-based approaches. We propose that any contestable automated system should be accompanied by a formal specification that describes in an unambiguous language the constraints that each constituent agent-module of the system needs to fulfil. This formal specification effectively corresponds to the organisation's *legal-compliance contract*, and includes all necessary legal and consumer protection requirements. When a system's decision is contested in a certain context, this is taken as a request to verify that the system indeed operated in line with its accompanying formal specification in that particular context. Verification is achieved by examining the system's (and each agent-module's intermediate) behaviour while monitoring for the violation or fulfilment of the constituent provisions of the specifications.

Since the contesting procedure is an examination of a decision already taken, software development practices that ensure *traceability* become fundamental. Furthermore, to ensure that all the relevant factors for the review of the decision are being preserved, this should be done in conjunction with standardised *elicitation* and *interpretation* processes to identify the relevant policy that the system is mandated to adhere to and to translate it into specific constraints on the system. These requirements are part of designing intelligent systems responsibly[8], and align with the push for relating high-level governance, including legal and ethical considerations, with concrete system functionalities [16].

3   Compliance Contract

We propose that any contestable automated system should be accompanied by a formal specification that describes in an unambiguous language the constraints that each constituent agent-module of the system needs to fulfil. Our proposed approach includes the following steps: 1. *norm management*, 2. *norm formalisation*, and 3. *negotiation and validation*. Each of these stages is further broken down into explicit steps, described in this section. The end-product of this process is the organisation's compliance contract, which can then be used for monitoring specific decisions in case of contest.

To illustrate our method, we will use the real-life example of Lufthansa's automated pricing algorithm, which increased prices up to 30% immediately following the bankruptcy of competitor Air Berlin [4]. Following consumer complaints of abusive monopoly, the German consumer-protection regulator, Bundeskartellamt, conducted an investigation. Lufthansa's initial response was that the algorithm acted autonomously, but Bundeskartellamt made it clear that even though Lufthansa was cleared of wrongdoing, the fact that price increases were the result of an automated algorithm had no bearing on their decision.

Norm Management. Building concrete specifications for a compliance contract starts, similarly to a 'traditional' software life cycle, with the *norm management phase*. Inspired by the *IEEE Recommended Practice for Software Requirements Specification* [1], we propose a two-step process: *elicitation* followed by *interpretation*. Each of these phases necessarily involves the participation of both the software development team and the legal department of the organisation, whose different areas of expertise will be fundamental in obtaining norms that are both implementable and legally sound.

The **elicitation stage** takes place by consulting governance, i.e. standards and legislation relevant to the system. The purpose of this stage is not to set the norms at once, but rather to identify and list the relevant policy that the system is mandated to adhere to. The produced list of rules and guidelines provide the high-level policy that not only the software deliverable itself, but also its development, deployment, and usage processes need to follow. In the case of an airline pricing system, relevant laws include the anti-monopoly and consumer-protection regulations. Moreover, laws such as non-discrimination should also be followed by the system. For example, in the case of Lufthansa's pricing algorithm, German anti-monopoly laws clearly apply.

The standard practice for setting airline ticket prices is to have similar seats divided in tiers, where each tier is in a more expensive preset price range than the previous one. The first seats sold belong to the first tier, and only when all of them are sold the more expensive seats of the second tier are made available to buy. Thus, price steadily increases as the plane fills up. In the case of a competitors' bankruptcy, airlines are not allowed to capitalise on it by imposing extreme price increases or selling only the most expensive tiers. Lufthansa was cleared from wrongdoing by demonstrating two points: (1) that only the comparatively more expensive booking tiers were available as the cheaper booking classes were imminently booked, and (2) that the price range for each tier was comparable to previous years' prices and not illegally increased. These requirements set out by Bundeskartellamt would be clearly identified at this stage, and set down as the basis for the compliance contract.

In order to interpret these rules into concrete checkable norms, abstract concepts such as *"comparable to previous years' prices"* must be turned into concrete computable requirements. Thus, the **interpretation stage** entails a translation of high-level governance and legal requirements into concrete norms specifying the constraints that the system needs to fulfil, taking into account its purpose and the context of its deployment. The resulting norms should be comprehensive enough so that fulfilling them can prove that the system is adhering to the ethical and legal policy of its developers' organisation. The shift from abstract to concrete necessarily involves careful consideration of the context identified in the previous phase. In this sense, the implementation of each requirement will vary from context to context the same way it can vary from system to system. In our simple example, an acceptable set of concrete norms that the company could set that would satisfy the consumer protection agency's concerns over the anti-monopoly regulations would be given by: (1) "cheaper tiers must be fully booked before more expensive tiers are made available" and (2) "the pricing range of a tier does not differ by more than 30% from the average price of the same tier on the same route on the same day in the previous 5 years".

Formalisation. This phase entails the formal specification of the constraints for each of the component agents. This step requires a further concretisation of the norms: they need to be formulated in a way that makes them operational and allows for the detection of violations. This requires linking the concepts contained in the rules with a rule-based language that will determine the normative framework [2]. The formal normative system obtained in this stage will constitute the organisation's proposed *compliance contract*.

An appropriate language for this purpose needs sufficient expressiveness to model the relevant legal requirements and policies, while allowing for compliance with these requirements to be monitored and tracked. Many existing approaches to norm monitoring in the MAS literature take an *enforcement* point of view, in which a monitoring system is an *observation* mechanism, that can log norm violations provided it can access the relevant information [11,15]. This mechanism is particularly developed for scenarios where each participant and component of the system has a well-defined purpose (such as buyer or seller) with clear actions available for each role (such as buy, sell, negotiate, concede) and has been successfully applied in contexts like marketplaces [13]. This type of encoding is therefore a proposed approach in this type of well-bounded scenario.

In heavily regulated scenarios, powerful expressive languages to capture the semantics of the regulations and their interactions are needed. To monitor adherence, these must be combined with a useful representation of the computation and run-time events of the decision being observed. A similar challenge is found in the case of *automated compliance checking* of business processes. Languages for automated compliance checking provide both a formalism to model and reason with regulations, and formal representations of processes [7,9]. Our proposed contesting procedure, likewise, requires monitoring adherence to regulations, but for determined and completed instances of a computation rather than for verifying adherence of processes. For this reason, we propose that automated compliance checking methods and languages could be usefully adapted to this framework.

Negotiation and Validation. This stage facilitates an open discussion of the proposed compliance contract with representatives of all groups of internal stakeholders; from product managers to software developers to the quality assurance engineers to legal experts. Where possible, external stakeholders—such as users and regulators—should also be consulted. These discussions aim to validate the norms to ensure their accurate interpretation of relevant legislation and their acceptance. The approval of the relevant regulators is particularly desirable, as their acceptance of the norms as a compliance contract entails that showing that the norms where adhered to is enough to dismiss a complaint under the grounds that the decision is fully legal. If possible, a negotiation and validation phase would occur after each phase of the process of obtaining the compliance contract, to maintain maximum transparency.

4   Examining a Contested Decision Under Monitoring

To adequately examine the original decision-taking under the compliance contract, both the inputs that the target process received and the 'state of the world' that held when the original decision was taken must be recorded. In the same vein, depending on the constraints imposed by the norms, the occurrence of certain events will need to be tracked and recorded as well. In the case of our example, knowing when a tier has been sold out, knowing which prices have been set for each tier through time and when seats from a certain tier were put on sale is indispensable to ascertain whether the criteria set by Bundeskartellamt were followed. Awareness of this trace of events is fundamental whether it is a human or an artificial agent that makes the determination of whether rules were followed. Furthermore, if the decision-taking algorithm is adaptive (for example learning from new data and adapting its behaviour) then it is the version that held at the time of the original decision that should be evaluated. Both of these challenges can be addressed with version control and thorough record keeping. Like formal specifications, version control is part of software engineering: even for machine learning approaches, advanced forms of version control including record keeping of data is recommended and increasingly used [3]. This practice ensures *traceability* and, therefore, reproducibility and auditability – as in the context of a contested decision.

The compliance contract could of course be used to check every decision for compliance with the specifications, or even to forcibly enforce adherence to norms. For example, the system could be endowed with norm-reasoning mechanisms forcing it to act upon the specified norms [10]. This could however considerably slow down the computation, and be expensive in terms of resources. Indeed, at each decision and action, the system would need to check whether a norm applies, and then how to act upon it. To assess the former, it may even need to access extraneous information about the state of the world. If an organisation is willing to pay this cost, this regimentation approach could be deployed for every decision, or perhaps for every *critical* decision as a safeguard. However, it may be preferable cost-wise to use monitoring specifically in the case of contests, and bear the cost of sanctions instead when norms have been violated.

5   Discussion and Future Work

Whenever a decision process takes place that has individual or social consequences, the right to contest the said decision is a well-established democratic right. In this paper we focused on *contestability* of decisions through the application of well-established software engineering and rule-based policy modeling techniques.

An important requirement for our proposed approach is that the norms identified in the elicitation and interpretation stages should be captured accurately in a computational language that can be used for specification and automated monitoring. If the normative framework is very complex, such as cases where great knowledge about the state of the world is required or when reasoning about causes and consequences is necessary, this can become a challenge. Research on how to completely capture regulatory frameworks is ongoing, involving the fields of policy modeling, normative reasoning and knowledge representation amongst others. For this reason, we expect this approach to work best in cases where the regulation is very clear and focused on the behaviour of the system itself, with limited dependence on the outside world. The range of application of our proposed approach will keep increasing, as more approaches are developed for increasingly complex normative frameworks.

An additional cornerstone of our proposed approach is the requirement of exhaustive record-keeping, to make decisions examinable. Although such good software development practices should be standard, they could prove technically challenging for some applications, or could interfere with other requirements such as data protection and privacy. Our proposed approach is versatile enough to still be applicable in such cases: by re-computing the decision under the monitoring agent, rather than operating with a record of events, certain norm violations could still be identified.

We believe our proposal opens new interesting research questions for further examination. First and foremost, it promotes a new avenue of research for rule-based representations of complex norms. While we have only begun to consider monitoring approaches, there is a need to conduct real-world implementations to identify real-world needs. Furthermore, looking beyond the implementation details, we call upon an exploration on how contestability and explainability differ in terms of costs, system requirements and trust calibration for naive and expert users, and advocate the development of concrete methodologies oriented specifically to contestability.

Acknowledgments. A. Theodorou was supported by the European Union's Horizon 2020 research and innovation programme under grant agreement no. 825619 (AI4EU project).

A. Aler Tubella and V. Dignum were supported by the Wallenberg AI, Autonomous Systems and Software Program (WASP) funded by the Knut and Alice Wallenberg Foundation.

L. Michael was supported by funding from the EU's Horizon 2020 Research and Innovation Programme under grant agreements no. 739578 and no. 823783, and from the Government of the Republic of Cyprus through the Directorate General for European Programmes, Coordination, and Development.

References

1. IEEE Recommended Practice for Software Requirements Specifications. IEEE Std 830-1998, pp. 1–40 (1998)
2. Aldewereld, H., Dignum, F., García-Camino, A., Noriega, P., Rodríguez-Aguilar, J.A., Sierra, C.: Operationalisation of norms for electronic institutions. In: Noriega, P., Vázquez-Salceda, J., Boella, G., Boissier, O., Dignum, V., Fornara, N., Matson, E. (eds.) COIN -2006. LNCS (LNAI), vol. 4386, pp. 163–176. Springer, Heidelberg (2007). https://doi.org/10.1007/978-3-540-74459-7_11
3. Bryson, J.J., Theodorou, A.: How society can maintain human-centric artificial intelligence. In: Toivonen, M., Saari, E. (eds.) Human-Centered Digitalization and Services. TSS, vol. 19, pp. 305–323. Springer, Singapore (2019). https://doi.org/10.1007/978-981-13-7725-9_16
4. Bundeskartellamt: No proceeding against Lufthansa for abusive pricing. Technical report, Bonn, Germany (2018)
5. Citron, D.K., Pasquale, F.: The scored society: due process for automated predictions. Washington Law Rev. **89**(1), 1–33 (2014)
6. Crawford, K., Schultz, J.: Big data and due process: toward a framework to redress predictive privacy Harms. Boston College Law Review. Boston College. Law School, vol. 55, no. 1, p. 93 (2013)
7. De Vos, M., Kirrane, S., Padget, J., Satoh, K.: ODRL policy modelling and compliance checking. In: Fodor, P., Montali, M., Calvanese, D., Roman, D. (eds.) RuleML+RR 2019. LNCS, vol. 11784, pp. 36–51. Springer, Cham (2019). https://doi.org/10.1007/978-3-030-31095-0_3
8. Dignum, V.: Responsible Artificial Intelligence: How to Develop and use AI in a Responsible Way. Springer, Switzerland (2019). https://doi.org/10.1007/978-3-030-30371-6
9. Governatori, G., Hashmi, M., Lam, H.-P., Villata, S., Palmirani, M.: Semantic business process regulatory compliance checking using LegalRuleML. In: Blomqvist, E., Ciancarini, P., Poggi, F., Vitali, F. (eds.) EKAW 2016. LNCS (LNAI), vol. 10024, pp. 746–761. Springer, Cham (2016). https://doi.org/10.1007/978-3-319-49004-5_48
10. Jensen, A.S., Dignum, V., Villadsen, J.: The AORTA architecture: integrating organizational reasoning in *Jason*. In: Dalpiaz, F., Dix, J., van Riemsdijk, M.B. (eds.) EMAS 2014. LNCS (LNAI), vol. 8758, pp. 127–145. Springer, Cham (2014). https://doi.org/10.1007/978-3-319-14484-9_7
11. King, T.C., et al.: Automated multi-level governance compliance checking. Auton. Agent. Multi-Agent Syst. **31**(6), 1283–1343 (2017). https://doi.org/10.1007/s10458-017-9363-y
12. Kroll, J.A.: The fallacy of inscrutability. Philos. Trans. R. Soc. A Math. Phys. Eng. Sci. **376**(2133) (2018)
13. Michael, L., Parkes, D.C., Pfeffer, A.: Specifying and monitoring economic environments using rights and obligations. Auton. Agent. Multi-Agent Syst. **20**(2), 158–197 (2010)
14. Miller, T.: Explanation in artificial intelligence: insights from the social sciences. Artif. Intell. **267**, 1–38 (2019)
15. Modgil, S., Faci, N., Meneguzzi, F., Oren, N., Miles, S., Luck, M.: A framework for monitoring agent-based normative systems. In: Proceedings of the International Joint Conference on Autonomous Agents and Multiagent Systems, AAMAS, vol. 1, pp. 126–133 (2009)

16. Poel, I.: Translating values into design requirements. In: Michelfelder, D.P., McCarthy, N., Goldberg, D.E. (eds.) Philosophy and Engineering: Reflections on Practice, Principles and Process. PET, vol. 15, pp. 253–266. Springer, Dordrecht (2013). https://doi.org/10.1007/978-94-007-7762-0_20
17. Wachter, S., Mittelstadt, B., Russell, C.: Counterfactual explanations without opening the black box: automated decisions and the GDPR. Harvard J. Law Technol. **31**, 841 (2017)

On Defining Rules for Cancer Data Fabrication

Juliana K. F. Bowles[1](✉) (iD), Agastya Silvina[1](iD), Eyal Bin[2], and Michael Vinov[2]

[1] School of Computer Science, University of St Andrews,
St Andrews KY16 9SX, UK
{jkfb,as362}@st-andrews.ac.uk
[2] IBM Research Laboratory, Haifa, Israel
{bin,vinov}@il.ibm.com

Abstract. Data is essential for machine learning projects, and data accuracy is crucial for being able to trust the results obtained from the associated machine learning models. Previously, we have developed machine learning models for predicting the treatment outcome for breast cancer patients that have undergone chemotherapy, and developed a monitoring system for their treatment timeline showing interactively the options and associated predictions. Available cancer datasets, such as the one used earlier, are often too small to obtain significant results, and make it difficult to explore ways to improve the predictive capability of the models further. In this paper, we explore an alternative to enhance our datasets through synthetic data generation. From our original dataset, we extract rules to generate fabricated data that capture the different characteristics inherent in the dataset. Additional rules can be used to capture general medical knowledge. We show how to formulate rules for our cancer treatment data, and use the IBM solver to obtain a corresponding synthetic dataset. We discuss challenges for future work.

Keywords: Cancer data · Synthetic data · Constraint solvers · Fabrication rules

1 Introduction

Data accuracy is crucial for being able to trust the results obtained from any machine learning models. Previously, we have developed machine learning models for predicting the treatment outcome for breast cancer patients that have undergone chemotherapy at a health board in Scotland [12], and developed a monitoring system for their treatment timeline showing interactively the options and associated predictions [13]. Available cancer datasets, such as the one used in our work, are often too small to obtain significant results, and make it difficult to explore ways to improve the predictive capability of the models further.

This research is partially funded by the Data Lab, and the EU H2020 project Serums: Securing Medical Data in Smart Patient-Centric Healthcare Systems (grant 826278).

V. Gutiérrez-Basulto et al. (Eds.): RuleML+RR 2020, LNCS 12173, pp. 168–176, 2020.
https://doi.org/10.1007/978-3-030-57977-7_13

Within the options available with machine learning and deep learning, we often require substantially more data than we can get access to. Even though we have direct access to the oncology dataset within the local health board, it is not easy to extract the required quantity of data for developing our model. Indeed, there may not be enough data available to perform a suitable analysis.

We explore an alternative approach to enhance our cancer dataset through synthetic data generation. This approach gives us enough data to design proof-of-concept enhanced prediction models. From our original dataset, we extract rules to fabricate data. These rules must formulate exactly the characteristics of the original dataset. Further rules can be added to capture general medical knowledge and information that a small dataset may not contain. This paper shows how to formulate all required rules for our cancer treatment data, which will enable us to obtain a corresponding synthetic dataset. An added complexity in our dataset is the relationship between different events throughout the treatment of a patient. Hence, to generate realistic synthetic datasets, we have to be able to capture accurately the various constraints associated to a treatment as well as possible relationships between events. We will show that the IBM Data Fabrication Platform allows us to capture these complex constraints as needed.

This paper is structured as follows: Sect. 2 motivates our approach, presents related work, and describes the structure of the original dataset and some restrictions on what is involved in a chemotherapy treatment for a given patient. Section 3 gives a brief description of the IDM data fabrication platform, and shows how to obtain the rules for our cancer treatment dataset. We conclude in Sect. 4 with a discussion of future work.

2   Motivation, Related Work and Cancer Data

Obtaining accurate toxicity prediction models in cancer care is vital, as it can help identify treatments that are not suited to a patient, and thus improve their outcome overall. However, cancer treatment data, and healthcare data in general, may be limited or difficult to access due to its sensitive and private nature.

There are advantages of using synthetic data in the healthcare domain. Fabricated data allows us to start building models without the need to access real data. We can fabricate large-scale datasets quickly, which allows us to improve the model to resist over-fitting (often a problem with small datasets). Furthermore, the use of synthetic data enables us to simulate outlier events (e.g., rare diseases). Note that we later need to retrain the model with the real dataset.

One option to generate fabricated data involves the use of an existing dataset and imputing the values for a desired field. Rubin [11] proposed the idea of using multiple imputations for all the data-points in the dataset to generate a (partial or complete) synthetic dataset. In statistics, imputation is the process of replacing missing data with substituted values. Given enough data and iterations, it is possible to generate a synthetic dataset for specific purposes. With the rise of machine learning in data mining, Reiter et al. [5,9] extend the idea of using multiple imputers by using several machine learning algorithms to generate synthetic data. There are many data synthesisers [6] available with machine learning models (e.g., linear regression, random forest, decision tree, neural networks) in their backbone. However, machine learning is not well suited for this task: we need sufficient data to be able to infer a pattern in the dataset, and machine learning cannot capture data sequences accurately. Data sequences arise in a cancer dataset, where every entry corresponds to a patient event (e.g., hospital visit, treatment), and several events form an ordered sequence in the treatment.

Generating data with potentially complicated dependencies, requires the use of solvers, such as *constraint satisfaction problem* (CSP) solvers [14] or *satisfiability modulo theories* (SMT) solvers [8]. As an example, there is a solution that generates data for form-centric applications using an SMT solver [2]. Although this may avoid many of the challenges of other data formats, such as relational databases with complex topologies and hierarchical structures, the solution uses workarounds which can introduce an under approximation of the solution space, thus yielding additional complications to the solver. These complications affect the performance and the scalability of the technology, as well as the quality of its results. In our approach we use the IBM solver which avoids these issues [4].

We use a cancer dataset extract from a Scottish health board from 2014 to 2016, consisting of Scottish Morbidity Records[1] which includes *SMR01* (hospital admission data), *SMR06* (cancer registry), and *Charlson Comorbidity Index* (categorising the coexistence of a chronic condition with cancer [10]); National Records of Scotland (e.g., *Data on Deaths*); the Oncology DCO database which includes *Demographics* (e.g., date of birth, gender, ethnicity), *Diagnosis* (e.g., cancer stage and site), *Surgery* and *ChemoCare* (e.g., chemocare_general and chemocare_toxicity). In addition, note that a patient in Scotland is uniquely identified by a *Community Health Index* (CHI).

A cancer patient may be given a series of different treatments, known as a treatment pathway. New patients undergo different sets of tests (e.g., MRI, CT SCAN) to determine the type of cancer and the first treatment to be given. There are several types of primary and follow-up treatments, but we focus on chemotherapy treatments here. Chemotherapy uses one or more anti-cancer drugs as part of a standardised chemotherapy regimen, and may be given with a curative intent, or with a palliative intent where the aim is to prolong life or to reduce symptoms. Overall the treatment is very aggressive and it affects the toxicity levels of the patient, particularly in case of comorbidities. Predicting toxicity levels is thus important throughout the treatment in order to be able to adjust it for the wellbeing of the patient. The general pattern of chemotherapy, important to define correct rules for data fabrication, is given below:

- A patient can only be treated with one intention or purpose of the treatment, such as, curative, palliative, adjuvant (an add-on therapy).
- After a specific time has passed, in case of cancer relapse, the patient might be given another treatment with a different intention.
- Each intention has several different regimens.
- Each regimen has several different drugs.

---

[1] See https://www.ndc.scot.nhs.uk/National-Datasets/ for Information on SMR datasets.

- The treatment may last for several weeks or months that is given in cycles. Hence, each regimen may have more than one cycle.
- A patient may be given several regimens at a time.
- Some regimens may belong to one protocol.

3   The IBM Data Fabrication Platform and Cancer Rules

We use the IBM Data Fabrication Platform (DFP) to generate synthetic data in our EU H2020 project Serums [7]. DFP is based on rule-guided fabrication whereby the data and metadata logic is extracted from the underlying real data or its description and is modelled using rules that the platform provides. DFP allows for new rule types to be added by users. Once a user requests the generation of a certain amount of data into a set of test databases or test files, the platform ensures that the generated data satisfies the modelled rules as well as the data consistency requirements. The platform is capable of generating data from scratch which we do for our dataset. We define the rules, type of data, volume of data, and the relationships among different columns in the dataset. The rule types include:

- Constraints: domains, mathematical functions, arithmetical relations, string relations, regular expressions.
- Knowledge: chosen from existing data sources.
- Analytics: value and pattern distributions, smart classifications.
- Transformations: constraints describing relations between targets and sources, can be bundled to transform tuples.
- Programmatic rules: user-defined code/script functions that generate target values.

Once the user has defined the data sources and rules, the solution builds the fabrication task, maintaining the referential integrity of data based on database constraints or applied constraints. Here, the constraints are solved by the solver and the solution is used to obtain the fabricated dataset [1]. The output can have multiple formats/extensions.

In order to generate fabricated data, we need to provide the constraints of the variables within the domain including the data fields and ranges of values. After specifying the constraints, the solver finds solutions by constraint propagation and search. Every time the solver generates a solution to all given rules (constraints), this solution is an instance in our dataset. Running the solver an indefinite number of times will give us a fabricated dataset which satisfies all the provided constraints. In case of inconsistencies in rules, no solution can be generated, but it indicates which rules are in conflict and these can be corrected.

Rules are formulated following the syntax accepted by the solver, which includes conditions, dependencies between fields, mathematical equations, ordering, and Boolean conditions. We can express weighted/probability, normal, and random distributions to determine the value of our fields.

Rules may result from a combination of medical knowledge and information extracted from the real dataset. Consider the rule below. If it is known that the cancer has metastasised into site *C34.9* we set *pulmonary_flag* to 1. Otherwise, we use a weight distribution to set the value of *pulmonary_flag*. We infer the weight distribution from the data extraction.

```
general.pulmonary_flag = (
  // Knowledge:
  (general.metastasis1 == 'C34.9' || general.metastasis2 == 'C34.9'
          || general.metastasis3 == 'C34.9') ? 1 :
  // From extraction:
  randomWeightedValue(general.pulmonary_flag,1200? 0, 120 ? 1). )
```

In Scotland, patients have a unique identifier given by the Community Health Index (CHI). The CHI has 10 digits consisting of the date-of-birth (*DDMMYY*) followed by a three-digit sequence number and a check digit. The ninth digit is always even for females and odd for males. To generate a proper CHI for patients we have to model this definition through several rules. For instance,

```
allDiff(from(general), general.chi)
```

specifies that every CHI is unique. The next rule specifies the structure of a CHI,

```
general.chi = concat(dateToString(general.DOB,DMy),
   intToString(general.D7),intToString(general.D8),
   intToString(general.D9),intToString(general.D10))
```

where the last four digits follow specific constraints. Here D7,D8,D10 are arbitrary, e.g., `0 <= general.D7 <= 9`, and D9 is used to indicate gender, which in our case has a 0.99 probability of being female given by:

```
randomBool(99)?general.D9 = {0,2,4,6,8}:general.D9 = {1,3,5,7,9}
```

We specify the first *incident date* or diagnosis date, to be between 2014 and 2016 by using the *equality-inequality* relation:

```
currentDate-(6*365)<general.incidence_date<= currentDate-(4*365)
```

We can use regular expressions to capture a postcode, and assign constants to fields such as cancer site, `general.site = 'C50.9'` to indicate breast cancer. We perform summation to populate the Charlson Comorbidity Index [10]. There are field values which influence other field values, and can be captured through implication (if there is not a first metastasis there cannot be a second or third).

```
(general.metastasis1 is Null -> general.metastasis2 is Null) &&
    (general.metastasis2 is Null -> general.metastasis3 is Null)
```

To populate some fields we check whether we can use a normal distribution or add another correlation between fields from inspecting the original dataset. For instance, for the BMI we use the probability distribution to determine the category (e.g. underweight, normal, overweight) and then use a normal distribution to populate the exact BMI value for the patients in each category.

Some patients may have more than one hospital admission (recorded in the dataset *SMR01*) during their cancer care, for example, when they experience side-effects as a result of their treatment. Here, we create a new table for the patient admission and use the CHI as a reference to the general table. First, we specify the admission rate to fabricate the admission data. The rule is as follow:

```
numOf(from(smr01s), smr01s.chi = general.chi) =
  randomWeightedNumber(500 ? 1,300 ? 2,200 ? 0)
```

stating that 50% of patients have one admission, 30% have two and 20% patients have none. Since the admission date is time based (sequential), we create another helper field, *elapsed_days*. The admission date depends on both.

```
smr01s.admission_date = (smr01s.incidence_date + smr01s.elapsed_days)
```

The *elapsed_date* has a monotonically increasing value as follows:

```
monotonic(from(smr01s), per(smr01s.chi), smr01s.elapsed_days,
     {normalDistributionNumber(110.4, 17.2)}, randomNumber(14,100))
```

The first value for *elapsed_days* is populated using a normal distribution with 110.4 as the *mean* and 17.2 as the *variance*. The next instance of *elapsed_days* increases by a random number between 14 to 100 days. Because the admission date is calculated by adding *elapsed_days* to *incidence_date*, its value increases sequentially. With this, we can fabricate a patient's admission event.

The next dataset we fabricate is the chemotherapy treatment dataset, where the main challenge is capturing the relation between data that belongs to the same patient. Briefly, a patient may have more than one intention, and each intention may have more than one regimen. Each regimen has more than one cycle and so on. To capture this relation, we created five helper tables (i.e., *patients*, *intentions*, *regimens*, *cycles*, and *drugs*). There are similarities between these helper tables. We create *patients* as the reference point. We create *intentions* to model the condition where each patient may have one or more intentions. Similarly, *regimens* is created to model the condition where each intention may have one or more regimens (i.e., *cycles* and *drugs* have the same purpose). Each helper table has foreign keys to each other (e.g., *patient_id*, *intention_id*).

The *patients* table has the demographic information during the treatment, with values assumed to be relatively constant, such as *CHI*, *height*, *hospital*, *tumour_group*. The *patients* table acts as the proxy to the *general* where *CHI* is used as the foreign key. The ratio between the data in the *patients* and *general* table is set to one. We also have the *first_intention* field in this table, used as the reference for populating the intention value. We use *randomWeightedValue* to populate this field. By counting the number of each intention occurring in the first cycle, we can get the weight value. The rule for the *first_intention* is shown below:

```
patients.first_intention = randomWeightedNumber(
  350? 'Adjuvant',
  200? 'Palliative',
  180? 'Neo-Adjuvant',
  15? 'Durable Remission',
  5? 'Curative')
```

The ratio between the *patients* and the *intentions* tables is determined by the *first_intention* because some intentions may or may not have follow up treatments. We specify the *intentions.ratio* rule as follow:

```
numOf(from(intentions), intentions.patient_id = patients.patient_id)=
(intentions.first_intention == 'Adjuvant'?randomWeightedNumber(15?2:85?1),
intentions.first_intention == 'Durable Remission'?1,
intentions.first_intention=='Neo-adjuvant'?randomWeightedNumber(60?2,40?:1),
intentions.first_intention == 'Palliative'?1,
intentions.first_intention == 'Curative'?1)
```

The *first_intention* field determines the value of the next instance of *intention*. Similarly to the *patients*, we have a field *first_regimen*. The value of this field depends on *intentions.intention* and has the same function like the field *first_intention* (i.e., this method is repeated to capture the sequence behaviour for *cycles* and *drugs*).

To populate the treatment appointment date we use a similar rule (as for instance for patient hospital admission) as mentioned before. We have the *appointment_date* field in *intentions* to populate the first *appointment_date* for each intention. In the *intentions* table, we set elapsed days based on the regimen ratio, cycle ratio and regimen interval days to prevent the overlap between appointment dates for each regimen.

In the regimens, we have another *elapsed_day* field to determine the date of the first regimen. The starting date for the *regime.elapsed_day* is taken from the *regimen.init_appointment_date*. The *regimen.init_appointment_date* equals the *intention.appointment_date*. The rule for the *regimen.elapsed_day* is as shown below:

```
monotonic (from(regimens),per(regimen.intention_id),regimen.elapsed_days,
     {cycle_ratio*regimen_interval_days},regimen.init_appointment_date)
```

Unlike *intentions* and *regimens*, we have the *cycle_ratio* in the *regimens* because we need to know the number of cycles for determining the correct elapsed days between regimens.

Finally, to populate several fields like the toxicity outcome, *regimens* and *performance status*, we integrate a simple Markov model into the rules (the value of the current fields depends only on its previous value). We use the previous value because we have observed a high correlation, based on the Pearson standard of correlation [3], between the previous value and the current value.

4 Conclusions and Future Work

We presented some of the rules describing the characteristics of our cancer treatment dataset which are fed to the IBM Data Fabrication Platform to generate synthetic data. The rules describe the expected range of values within a column, relationships between columns, and - more significantly - relationships between rows where these describe different events in the treatment of the same patient. An accurate set of rules is essential to generate realistic data, and we need to evaluate how realistic the synthetic data is. Machine learning can be useful to establish this to some extent, but was outside the scope of the present paper.

Although synthetic data is valuable it is not a replacement of real data. If all the features present in a dataset have been incorporated into a synthetic dataset, then the later may in fact have the same biases as the original dataset. However, we believe that an added advantage of using the IBM Data Fabrication Platform comes from the ability to generate rules derived from a combination of domain knowledge directly (in our context this includes information from clinical guidelines, clinical studies as well as medical practice) and features extracted from real data. This flexibility, may consequently lead to a synthetic dataset less prone to biases inherent in real data specially when real datasets are small.

References

1. Adir, A., Levy, R., Salman, T.: Dynamic test data generation for data intensive applications. In: Eder, K., Lourenço, J., Shehory, O. (eds.) HVC 2011. LNCS, vol. 7261, pp. 219–233. Springer, Heidelberg (2012). https://doi.org/10.1007/978-3-642-34188-5_19
2. Adorf, H.-M., Varendorff, M.: Constraint-based automated generation of test data. In: Winkler, D., Biffl, S., Bergsmann, J. (eds.) SWQD 2014. LNBIP, vol. 166, pp. 199–213. Springer, Cham (2014). https://doi.org/10.1007/978-3-319-03602-1_13
3. Akoglu, H.: User's guide to correlation coefficients. Turk. J. Emerg. Med. **18**, 91–93 (2018)
4. Bilgory, E., Bin, E., Ziv, A.: Solving constraint satisfaction problems containing vectors of unknown size. In: Beck, J.C. (ed.) CP 2017. LNCS, vol. 10416, pp. 55–70. Springer, Cham (2017). https://doi.org/10.1007/978-3-319-66158-2_4
5. Caiola, G., Reiter, J.P.: Random forests for generating partially synthetic categorical data. Trans. Data Privacy **3**, 27–42 (2010)
6. Dandekar, A., Zen, R.A.M., Bressan, S.: Comparative evaluation of synthetic data generation methods. In: Proceedings of ACM Conference (Deep Learning Security Workshop) (2017)
7. Janic, V., Bowles, J.K.F., Vermeulen, A.F., et al.: The serums tool-chain: Ensuring security and privacy of medical data in smart patient-centric healthcare systems. In: IEEE International Conference on Big Data (IEEE Big Data 2019) (2019)
8. de Moura, L., Bjørner, N.: Satisfiability modulo theories: introduction and applications. Commun. ACM **54**(9), 69–77 (2011)
9. Reiter, J.P.: Using CART to generate partially synthetic public use microdata. J. Official Statist. **21**, 441–462 (2005)
10. Roffman, C.E., Buchanan, J., Allison, G.T.: Charlson comorbidities index. J. Physiotherapy **62**, 171 (2016)
11. Rubin, D.B.: Discussion statistical disclosure limitation. J. Official Statist. **9**, 461–468 (1993)
12. Silvina, A., Bowles, J., Hall, P.: On predicting the outcomes of chemotherapy treatments in breast cancer. In: Riaño, D., Wilk, S., ten Teije, A. (eds.) AIME 2019. LNCS (LNAI), vol. 11526, pp. 180–190. Springer, Cham (2019). https://doi.org/10.1007/978-3-030-21642-9_24

13. Silvina, A., Bowles, J., Hall, P.: Combining patient pathway visualisation with pre-
    diction outcomes for chemotherapy treatments. In: 12th International Conference
    on eHealth, Telemedicine, and Social Medicine, pp. 108–113. IARIA (2020)
14. Tsang, E.: Foundations of Constraint Satisfaction. Academic Press, Cambridge
    (1993)

On the Formal Representation of the Australian Spent Conviction Scheme

Guido Governatori[1,2]([⊠]), Pompeu Casanovas Romeu[2,3], and Louis de Koker[2]

[1] Data61, CSIRO, Eveleigh, Australia
guido.governatori@data61.csiro.au
[2] Law School, La Trobe University, Melbourne, Australia
[3] Institute of Law and Technology, Autonomous University of Barcelona,
Barcelona, Spain

Abstract. We discuss how to use Defeasible Deontic Logic to provide
a formal representation of the Commonwealth of Australia spent conviction schema (Part VII C of the Crimes Act (1914)). The formalisation is
directly written and implemented in Turnip (a modern implementation
of Defeasible Deontic Logic).

1 Background: Spent Conviction

A "spent conviction" is a conviction that becomes hidden from public view after
a set period of time but, depending on certain factors, still remains accessible
for specific (public) purposes by specific interested parties. These schemes are
mainly focused on convictions for less serious crimes and generally do not extend
to convictions for violent sexual offences. The set period of time is also extended
where the person has re-offended during the set period.

Australia has a spent conviction scheme operating at a Commonwealth level
and Territories and States also have schemes, but the nature and rules of these
schemes differ. Each regime has exemptions which permit the lawful disclosure
of spent convictions in certain limited circumstances. These exemptions usually
relate to employment in particularly sensitive positions (e.g., on application for
appointment as a police official, teacher, or childcare worker). In this sense,
unless an ex-offender falls within an exemption, spent conviction schemes operate
to encourage the rehabilitation of ex-offenders and to reduce the potential for
ongoing punishment or discrimination against them [6]. The paper focuses on
elements of the Commonwealth spent conviction scheme National Crime Check
describes a "spent conviction" as follows for purposes of this scheme:

A "spent conviction" is a conviction of a Commonwealth, Territory, State or
foreign offence that satisfies all of the following conditions: (i) it is 10 years since
the date of the conviction (or 5 years for juvenile offenders); AND (ii) the individual was not sentenced to imprisonment or was not sentenced to imprisonment
for more than 30 months; (iii) AND the individual has not re-offended during
the 10 years (5 years for juvenile offenders) waiting period; (iv) AND a statutory

© Springer Nature Switzerland AG 2020
V. Gutiérrez-Basulto et al. (Eds.): RuleML+RR 2020, LNCS 12173, pp. 177–185, 2020.
https://doi.org/10.1007/978-3-030-57977-7_14

or prescribed exclusion does not apply. (A full list of exclusions is available from the Office of the Australian Information Commissioner).[1]

Exchanges of criminal records data among the jurisdictions in Australia are coordinated by and through the Australian Criminal Intelligence Commission (ACIC). It manages the processes and provides the system through which Australian police agencies and accredited bodies submit nationally coordinated criminal history checks. The ACIC operates the National Police Checking Service that assists organisations to screen and make informed decisions for example about prospective employees and volunteers, visa and citizenship applications and work-related due diligence relating to national security. The service is used by 251 accredited agencies and bodies. During the period 2017–18 the number of checks processed increased by 11.1% to 5.29 million, and 1.49 million checks were referred to police agencies for further assessment to determine whether the information may be disclosed in accordance with their spent convictions legislation and/or information release policies.[2] The aim of the paper is to explore the possibilities to automatise or, better, semi-automatise the service described above. The extensive number of checks referred to police agencies is directly linked to the complexity of the regime and inconsistencies among the different jurisdictional schemes. Accordingly, the objective of this work was to produce a proof of concept to partially model project use case solutions relating to the Spent Convictions Scheme, to lessen the current pressure on officials who need to process the checks.

For the modelling required to implement the proof of concept we selected Part VIIC (Pardons, Quashed Convictions and Spent Conviction) of the *Crimes Act 1914* (Cth). Modelling of the Part of the Act we selected Defeasible Deontic Logic (DDL) for its ability:

- to integrate reasoning with exceptions,
- to model deontic concepts such us obligations, permissions, prohibitions, and
- to represent both prescriptive norms and definitional norms.

All such elements are present in the Commonwealth spent conviction scheme as set out in the *Crimes Act 1914* (Cth). The aim of the modelling was to understand to what extent formal models are suitable to represent legislation and if they offer suitable environment to support legal decision. The encoding of the selected section was done in the Turnip language and reasoner that implements DDL. The encoding was then tested with a few examples to provide an initial, small scale, validation of the approach.

2　Defeasible Deontic Logic

In this section we provide a brief outline of Defeasible Deontic Logic, for the full details of the logic see [4]. DDL is an extension of the Defeasible Logic [1] and [5]

---

[1] https://www.nationalcrimecheck.com.au/resources/spent_convictions_information.

[2] ACIC. Annual Report 2017–18 https://www.acic.gov.au/25-national-information-and-intelligence-sharing-services-0.

combining defeasibility for the natural handling of exceptions, deontic modalities for modelling legal provisions about obligations, prohibitions and permissions, and a non-classical compensation operator to model obligations in force after a violation. Also, DDL has been used for applications in the legal domain [3].

In DDL a rule is an IF...THEN...statement where the IF part encodes the condition of applicability of the rule (where in general a rule corresponds to a norm or a part of a norm), and the THEN part models the effect of the norm. Rules can then be divided in constitutive rules that are used to provide the definitions of the terms used in a normative document, and normative rules that give the conditions (IF part) under which legal requirements (i.e., obligations, permissions, prohibitions, ...), THEN part, are in force. In DDL rules can be further classified according to their strength: thus we have strict rules, defeasible rules and defeaters. A strict rule is a rule in the classical sense. Defeasible rules are rules subject to exceptions: the conclusion of the rule holds unless there are other (applicable) rules (for the same conclusion) that defeat the rule. Finally, defeaters are a special kind of rules, they do not support conclusions, but prevent the conclusion to the opposite.

Constitutive rules are rules in standard defeasible logic, while for normative rules we consider prescriptive rules (setting when something is obligatory/forbidden) and permissive rules (rules making something explicitly permitted derogating rules for prohibitions or obligations to the contrary). Normative rules have the following form:

$$r: A_1, \ldots, A_n \hookrightarrow_\Box C_1 \odot \cdots \odot C_m$$

where $A_1, \ldots, A_n$ are the conditions of applicability of the rule and are expressed as literals or deontic literals (a literal in the scope a deontic modality: obligation O or permission P), $\Box$ is one of the deontic modalities, and the C_i are literals ($C_1 \odot \cdots \odot C_m$ is called a reparation chain). The mode of the rule $\Box$ determines the scope of the conclusion. In case the mode is O the meaning of the right-hand side of the rule is that when the rule applies OC_1 is in force (C_1 is obligatory), and if it is violated, i.e., $\neg C_1$ holds, then OC_2 is in force (C_2 is obligatory), and C_2 compensates for the violation of OC_1. We can repeat the reasoning when OC_2 is violated. The reasoning mechanism of DDL extends the proof theory of Defeasible Logic [1] and it is based on an argumentation like schema. To prove a conclusion, there must be an applicable rule for the conclusion we want to prove. A rule is applicable if all the elements of the antecedent of the rule hold (have already been proved). In addition, all counter-arguments are either rebutted or defeated. A counter-argument is a rule for a conflicting conclusion (the negation of the conclusion, or in case of deontic conclusions, conflicting deontic modalities). A counter-argument is rebutted if some of its premises do not hold (we proved that the premises do not hold) and the counter-argument is defeated when the rule is weaker than an applicable rule for the conclusion. For reparation chains, in addition to the normal defeasibility conditions, to prove OC_k we require that for all the elements before it in the chain, we are able to prove OC_l and $\neg C_l$.

Turnip[3] is a modern (typed) functional programming implementation of DDL written in Haskell. The aims of Turnip is to provide a reference implementation of DDL and at the same time to offer features to facilitate the encoding of norms as rules. Turnip requires that the terms used in a set of rules are defined before they are used, where the definition of a term has the following form:

```
Type Name description_string
```

where **Type** is either a Boolean (**Atom**, string, numeric, date, datetime or duration. The description string is optional, and its main use is to provide the meaning of the term in natural language. Arithmetic operators (i.e., **+, -, *, /,**) can be used for numeric terms and values and comparison operators (i.e., **==, !=, <, <=, >, >=**) to create boolean types from numeric and duration terms. Also, Turnip provides conversion functions (e.g., **interval, toDays, after**) to operate on dates, times and duration terms. For example, the **interval** function takes two dates as input and returns a duration. Consider the snippet

```
case.date  := 2019-09-01
conviction.date := 2010-12-03
interval(case.date,conviction.date)>=5y
```

where we use the assignment operator **:=** to give values to two terms of type date; then, we use the **interval** operator to compute the duration (time elapsed between the two dates), and we compare it with a given duration (5 years). Rules consist of a label (optional), a condition list, an arrow and a conclusion list.

```
label: condition_list => conclusion_list
```

where the arrow determines the type of rule (strict, defeasible or defeaters). Rules are meant to represent norms and it is reasonably common that a norm prescribes multiple (simultaneous) effects; similarly, the same effect can be prescribed by different norms. To ease the effort of writing the rules encoding such norms, the condition list can be either a conjunction (**&**) or a disjunction (|) of Boolean, while the conclusion list is either an assignment, a single Boolean, a conjunction of assignments, or a conjunction of Boolean. For the Boolean expression Turnip, in addition to Atom, their negation ~, and expression constructed from numeric and temporal expression allows for deontic expressions, where a deontic expression is obtained from the combination of one the following deontic modalities [O], [P], [F], [E] (standing, respectively for Obliged, Permitted, Forbidden, Exempt) and an atom. For the modalities, notice that: [F]A is equivalent to [O]~A (and ~[P]A) and [E]A is equivalent to [P]~A.

3 Formal Modelling of the Spent Conviction Schema

The encoding of Part VIIC requires the extraction of the terms (or atoms in DDL parlance), corresponding to the concepts, used in the legislation. While the Turnip language supports different data types (e.g., Boolean, numeric, date and time, duration, ...), for the encoding of this part we only needed to use

---

[3] An online environment to run Turnip rulesets, with samples of the features it offers is available at http://turnipbox.netlify.com/.

Boolean, duration and date. The representation of each atom comes with its textual description providing the meaning in natural language of the term. The atoms encode either factual information relevant for a case (e.g., the date when a person was convicted for an offence, or the whether a person was convicted or found guilty of an offence) or for information that can be obtained based on the conditions defined in the Act (whether the waiting period for an offence ended). For example, we can create the following atoms

```
Date  conviction.date "the date when the person was convicted"
Date  case.date "the date when the current case is dealt with"
Atom  minor "the person was a minor when the offence was dealt with"
Atom  WaitingPeriodEnded "the waiting period for the offence ended"
```

that can then be used by the following constitutive rules

```
wp1:  interval(conviction.date,case.date)>=5y & minor
      => WaitingPeriodEnded
wp2:  interval(conviction.date,case.date)>=10y  => WaitingPeriodEnded
```

encoding the definition of waiting period given in Division 1 of Part VIIC, namely:

> waiting period, in relation to an offence, means:
> (a) if the person convicted of the offence was dealt with as a minor in relation to the conviction–the period of 5 years beginning on the day on which the person was convicted of the offence; or
> (b) in any other case–the period of 10 years beginning on the day on which the person was convicted of the offence.

Similarly, Section 85ZM on the meaning of conviction and spent conviction, i.e.:

> (1) For the purposes of this Part, a person shall be taken to have been convicted of an offence if:
> (a) the person has been convicted, whether summarily or on indictment, of the offence;
> (b) the person has been charged with, and found guilty of, the offence but discharged without conviction; or
> (c) the person has not been found guilty of the offence, but a court has taken it into account in passing sentence on the person for another offence.
> (2) For the purposes of this Part, a person's conviction of an offence is spent if:
> (a) the person has been granted a pardon for a reason other than that the person was wrongly convicted of the offence; or
> (b) the person was not sentenced to imprisonment for the offence, or was not sentenced to imprisonment for the offence for more than 30 months, and the waiting period for the offence has ended.

can be encoded by the following atoms and (constitutive) rules:

```
Atom Person "an individual not a body corporate"
Atom ConvictionVII "a conviction according to Part VII"
Atom Conviction "a person has been convicted for an offence"
Atom Guilty "a person has been charged and found guilty"
Atom Discharged "a person has been discharged without a conviction"
Atom OtherOffence "a person has not been found guilty, but the court
  has taken it into account (for the conviction) for another offence"
```

```
s85ZM_1a: Person & Conviction => ConvictionVII
s85ZM_1b: Person & Guilty & Discharged => ConvictionVII
s85ZM_1c: Person & OtherOffence => ConvictionVII
```

where the ConvictionVII atom corresponds to the "institutional" fact that an
event counts as a conviction for the purpose of applying Part VIIC to that event.

```
Atom SpentConviction "a conviction is considered spent"
Atom Pardon "a person has been granted a pardon"
Atom Imprisonment "a person was sentence to imprisonment"
Duration imprisonment_term "the length of the imprisonment"

s85ZM_2a: ConvictionVII & Pardon => SpentConviction
s85ZM_2b1: ConvictionVII & ~Imprisonment & WaitingPeriodEnded
    => SpentConviction
s85ZM_2b1: ConvictionVII & imprisonment_term <= 30m
    & WaitingPeriodEnded => SpentConviction
```

As one can notice, the rules in DDL bear a close resemblance with the textual
provisions they are meant to encode. For examples of prescriptive rules we can
consider the rules encoding Section 85ZS(1a-b)

(1) Subject to Division 6, but despite any other Commonwealth law or any State
    law or Territory law, where, under Section 85ZR, a person is, in particular
    circumstances or for a particular purpose, to be taken never to have been
    convicted of an offence:
    (a) the person is not required, in those circumstances or for that purpose, to
        disclose the fact that the person was charged with, or convicted of, the
        offence;
    (b) it is lawful for the person to claim, in those circumstances, or for that
        purpose, on oath or otherwise, that he or she was not charged with, or
        convicted of, the offence;

```
s85ZS_1a: Person & PardonOrWronglyConvicted
    => [E] Disclose.charged & [E] Disclose.conviction
s85ZS_1b: Person & PardonOrWronglyConvicted
    => [E] Oath.not_charged & [E] Oath.not_conviction
```

Section 85ZW on Effect of right of non-disclosure

(b) anyone else who knows, or could reasonably be expected to know, that
    Section 85ZV applies to the person in relation to the offence shall not:
    (i) without the person's consent, disclose the fact that the person was charged
        with, or convicted of, the offence to any other person, or to a Com-
        monwealth authority or State authority, where it is lawful for the first–
        mentioned person not to disclose it to that other person or that authority;

is then encoded as follows:

```
Atom ExpectedKnow85ZV "the other entity knows or could reasonably be
    expected to know that Section 85ZW applies"

s85ZW_b: OtherEntity & ExpectedKnow85ZV & [E]Disclose.convictionInfo
    => [F] OtherDisclose.conviction & [F] OtherDisclose.charged
```

As Section 85ZS(1) recites, there are exemptions to the provisions allowing a person the right of non-disclosure (and preventing other entities to disclose such information). For instance, one can consider Subdivision B of Section 6, where Section 85ZZH Exclusions (a) and (g) provide that:

Division 3 does not apply in relation to the disclosure of information to or by, or the taking into account of information by a person or body referred to in one of the following paragraphs for the purpose specified in relation to the person or body:

(a) a law enforcement agency, for the purpose of making decisions in relation to prosecution or sentencing or of assessing:
   (i) prospective employees or prospective members of the agency; or
   (ii) persons proposed to be engaged as consultants to, or to perform services for, the agency or a member of the agency;
   . . .
(g) Commonwealth authority, for the purpose of assessing appointees or prospective appointees to a designated position;

These provisions can be modelled by the following DDL rules:

```
s85ZZHa_2: LawEnforcementAgency & PurposeOfEngagementWithAgency ->
    [O] Disclose.charged & [O] Disclose.conviction &
    [P] OtherDisclose.conviction & [P] OtherDisclose.charged
s85ZZHh: CommonwealthAutority & PurposeOfEngagementWithAgency =>
    [O] Disclose.charged & [O] Disclose.conviction &
    [P] OtherDisclose.conviction & [P] OtherDisclose.charged
```

where **CommonwealthAutority** and **LawEnforcementAgency** are defined by constitutive rules based on the definition of the terms in Section 85ZL. Similarly, **PurposeOfEngagementWithAgency** can be defined by an auxiliary constitutive rule based on the conditions in 85ZZH(a)(ii).

The rules for Section 85ZS and Section 85ZZH are in conflict with each other, DDL provides a mechanism (called superiority relation) to solve the conflict. Specifically, rule s85ZZHa_2 overrides rule s85ZS_1a (same for rule s85ZZHh):

```
s85ZZHa_2 >> s85ZS_1a
s85ZZHh >> s85ZS_1a
```

Thus, in case both rules apply, i.e., a person who received a pardon for an offence, seeking to work for the Australian Federal Police has to disclose the conviction. Consider a case related to the vetting of Person A's appointment as a management consultant to the Australian Federal Police. Person A had two prior convictions for insider trading in 1998 and had been released on entering into a good behaviour bond for two years. For the sample case we have to determine (1) it there was a conviction, (2) whether the conviction has been spent or not, and in case the conviction is spent (3) to assess if any exclusions under Section 6 apply. Accordingly, we encoded the facts of the cases in Turnip as follows:

```
Person // Person A
Conviction // there was a conviction for insider trading
conviction.date := 1998-08-10 // when A was convicted
case.date := 2019-09-22 // when the case was examined
Guilty // A was found guilty
Discharged // A was discharged with 2y good conduct bond
```

```
~Imprisonment // A was discharged with 2y good conduct bond
proposedConsultant // A seeks to work as proposed consultant for
AustralianFederalPolice // the Australian Federal Police
```

based on the above facts, we obtain the following conclusions (excluding the given facts)

```
[O] Disclose.charged            CommonwealthAutority
[O] Disclose.conviction         ConvictionVII
[P] OtherDisclose.charged       LawEnforcementAgency
[P] OtherDisclose.conviction    SpentConviction
                                WaitingPeriodEnded
```

showing that the waiting period for the conviction ended and so the conviction is spent; but the person has to disclose the information for his application to work as consultant and other entities (expected to know the conviction) are permitted to disclose the information to the relevant authority or agency (in this case the Australian Federal Police).

The encoding for Part VIIC in Turnip, with the facts of the case, is available at https://turnipbox.netlify.com/fiddles/fcA5uXkUnQ0y4B9uVkIq.

4　Conclusions and Future Work

This paper reported on the formal representation of elements of the Australian Spent Conviction Scheme, developed in the course of research of the Australian government-funded Data to Decisions Cooperative Research Centre (D2D CRC). The project [2], which concluded in June 2019, focused on specific spent convictions use cases selected by the ACIC to produce a proof of concept on Compliance through Design (CtD) modelling [7].

The main conclusion is that the modelling of the Spent Convictions scheme can be used to process the most common cases at the federal level. The encoding has proved to be consistent both at the formal and empirical levels in the most common cases. But its implementation with legal effects in more complex scenarios would require embedding it into a broader legal context. This alignment between the extracted rules with the legal conceptual analysis for decision-making purposes at Commonwealth and State and Territory levels constitute the challenge that we are going to face in the immediate future.

References

1. Antoniou, G., Billington, D., Governatori, G., Maher, M.J.: Representation results for defeasible logic. ACM Trans. Comput. Log. **2**(2), 255–287 (2001)
2. Casanovas, P., et al.: Summary Legal and Technical Report on Spent Convictions. D.C3.7. DC25008, July 2019. https://doi.org/10.5281/zenodo.3271525
3. Governatori, G.: Practical normative reasoning with defeasible deontic logic. In: d'Amato, C., Theobald, M. (eds.) Reasoning Web 2018. LNCS, vol. 11078, pp. 1–25. Springer, Cham (2018). https://doi.org/10.1007/978-3-030-00338-8_1
4. Governatori, G., Olivieri, F., Rotolo, A., Scannapieco, S.: Computing strong and weak permissions in defeasible logic. J. Philos. Log. **42**(6), 799–829 (2013)

5. Governatori, G., Rotolo, A.: Logic of violations: a Gentzen system for reasoning with contrary-to-duty obligations. Australas. J. Log. **4**, 193–215 (2006)
6. Paterson, M., Naylor, B.: Australian spent convictions reform: a contextual analysis. UNSW Law J. **34**, 939 (2011)
7. Stumptner, M., et al.: An architecture for establishing legal semantic workflows in the context of integrated law enforcement. In: Pagallo, U., Palmirani, M., Casanovas, P., Sartor, G., Villata, S. (eds.) AICOL 2015-2017. LNCS (LNAI), vol. 10791, pp. 124–139. Springer, Cham (2018). https://doi.org/10.1007/978-3-030-00178-0_8

Author Index

Printed in the United States
By Bookmasters